8R   12°°

The Kind of Man I Am

Nichole Rustin-Paschal

THE KIND OF MAN I AM

Jazzmasculinity and the World

of Charles Mingus Jr.

Wesleyan University Press   Middletown, Connecticut

Wesleyan University Press

Middletown CT 06459

www.wesleyan.edu/wespress

Manufactured in the United States of America

Designed by Mindy Basinger Hill | Typeset in Minion Pro

The excerpt from William Matthews, "Mingus in Diaspora," from *Search Party: Collected Poems of William Matthews*, © 2014 by Sebastian Matthews and Stanley Plumly, is reprinted by permission of Houghton Mifflin Harcourt Publishing Company. All rights reserved.

"God Must Be a Boogie Man," words and music by Joni Mitchell, Copyright © 1979 Crazy Crow Music. All rights administered by Sony/ATV Music Publishing, 8 Music Square West, Nashville, TN 37203. All rights reserved. Used by permission of Alfred Music.

Portions of the introduction appeared in "Self-Portrait: On Emotion and Experience as Useful Categories of Gender Analysis in Jazz History," ed. Wolfram Knauer, in *Jazz Debates/Jazzdebatten*, Darmstadt Studies in Jazz Research, vol. 13 (Jazzinstitut Darmstadt, 2014): 119–48.

Publication of this book was supported by a grant from the H. Earle Johnson Fund of the Society for American Music.

Library of Congress Cataloging-in-Publication Data

Names: Rustin-Paschal, Nichole.

Title: The kind of man I am: jazzmasculinity and the world of Charles Mingus Jr. / Nichole Rustin-Paschal.

Description: Middletown, Connecticut: Wesleyan University Press, [2017] | Series: Music/culture | Includes bibliographical references and index. | Identifiers: LCCN 2017012818 (print) | LCCN 2017013371 (ebook) | ISBN 9780819577573 (ebook) | ISBN 9780819577559 (cloth: alk. paper) | ISBN 9780819577566 (pbk.: alk. paper)

Subjects: LCSH: Mingus, Charles, 1922–1979. | Jazz musicians—United States. | Jazz—History and criticism. | Masculinity in music. | Music and race—United States—History—20th century.

Classification: LCC ML418.M45 (ebook) | LCC ML18.M45 R87 2017 (print) | DDC 781.65092—dc23

LC record available at https://lccn.loc.gov/2017012818

5   4   3   2   1

For my sonshine, AKIL

CONTENTS

PREFACE

This is almost my time.
Charles Mingus Jr.

Charles Mingus Jr., the youngest child of Harriet and Charles Mingus, was born on April 22, 1922, in Nogales, Arizona. The Mingus family, including Charles Jr.'s two older sisters, Vivian and Grace, moved west a few months later, settling in Watts, then a suburb of Los Angeles. Mingus Sr., with his light skin and blue eyes, had been born and raised in North Carolina, of black and white parentage. The Texas-born Harriet was of mixed Chinese, European, and African heritage. Not long after their arrival in Watts, Harriet died from chronic myocarditis at the age of thirty-four. Mingus Sr., who had enlisted in the U.S. Army in his late thirties, retired as a sergeant and resumed working as a postal employee. He also remarried. Mingus Sr.'s new wife, Mamie Carson Mingus, was a migrant from South Carolina of mixed Native American and African ancestry. Her son Odell took the Mingus surname.

An "old man's son," Mingus Jr. resembled his father in many respects. Physically, they shared round faces, the cheeks giving way to jowls as they aged, though Mingus did not possess his father's fair coloring. In terms of personality, both expressed explosive anger—verbally and physically. Mingus tended to direct his ire at those he considered to be acting unjustly and disrespectfully toward himself and the music he devoted his life to creating and performing; Mingus Sr. could often be abusive to his wife and children.

Charles Mingus often dwelt on his family's mixed-race heritage and on how his father's beliefs had shaped his home life. He was frank about race and racial difference, keenly aware of how gradations of color dictated opportunity and expectations in American society. Mingus confronted those societal limitations from childhood through adulthood, always with a sense that things would have worked out differently for him had he been just a bit lighter in complexion. He also reproved himself for feeling this way, acknowledging racism as an insidious structural and internalized system that affected people—regardless of color—in wide-ranging ways, including the ability to listen empathetically to music.

Mingus began his musical education on the trombone, then moved on to the cello, the piano, and the bass. He earned a chair in the Los Angeles Junior Philharmonic, played in the Senior Symphony Orchestra at Jordan High School, and pursued his burgeoning interest in jazz alongside many of his childhood friends. He took lessons from the bassist Red Callender, from the trumpeter, saxophonist, and clarinetist Lloyd Reese, and from Herman Reinshagen, a former New York Philharmonic bassist then teaching in Los Angeles.

At twenty-two, Mingus became a father himself. Charles Mingus III was born in 1944. Two years later, Mingus and his wife Jeanne would have a second son, Eugene, but the marriage ended shortly after Eugene's birth.

After failing a military physical and rejecting his father's advice that he find work at the post office, Mingus set forth as a musician on Central Avenue, the hotbed of black musicking in Los Angeles. Along with childhood friends Buddy Collette and Britt Woodman, Mingus worked with numerous young jazz lions, including Miles Davis, Lee Young, Joe Comfort, Charlie Parker, Art Pepper, Oscar Pettiford, and Dexter Gordon. He performed with Louis Armstrong, Billie Holiday, Duke Ellington, and Lionel Hampton, with whom he made his first New York tour. Returning west, Mingus played in San Francisco and Oakland. When his music gigs temporarily dried up, he reluctantly took work at the post office. Joining vibraphonist Red Norvo and guitarist Tal Farlow allowed him to make a permanent move to New York in the early 1950s.

The fifties were a vibrant period for Mingus. After working with Norvo, Mingus performed with numerous musicians, among them Billy Taylor, Max Roach, Art Tatum, and Mal Waldron, in New York and other cities. After Mingus met drummer Dannie Richmond, the two launched a partnership that lasted over two decades. Mingus's second wife, Celia, whom he met while living in San Francisco, gave birth to their son, Dorian. Along with Max Roach and Celia, Mingus founded Debut Records, an independent label featuring musicians who embraced a modern approach to jazz. One of the label's earliest recordings documented the famous Jazz at Massey Hall Concert with Dizzy Gillespie, Bud Powell, Charlie Parker, Max Roach, and Mingus. In New York, Mingus organized workshops and collectives to advance musicians' ideas, and made lasting friendships with critics such as Nat Hentoff and Bill Coss.

Mingus also recorded for other jazz labels, including Atlantic, Columbia, Bethlehem, Impulse! and Candid, producing critically acclaimed albums featuring his interpretations of standards as well as his own compositions. In addition to a stunning trio album featuring Mingus, Max Roach, and Duke Ellington called *Money Jungle*, he released other notable recordings, such as *Tijuana Moods*, *Blues and Roots*, *Charles Mingus Presents Charles Mingus*, and *Pithecanthropus Erectus*. Mingus also began composing his autobiography, *Beneath the Underdog*, which would eventually be published in 1971. Additional forays into literature found Mingus backing poet Langston Hughes on the album *Weary Blues*, and performing with poet Kenneth Patchen. Jean Shepherd improvised a prose poem on Mingus's *The Clown*.

Mingus continued to compose and record during the 1960s, although some periods were more fertile than others. Daughter Carolyn and son Eric, named for Mingus's dearly admired friend and band member, saxophonist Eric Dolphy, were born during his marriage to Judy Mingus. As a result of emotional and mental exhaustion, as well as the disappointing trajectory he felt his career was taking, he retreated from performance. As the decade wore on, however, Mingus began recording and performing again, touring Europe, the West Coast, and playing regularly in New York at clubs like the Five Spot and the Village Vanguard. He appeared in the film *All Night Long*, a take on Shakespeare's *Othello*, and scored John Cassavetes's film *Shadows*. He met his fourth wife, Susan Ungaro, the week he learned of Eric Dolphy's sudden death.

The seventies continued to provide Mingus with creative opportunities and accolades. He received two Guggenheim awards, was elected to *Down Beat*'s Hall of Fame, and published *Beneath the Underdog*. Alvin Ailey created *The Mingus Dances* based on his compositions. Mingus toured Europe and the United States extensively, and was recognized at the White House. He signed a contract with Atlantic and produced a number of albums featuring new and old compositions. Just as Mingus appeared to be getting into a consistently productive groove, however, his health began to fail him, leading to a diagnosis of amyotrophic lateral sclerosis. By the late seventies, he was no longer able to perform on the bass, though he could still create music. His final collaboration, with Joni Mitchell, was released posthumously. In that project, Mitchell worked with Mingus on compositions and added lyrics to some of his classic pieces, like "Goodbye Pork Pie Hat."

Charles Mingus Jr. died on January 5, 1979, in Cuernavaca, Mexico. Musicians such as Toshiko Akiyoshi, Ted Curson, Jon LaPorta, Dannie Richmond, the Art Ensemble of Chicago, and Stanley Clarke wrote compositions expressing their regard for him. Sue Mingus has ensured that her husband's music will live on by managing the publishing of his compositions and the establishment of legacy bands; his papers have been archived at the Library of Congress.

Like other black musicians in the 1950s, Mingus articulated a complex conception of emotion and its relevance to his creative practice. Emotional life provided a source for musical ideas and meanings; musicians bent, shaped, and reimagined the significance of their feelings in their compositions and performances. They also drew on their experiences of difference—based on race, gender, sex, religion, art, and class—and contributed to redefinitions of masculinity. *The Kind of Man I Am: Jazzmasculinity and the World of Charles Mingus* threads the life and career of Charles Mingus with those of the jazzmen in his orbit and with the jazz culture they created.

The introduction frames the book's theoretical arc by exploring how the self-portrait figures in Mingus's music and life, as well as by examining how race, masculinity, and emotion give meaning to jazz and experiences within jazz. Drawing on my own experiences becoming a jazzman, I also consider gender difference and what it means to love jazz.

In the first chapter, I turn to Mingus's memoir, *Beneath the Underdog* (1971), documenting the sources of feeling he drew on to compose and perform, and describing his own expectations for music's ability to convey emotional complexity. The chapter explores how Mingus depicted the impacts of intraracial colorism, his emerging sexuality, his familial ties, and the demands of making a living on his music-making. Like his music, Mingus's words challenge the reader to dig below the surface of jazz culture and black masculinity. *Beneath the Underdog* emerges as a story about the emotional truths underpinning the realities of being a black jazzman.

In the second chapter I consider Mingus's evolving ideas about being a musician and composer—how he understood himself in relationship to wider, intersecting communities of musicians, and to others' expectations. As emotional truth becomes shorthand for racial authenticity, exclusivity, and power, who feels what and how they are able to feel become measures for masculinity, authority, and control. During a period when mainstream notions of masculinity were, more often than not, measured in terms of militarism, stoicism, and hardness, and white male vulnerability was being articulated by writers like Jack Kerouac and in films like *Young Man with a Horn* and *The Man in the Gray Flannel Suit*, black jazzmen filled a troubling role.[1] Black jazzmen were allowed, even expected to be both "emotional" and masculine as long as their emotionality conformed to stereotypes of racialized masculinity. Anger was defensible if it gave the music force and energy; humor was permissible as long as the performer was not a sexual threat. Black jazzmen, however, understood their "feelings" as a reflection of their position in society, not merely a performance persona.

The third chapter focuses on the story of Debut Records, the small independent music label owned by Charles Mingus, Max Roach, and Celia Mingus in the 1950s. By considering the business of becoming, in Dizzy Gillespie's words, "musical industrialists," I examine "the aesthetic responsibilities" Mingus and Roach undertook to provide an outlet for their own work and that of other musicians who they believed deserved an audience, along with their efforts to provide themselves with a sustaining source of income. I pay particular attention to Celia Mingus's experience of jazzmasculinity and her efforts to keep Debut afloat. By illuminating Debut as a source of empowerment for female jazzmen, as a demand for control of artistic practice, and as a vision of jazz modernity, I show how the label reflected Mingus's communitarian ideals of jazz.

In the fourth chapter, I extend my focus on women's jazzmasculinity by concentrating on pianist Hazel Scott, whom Mingus recorded on Debut. By letting Scott take an extended solo in *The Kind of Man I Am*, I demonstrate how black women perform gender difference and incorporate jazz culture's masculine values in their presentation of self.[2] Like Mingus, Hazel Scott is a compelling figure because her art drew from her determination to create in situations that often ignored or disrespected her humanity, mastery of form, and agency. The trajectory of Scott's career—from child prodigy to movie star to pariah then back to star—illustrates how women navigated the professional demands and the gendered cultural narratives of jazz.

The concluding chapter looks at Mingus through the eyes of other musicians and writers—including Al Young, Joni Mitchell, and Buddy Collette—whose experience of jazz was profoundly shaped by their relationship to him. Relationships with Mingus were tough—he didn't get his reputation as "Jazz's Angry Man" for nothing—but, more often than not, also rewarding. Given love, he gave love in return—on his own terms certainly, but love nevertheless. This final section of *The Kind of Man I Am* tells the story of Mingus as mentor and muse, illuminating the familial, musical, and social world that influenced one of the twentieth century's most important composers and musicians.

ACKNOWLEDGMENTS

This book is finally done. My thanks are many.

During the course of this journey from dissertation to book, I am proud to have received research support from New York University, the Gaius Charles Bolin Dissertation Fellowship from Williams College, the Huggins-Quarles Award from the Organization of American Historians, the University of Illinois at Urbana-Champaign, the University of Houston Black History Workshop, the Black Women and Work Collective, the Jazzinstitut Darmstadt, and the Historical Society of Southern California. I am incredibly thankful for the help I received from archivists at the Institute for Jazz Studies at Rutgers University, the Performing Arts Library at the Library of Congress, the Smithsonian, the Schomburg Center for Research in Black Culture, the NYPL-Performing Arts Library, and UCLA.

As a graduate student, I benefited from the grace and camaraderie of those in my cohort at NYU—Alicia Headlam Hines, Rick Treiber, Alondra Nelson, Thuy Linh N. Tu, Davarian Baldwin, Mabel Wilson, Donette Francis, Antonette Irving, Fanon Che Wilkins—and fellow travelers in that journey—Lucinda Holt, Scott Brown, Maxine Gordon, Jeffrey O. Green Ogbar, Grant Farred, Martha Jones, John L. Jackson, and Deborah Thomas. What I learned in graduate school, I learned from the best—Robin D. G. Kelley, Tricia Rose, Lisa Duggan, Andrew Ross, Wahneema Lubiano, Fred Moten, Manthia Diawara, Kobena Mercer, Arnold Rampersad, and Kevin Gaines.

My colleagues at Williams College and the University of Illinois at Urbana-Champaign were fantastic. I'd especially like to thank Regina Kunzel, Dianne Pinderhughes, and Kathy Perkins for modeling engaged scholarship, teaching, mentorship, and friendship. In addition, I heartily thank Barrington Edwards, Jessica Millward, Gabriel Solis, John Jennings, Fanon Che Wilkins, Cynthia

Oliver, Assata Zerai, Damion Thomas, Minkah Makalani, David Roediger, Kenda Mutongi, David L. Smith, Craig Steven Wilder, Cheryl D. Hicks, Pat Gill, Cliff Christians, William Berry, Alice Deck, Angharad Valdivia, Cameron McCarthy, and Desiree Yomtoob (amazing spirit and researcher!).

My journey in jazz has been adventurous and full of good cheer. The friends and colleagues I have made because of jazz are without a doubt beyond category: John Gennari, Eric Porter, Krin Gabbard, Bernie Gendron, Farah Jasmine Griffin, Salim Washington, Robert O'Meally, Robin D. G. Kelley, Elsa Barkley Brown, Sharon Harley, Sherrie Tucker, Tami Albin, Monica Hairston-O'Connell, Richard Pierce, Jennifer Griffith, Lara Pellegrinelli, Steven Isoardi, John Gill, João H. Costa Vargas, Gabriel Solis, Wolfram Knauer, Kellie Jones, Guthrie P. Ramsey, Tony Whyton, James Miller, Karl Miller, Nicholas Gebhardt, Martin Niederauer, George E. Lewis, Mark Anthony Neal, Gayle Wald, Ingrid Monson, Walter van de Leur, Andy Jaffee, Gary Funston, Kathy Mallory-Jones, Tony Haywood, Penny Von Eschen, Kevin Gaines.

Hear the drumroll for these friends and readers who kept me focused on the end goal and were as excited as I was, if not more so, to see me wrestle my thoughts on Mingus into the book you hold now. Sherrie Tucker—an angel on earth!—inspires me with her brilliant mind, her generosity, her laughter, and her gently insistent demands to get the writing done. Thank you! Without her, I couldn't have done it. Lucinda Holt, my deuce, steered and cheered me through the revision process, helping me focus on what I had done right and what could be made much, much better. Thank you! Karima Rustin, my sister, is my fiercest cheerleader and I love her. Thank you! Robin D. G. Kelley launched me on this journey with love, encouraging me to write as best and as fully as I could about Mingus; without his example as a writer, historian, teacher, and dear friend, the book and I would be all the poorer. Thank you!

Wesleyan University Press is a dream! Thank you to the series editors: Sherrie Tucker, Deborah Wong, and Jeremy Wallach. Thank you to Suzanna Tamminen, Parker Smathers, Peter Fong, Susan Abel, Mindy Basinger Hill and Marla Zubel. Thank you as well to the wonderful anonymous readers who provided much-needed critical advice on the work. I'm grateful for the time and care they gave my manuscript. What I've done well here is because of them.

I can't overstate how much I have loved and relied on my friends and family to get through the research and writing. Their support and generosity made it possible. Thank you Karima Rustin, Myisha Gomez, Ahman Rustin, LaRicke Blanchard, Tony Haywood, Christopher Allen, Lucinda Holt, Lena Holt, Anastasia

Rowland-Seymour, Hannah Rowland-Seymour, Evan Rowland-Seymour, Phillip Rowland-Seymour, Lydia Holt, Snorri Sturluson, Andri Snorrison, Nicholas Snorrison, Helena Paschal, Christina Paschal, Mary Guy, Khadijah DeLoache, Mike Lee, Amanda Lee, Kaylynn Lee, Laura Lee, Lexi Lee, Tara Roberts, Sheryl Wright, Jackie Modeste, Michelle Taylor, Harmony Wu, Amy Detjen Kline, Marc Rotenberg, Risa Golubuff, Kim Forde-Mazrui, Erin Kershner, Serena Gruia, Karen Green, Miller Susen, Tanya Stanciu, Paula Seniors, Luke Trimble, Jill Sullivan, Noreen Sugrue, Tim McCarthy, Kathy Flaxman, David Flaxman, James Harrigan, Rachel Unkefur, Sibley Johns, Allison Wright, Dennis Barnes, Capeton Rustin, Rose Reiter, Alan MacGregor, Myra MacGregor.

My heart breaks a little knowing that my grandmother, Daphne Rustin, whom I strive to be like every day, and my father, Carlton Rustin, for whom music was life, could not hold this book in their hands. I take comfort in knowing they believed I would do it. Love to my first dog, who happens to be the best dog, Levinas. A lifetime has been lived in the writing and that lifetime has been full of blessings. The best of them are Marlin D. Paschal and Akil Nicholas Paschal, without whom I wouldn't know myself.

The Kind of Man I Am

INTRODUCTION

"Self-Portrait"

It seems to me that [music] should come
from the heart, even if it's composed.

Charles Mingus Jr.

Jazz is specific. It *is* what each musician feels as he plays;
and that concatenation of emotions comes from specific experiences
in each player's life. . . . Each player is his own prophet, and the messages
range from picaresque defiance to comfortable acceptance
of whatever values are negotiable at the moment.

Nat Hentoff

Charles Mingus Jr. had an unerring ability to title his compositions with names that were biting, romantic, and metaphorical ruminations on the potential meaning of the piece in question. The meaning he found in his "Self Portrait," for example, morphed over the years. Originally titled "God's Portrait," then "Self Portrait," "Portrait," and finally "Old Portrait," the composition evolved from depicting the tension between his despair at the dissolution of his first marriage and the pleasure he felt viewing the natural beauty of the countryside while traveling on a train, to the realization that he didn't "look like that portrait anymore." Mingus believed that honest emotional expression was tied inextricably to the demands of composition and performance. The Mingus of "Old Portrait" had changed from the one who initially composed it,[1] and the structure of the composition was elastic enough for him to reflect his maturing impressions about his life experiences in performance. He was a witness to life and his music life's testimonial. Mingus considered himself burdened with the responsibility of being both a chronicler and a critic, one who archived reality through the record of his music.[2]

"Just because I'm playing jazz," Mingus said, "I don't forget about *me*. I play or write *me*, the way I feel, through jazz, or whatever. Music is, or was, a language of the emotions. If someone has been escaping reality I don't expect him to dig my music. . . . My music is alive and its [*sic*] about the living and the dead, about good and evil."[3] Voluble, dynamic, romantic, and demanding, Mingus was a performer, writer, and composer who crafted luminous portraits in music. "Changing all the time," his music was a layered expression of his life as a black jazzman. His insistence that he was trying to "write me" expressed the complexity of the intellectual project of capturing his experience and communicating with his audiences. Mingus understood music as a structure of feeling that documented both individual and collective experience, and imagined new ways of being. Music is a universal system of emotional signs, "a kind of international language" through which "one can express his feelings about life, the world and conditions in it—the bad with the good."[4]

As Mingus's "Self-Portrait" implies, it is through the self's own experience that we make meaning about jazz as an art, as a way of living and a worldview, and as a site of gendered expectations about community and culture. Our experiences in jazz are profoundly shaped by how we are situated in relation to the music and culture. In jazz history and writings about jazz history, "experience" has been unassailable in its guise, as Ronald Radano notes, as the "real."[5] A slippery concept, experience is a "universal theme," the historian Martin Jay observes, a signifier "at the nodal point of intersection between public language and private subjectivity, between expressible commonalities and the ineffability of the individual interior."[6] Experience is "something which cannot be fully possessed by its owner."[7] It is of the subject but, for Mingus, it is not the subject himself.

Mingus pushed his musicians and his audiences to see music as an expression of community, of morality, of individuality. Musicians were most creative and affecting, he believed, when they were conscious of tradition, willing to experiment, and open to the challenges of embracing new ideas. Musicians who played with feeling understood how to link their emotions—and the truths they had learned from experience—into a cohesive musical expression; they mastered the performance of ideas, not just the performance of feeling. Jazz expresses both the individual experience of the musician performing—not just as a general idea, but as a day-in, day-out demand that the musician make music out of experience and emotion—and the collective work of musicians to give voice to communities.

Ever the optimist, Mingus wrestled with his disappointment over the fact that others did not share his idealized view of music. So he raged—against lazy musicians, nightclub poseurs, shady business owners, know-nothing critics, as well as himself—and he loved. Mingus is all about love: musical, familial, sexual, and spiritual. He poured his heart into mastering his instrument, the bass, into composing music, and into advocating for music and musicians. He yearned for passionate and nurturing relationships—and found them with lovers, wives, children, and friends. These people responded to the demands of his loving (and at times prickly) attention by themselves becoming more protective and supportive of his dreams. To express his fundamental belief that in music we find our individual divinity, he faithfully turned to music again and again.

The Kind of Man I Am delves into Mingus's ideas about being in jazz—and how his experiences as a black jazzman tested and emboldened his art-making—by reading his autobiography, tracing his development as a musician and composer, historicizing his experience as an independent record-label owner, and considering how he has been depicted as a site of memory, biography, and criticism. This book also explores the broader network of jazzmen who ushered jazz into the mainstream.

In the postwar period, when jazz was viewed as a metaphor for such wildly disparate concepts as democracy, truth, authenticity, and emotion, the jazzman was a symbol of interracial cooperation, a representative of the state, an assertion of modernity, and a way of being in the world.[8] Those who assumed authority in jazz, whether critics, musicians, fans, label owners, poets, or historians, used the language of emotion to categorize musicians, to define acceptable music behaviors, and to grade musicians' depths of emotional expressivity. These behaviors and value judgments were shaped by competing inter- and intraracial expectations of music as a social practice, as an opportunity for expressions of individuality, and as a representation of cultural traditions.

Through the language of emotion, jazzmen understood themselves as communicating values about aesthetics, about jazz as a social and political space, and about individual musicians and collective experience. Jazzmen understood their emotions as key to conceptualizing an ethical life in which ideals about collectivity, equality, and beauty were embraced and practiced across the culture.[9] Emotions are judgments, the philosopher Martha Nussbaum explains, that allow us to articulate how we interpret the world and our experiences in it. Embedded within the circulation of the trope of "emotions" for musicians of Mingus's generation is an ethics of feeling and moral suasion. "Emotions" are experiential, evaluative, self-referential.[10] Though not all jazzmen were successful in doing the "moral work" of rigorous self-examination necessary to benefit from the intelligence of the emotions,[11] they nevertheless aspired to a level of self-awareness that could disrupt the mores of mainstream society, particularly those that devalued emotional expressivity.

Emotions do both background and situational gender work that has real social impact as people interact with each other based on a "network of judgments at many levels of generality and specificity."[12] For some, emotion in jazz culture reveals evidence of traits typically associated with masculinity, including authority, creativity, truth-telling, self-determination, and authenticity. For others, like Mingus, emotions also included so-called feminine feelings of love, vulnerability, and melancholy. The language of "emotions," music, allowed for a collective, ever-evolving political language, capable of wrestling with the meaning of the contemporary moment.

The shorthand of "emotion" circulates in and through jazz culture primarily as a term inclusive of subjectivity and experience, rather than of physiological expressions of feeling.[13] Jazzmen's emotions are often richly imagined feelings of community, well-being, and selfhood. Though jazzmen used the language of emotion to describe what they valued about jazz music, musicians, and culture in terms of "feeling," the word "feeling" was usually intended as a "terminological variant" of emotion.[14] Jazzmen like Mingus described emotion through bodily effects when, at specific moments in their personal experience, the music came alive for them emotionally and intellectually. For others, bodily feeling marked jazz as a site of the primitive and of unmediated expression. Despite these warring conceptions, both camps viewed jazz as key for an individual's flourishing precisely because it articulated emotions and feelings that mainstream society diminished.

While we understand jazz as a distinctly male culture, there is a dearth of studies of race and masculinity as a combined category in jazz.[15] The extension of gender analysis to jazz history proves that women have long had a presence and influence on jazz music and culture and that their aesthetic judgments have been grounded in their experiences as women performing in male-dominated settings.[16] The analysis of race in jazz challenges ideas about racial authenticity and sound,[17] expands our understanding of how black musicians approach jazz as intellectual work,[18] and details how the seemingly democratic space jazz purported to be nevertheless reproduced many of the broader social restrictions and prejudices of segregation and racial bias defining twentieth-century U.S. society. In exploring how jazzmen describe their feelings about interacting with one another and about the music, we talk about jazzmasculinity and, by understanding that "race is everywhere in music," we talk about racialized jazzmasculinity and, in particular, the sway of black jazzmasculinity on politics, identity, and culture.

We also appreciate how much women were invested in the principles of jazzmasculinity, even as they reveled in their femininity. I am especially interested in how Hazel Scott and Celia Mingus found, in black jazzmasculinity, a creative space enabling them to embrace authority, freedom, and agency in the postwar period. By aligning these women's experiences with those of Charles Mingus, I show how one cannot possibly tell a story about jazz or jazz musicians without understanding how central women—with their separate and inseparable experiences—are to that story.[19] *The Kind of Man I Am* examines how racial and gender difference defines discourses about the music and participation in the culture for men and women, musicians and nonmusicians alike.

In jazz culture, a site of belonging and exclusion marked by emotions sticking to certain bodies, Mingus was "Jazz's Angry Man."[20] In the "affective economy" of jazz that could produce such a narrative, "'feelings' become 'fetishes,'" as Sara Ahmed observes, "qualities that seem to reside in objects, only through an erasure of the history of their production and circulation."[21] Mingus prized self-awareness—the continuous examination and reexamination of the self—as part of his creative intellectual labor. Likewise, he demanded openness and vulnerability in both his personal and professional relationships. His demands for self-awareness, from himself and others, caused numerous confrontations on the bandstand and in real life. Mingus's "anger" exposes the metalanguage of race, the double-voiced discourse Evelyn Brooks Higginbotham names as "serving the voice of black oppression and the voice of black liberation."[22] Whether deployed to celebrate or denigrate his nonconformity, the continued reinscription of his "anger" in critical, popular, and scholarly work serves to caricature and marginalize both his authority to tell his experience as a black jazzman and his importance as a jazz composer and performer. As I will demonstrate, Mingus discovered through music a community in which the love expressed between men (usually homosocial, sometimes homoerotic) was as sustaining and disruptive as "anger" could be to a career and a life. Mingus made love the source of his creativity and identity as a black jazzman.

As Tony Whyton argues, when we ignore the fact that people don't all experience jazz in the same way, we are often in danger of silencing the variety of uses to which jazz is put as a source of social and political identification.[23] Adding more voices, or more discussions of difference, means nothing if we ignore "the relational nature of those differences."[24] Ethnomusicologist Ruth Solie directs us to "interrogate" difference if we are to explore power, race, and gender in music culture and practice, including "the sites at which cultural forces permit or encourage resistance to the construction of difference," and "the differences that all of us understand and enact in daily life."[25] In *The Kind of Man I Am*, I interrogate the differences that inform jazzmasculinity. And, to craft an answer to Guthrie Ramsey Jr.'s question, "Who hears here?," I offer at least one method of capturing those dynamic and conflicting meanings in a way that presents, as Elsa Barkley Brown proposes, "everybody talking at once, multiple rhythms being played simultaneously."[26]

While experience is central to interpretations of jazz, those experiences are too often written as if they follow a set narrative of identification. Experience is a given, rather than a question. I want to explore how experience is both a site of analysis and a way of shaping meaning about experience. In the next section, I employ a cultural historical practice that embraces difference without reifying and naturalizing difference,[27] making my work both reflective and reflexive, putting "experiential and critical knowledge" in "dialogic tension."[28] Through my own self-portrait, I show how and why I came to have feelings about jazz and about Mingus in particular. Because my experience of Mingus is complicated by my identity as a black feminist, to document that experience is to expand the critical language for writing about jazz history. It is also—as Mingus would have demanded—an engagement that risks its authority by being honest about its emotional investments in the work.

"THERE IS NO GUILT IN LOVE"

I'm going to write a book and when I sell it I'm not gonna play
any more for money. I'll compose and now and then rent a ballroom
and throw a party and pay some great musicians to play a couple of things
and improvise all night long. That's what jazz originally was, getting
away from the usual tiddy, the hime, the gig.

Charles Mingus Jr.

The young mose who keeps the fay boys all shook these days is a bass
fiddle player named Charles Mingus, who can out talk, out analyze, out
intellectualize, and out fiddle just about anybody around.

Albert Murray

Charles Mingus once described himself as a frustrated pianist.[29] I am in reality
a frustrated poet (the title of this section is from Amiri Baraka).[30] When I was
growing up in the Bronx, being introduced to jazz through films—from Diana
Ross playing Billie Holiday in *Lady Sings the Blues* to the 1940s and 50s musicals
in regular rotation on WPIX Channel 11—I did not imagine my youthful interest
becoming a professional one. It was stories and poetry that I dreamed of writing
and publishing. In my childhood, soul and rhythm and blues provided the pulse
in our apartment, not jazz. But as I continued to seek my place in the world, jazz
became my personal thing, like the late Frankie Crocker on WBLS signing off
each night with James Moody's "Moody's Mood for Love."[31] Jazz compelled me
to think about sound and its infinite layers; the music drew me in with its aural
complexity, its articulation of humor, tragedy, anger, and love.

I grew increasingly obsessed with Billie Holiday, Miles Davis, and Wynton
Marsalis. Each of them shaped my development as an intellectual and an individual, influencing my approach to thinking about jazz as a site of gendered and
racial experience. Succumbing to the desire for completeness, I began "collecting" jazz in middle school and continued throughout high school, with the bulk
of my cassettes weighted toward the music of those three artists. Writing this,
I laugh at the thought of how some jazz authorities might become alarmed by
the dissonant pairing of "collecting" and "cassettes." And yet, it was as a collector that I understood myself to be an authentic jazz fan. Authentic in the sense
that I was immersing myself in the body of work of musicians whose sounds
expressed concepts that I was not yet able to articulate but with which I could

identify. Indeed, if I was at all concerned about my lack of authenticity as a jazz fan, it was not because I was black and female, but because I was young. My age, I thought, would mark me as a jazz novice at best and an outsider at worst.

As Marsalis was rocketing to fame in the 1980s and 90s, his status as a Young Lion rewarded my identification as a fan. I hung on his every word and melody (or almost every). His *Majesty of the Blues* introduced me to jazz polemic and mythology as an emotional framework for thinking about jazz. The tone of the notes—prophetic, insistent, euphonic—reverberated with the tradition of the persona of a preacher in the black church. In the liner notes I recognized the interplay between words and music; they illuminated the ability of musicians to perform in both written and musical texts. Rooting jazz with cultural capital and a theoretical perspective, Marsalis has insisted that jazz is heroic, black, masculine, philosophical, passionate, ethical. Other writers in the jazz canon have echoed these themes in their explorations of the music. Ever since reading his notes, I have been working to find how else to write about jazz.

At the same time I was developing a passion for jazz, I was identifying as a writer with Langston Hughes. Through my high school's library, I devoured his poetry and fiction. The multiplicity of voices and personas Hughes inhabited taught me that the artist's greatest gift and genius was imagination, the ability to situate oneself in a completely different skin and communicate what one learned there. The poet who wrote "To Artina," "A Dream Deferred," and "I, Too, Sing America," was one and the same, making each persona he assumed (the ardent lover, the despairing urban dweller, the marginalized American) believable, accessible. I knew the poems reflected some kernel of Hughes's identity, but I never imagined that he revealed his truest self in them. If nothing else, I believed there was a Hughes one step removed from the poems; he was a historian writing down and archiving his observations of the experience of the everyday and the everyman. His language and images were vivid; the streets and people he described were very much a part of my daily life. Because of Hughes I saw the possibilities of language for rendering my experience and understanding its import. Because of Hughes I appreciated jazz as nonverbal poetry, a medium for musicians to tell stories, to dramatize and evaluate their everyday lives. Marsalis and Hughes led me to thinking of jazz as narrative, as the musician's articulate, impassioned, and reasoned interpretation of the world he encounters. As Amiri Baraka explains, "Music, as paradoxical as it might seem, is the result of thought."[32]

My commitment to jazz grew while I was an undergraduate at Amherst College, where, for nearly four years, I hosted a weekly jazz show on our AM radio station, WAMH. Technologically primitive and located in the basement of one of our dorms, the station was rich in music and completely independent in its programming. Once I had learned how to operate the controls, I received my license and was left to the mysteries and challenges of choosing my music. I prowled unscientifically among the stacks of LPs, planning each show. Sometimes I chose songs based on the appeal of the title (like Max Roach's "Nommo"), or of the performer's instrument (the bass was my favorite); other times I relied on the albums of a recommended artist. Though my knowledge of the music broadened exponentially during those four years, I remained a jazz innocent, so much so that, in 1994, when I came across a copy of Billie Holiday's autobiography, *Lady Sings the Blues*, at a book stall across from the Apollo Theater on 125th Street in Harlem, I seized it as if it were a rare and precious thing. It was only when I began to study jazz as a scholar that I realized *Lady Sings the Blues* had been continuously in print and I was in no danger of being unable to enjoy it. And yet, that experience of accessing the past, of consuming the words of someone I had long admired, remains with me as a feeling of excitement and wonder. That book led to the first paper I ever presented at an academic conference; Holiday's music spurred me to explore issues of gender, racial difference, and political consciousness in American cultural history.

While in college, I also began to see live jazz performances for the first time. Growing up I had been thrilled by the ballet of the Dance Theater of Harlem and the modern work of Alvin Ailey. I also had danced in recitals at Alice Tully Hall at Lincoln Center, sung in my high school chorus, and published poetry in my high school literary magazine. Yet it was not until I reached the Pioneer Valley that the doors of live music opened to me. Through buying my own tickets to shows, I became (in a small way) a patron of the arts—which has since become a part of my adult practice, my way of seeing myself. Those college years also marked the flowering of my attempts to integrate art patronage, my own practice of art, and my intellectual interests. During that time I published my creative writing and nonfiction, I shot films on Super 8 and edited them, I drew and painted still lifes, I sang in the gospel choir, I stepped with my sorority chapter, I wrote a thesis about Spike Lee's films. I began to think systematically about the importance of black art and cultural practice.

My growing recognition of myself as an intellectual was tied to my attendance at live music performances by Koko Taylor, Joe Sample, Take 6, the Preservation Hall Jazz Band, Max Roach, and others. Two jazz performances in particular informed my choices about pursuing the study of black music. The first jazz concert I attended on my own was Miles Davis at Smith College's Aaron Davis Hall in the fall of 1990. Though I was buried somewhere close to the back of the auditorium, Davis, whose music comprised a third of my personal jazz collection, seemed tantalizingly close. I do not remember why Miles Davis first appealed to me though I do recall that it was his electronic music that I initially collected. In high school, I had shared an interest in Davis with a friend; he named *Bitches Brew* as his favorite album, while I claimed *Amandla*.[33] Not long after the concert, Davis died. Though I don't remember the selections he performed, I do remember the impact of his presence on stage, and the thrill of seeing him with my own eyes. Miles Davis was the first living jazz musician that I had taken an interest in—and a legend to boot. I had no expectation that Davis would perform his past hits, and I doubt that I could have recognized them at the time. I did begin to wonder more about his musical past, however, about the continuity of his singular sound over the years. Perhaps it was the influence of Wynton Marsalis or the LPs at WAMH that led me into Davis's songbook, to *Kind of Blue* and *Sketches of Spain*, but ever since I have been listening backwards in both the history of Davis and the history of jazz.

The first time I saw Marsalis live was in 1991, when my best friend and I went to the Iron Horse in Northampton, Massachusetts, to hear his septet. The audience was densely clustered around the stage, and we were probably the only black women in the place. Charming, charismatic, and swinging, the all-male septet and its performance connected me to the "authentic jazz experience," the one rooted in small nightclubs and celebrated in jazz literature. Critic Burnett James argues that live music is preferable to a mechanical recording, which is "in a sense a fossilized performance—that is to say, it must inevitably lack something of that sentient fluidity, the subtle overtones prompted by a sudden emotional response to a live audience, above all the immediacy of personal contact and communication."[34] Here James articulates one of the central tenets of jazz criticism. Authentic fans prefer live music. Similarly, the musician's experience is privileged in the live setting—the proximity of the audience acts as a creative catalyst, stimulating communication between musician and the muse.

Marsalis has written of the emotional, creative intensity of the nightclub gig: "Small places, man. The people all around you, making all kind of noise and grooving. It just inspires the band. Folks in the audience let the sound wash all over them."[35] In the way that the musicians played to us at that long-ago concert, I also realized that gender could mark me as a fan, that it could render me passive and silent, and that it could both feminize and sexualize my participation in that "authentic jazz experience." As Marsalis explains in *To a Young Jazz Musician*, "Just like that first real good slow dance you ever have, when you get to just rub all over against a girl and you can't believe it. You feel like you can crawl inside her. And you don't ever want it to stop. Ebbing and flowing, you're trying to become one. It's unpredictable, giddy, the feeling of coming together with somebody else. Immeasurable joy. And you're doing it in time. You better enjoy it. You better, because it's unrelivable. That's jazz."[36]

Marsalis's book is structured as a series of letters to a fictional disciple, a young jazz musician. In those letters, he teaches that jazzmasculinity is primarily the aesthetic expression of the musician's own heterosexual power and pleasure. Jazz is grounded in heteronormative experiences of homosociality. At the same time, jazz is, Marsalis writes, an aesthetic that requires swinging in time, expressing a unique identity and voice, embracing checks and balances, challenging the listener, and pursuing freedom in the bounds of structure.

Under the sway of these competing norms of black jazzmasculinity, I made the decision to enter graduate school. The appeal of studying authentic jazz experience was linked to my abiding interest in African American cultural practices, and my increasing identification with black feminism, particularly the work of bell hooks, who moved my voice from margin to center and taught me oppositionality. Not only do black women have important and necessary things to say about their own experiences, hooks argues, they also have important and necessary things to say about the world as we live in it and make it. She insists on the responsibility of black women to be critical, to speak the truth, and to engage in dialogue with others across lines of racial, gender, and class difference. In feminist praxis, hooks sees men as "comrades in struggle" and masculinity as a relevant site of analysis. She recognizes that the study of culture provides a vehicle for resistance and witness, and that its accessibility offers an academic toehold for young and eager scholars seeking a critical and unique voice.[37]

In conceptualizing a research agenda, I considered exploring the sustaining metaphor of jazz as democracy, but I decided that was too unwieldy a dissertation topic. I chose instead to study bassist and composer Charles Mingus Jr., hoping that through him I could take the concerns of black feminism—race, gender, cultural politics, community—to the heart of jazz. Because of the relative paucity of literature about him at the time, I had little sense of others' enthusiasm for Mingus when I began the project. As more people learned I was pursuing this work, however, I discovered a vast network of fans; they offered me tales of their encounters with Mingus, and lauded me for undertaking the monumental task of writing about him.[38] When they asked me why Mingus, I responded truthfully—I was in love with him—even though a black male feminist scholar warned me against spreading this about. Because Mingus died when I was seven, I cannot claim that my crush developed after meeting him or hearing him perform live. The Mingus I fell in love with was written on paper, the one found in his autobiography, *Beneath the Underdog*.

Mingus seduced me with his jive talk; I laughed at his braggadocio. He had me at hello or, rather, that unforgettable line which opens his narrative: "In other words, I am three." *Beneath the Underdog* is orchestrated by a vulnerable hero both on a journey requiring battles with mythic dragons and on an unshakeable, hopeful search for love; it is simultaneously a composition, a beginning, an epitaph. Swept along on the raging current of Mingus's words, I surrendered to his narrative. Mingus seemed to be a man who believed in fate; perhaps (I hoped) he would think it fated that I, born in the year *Beneath the Underdog* was published, would come to be his champion, storming the walls of academia and jazz criticism with my scholarship.

Yes, that word "champion" well describes my mindset as I sat down to wrestle with my dissertation. I wanted to know how Mingus imagined himself as a man in the multiple worlds he occupied. I also wanted to rescue him from the margins of critical studies in jazz history and culture, thereby challenging some of the precepts of jazz historiography.[39] That was what I was planning after my second reading of *Beneath the Underdog*, a reading developed with archival research to solidify the claims I wanted to make about Mingus's significance for gender studies and jazz history. During my first reading, I'd had no idea that Mingus would become my research focus. Indeed, there were several times I had passed him by when browsing the stacks at Shakespeare & Co. on Broadway or the Barnes & Noble on Astor Place, searching for my next readings in a serendipitous series of memoirs, biographies, and fiction by black artists of the 1950s and 1960s. I remember his book as being the last of them (though perhaps he was really somewhere in the middle). Still, he was the one I committed to: Audre Lorde, Amiri Baraka, A. B. Spellman, Samuel Delany, Charles Mingus. Through their examinations of themselves, I could imagine the world these young black artists found themselves in and understand why they turned to literature and music as pleasurable, critical, and testimonial work. Having grown up in New York and attended schools in Greenwich Village, I had often walked the same streets they described as central to the flowering of their art, and I clung to those tenuous connections as I tried to find my own critical voice.

Working with *Beneath the Underdog* required that I question what autobiography told me about jazz music and culture. I knew I wanted to write about jazz, but why was it important to begin with the written word, for example, rather than music? When Mingus wrote the book he was in both semi-retirement and a deep depression. As a result, *Beneath the Underdog* is as much about Mingus's disillusionment with the jazz scene as it is about his love of the music. Just as Mary Lou Williams turned to religion to assuage her disappointment with contemporary jazz culture,[40] Mingus found in his writing a way to process his experiences and feelings about being a black musician. He wrestled with the racism of the business and of society, with musicians' attempts to escape through drugs, with his ego and his temper, with his desire and vulnerability. The primary framework for the memoir is a discussion with his analyst, allowing Mingus to look for, as Amiri Baraka himself sought in his own autobiography, "part of the answer to the question How did you get to be you?"[41]

Christopher Harlos argues that, for jazz musicians, autobiographies are often representative of efforts to "deconstruct the label *jazz* (denotatively and connotatively) as the binary other against which so-called 'serious' or 'legitimate' music was defined." More importantly, Harlos observes that "the turn to autobiography is regarded as a genuine opportunity to seize narrative authority," an opportunity for musicians to challenge precepts of jazz history.[42] In Mingus, both Harlos and I recognize a subject who finds in written text possibilities for "literary agency," for deploying the jazz musician's life as a metaphor for thinking through race, economics, culture, politics, and identity. In his autobiography Mingus grapples with "the function of artifice within the act of self-inscription."[43] He dons various personalities as a challenge to audiences seeking a definitive, single, subsumable subject. Mingus, as I will argue throughout this book, seeks something more than setting the record straight; rather, he is concerned with putting into language the themes he explores in his music, the world that he creates in melodies and harmonies, the emotions and consequences endured living in a racialized male body.

Mine is, indisputably, a black feminist project. I draw on my jazz heroes to enter the great jazz conversation, to understand how I am situated within the dialogues of those who have written about and thought about and played it. My self-portrait exemplifies the possibilities of using the jazzman as a gendered analytic of emotion and experience capable of disciplining jazz discourse. The self-portrait provides the grammar for what poet Elizabeth Alexander describes as a "language to talk about 'my people.'" Alexander imagines a language filled with metaphor and fact, realism and idealism, allowing her to explore and explain how her own "embodied experiences as a black woman in a certain era and geography shape [her] sense of the possibilities as well as the limitations of blackness and help [her] understand [her] self collectively."[44]

The language of emotion articulates collective and individual conceptions of jazz as a measure of racial and gender identity, belonging, and influence. In the expression of emotions such as disappointment, love, solidarity, and anger to describe the experience of jazz, we invest it with our collective values and our aspirations for a good life. In the image of the jazzman we see reflected our gendered expectations of what makes an artist. In the experiences of women who are jazzmen, we confront sharply drawn lines around who can embody authority, creativity, and authenticity. And through the experiences of black women who are jazzmen we understand the sway of black jazzmasculinity.

"THERE'S LOVE AS AN ANTIDOTE"

Like me, Mingus loved Billie Holiday.[45] They met when Holiday was in Los Angeles in the late 1940s. He writes in *Beneath the Underdog*:

> Oh, there's no way to describe how my boy feels when he's all tied up inside digging the mood conjured up by a Lady in Philharmonic Hall singing to an audience that's with her every note and innuendo and someone calls a tune that's great and Lady Soul who has already blessed the entire evening with her presence says, "You got it, Mingus, what's your 'Sophisticated Lady' like tonight?" Just pure music, no funny clothes or trick effects, 'cause Lady's elegant in dress and manner and mind. She *is* the song and the people are pleased and show it with their Bravos! and Encores! (314)

Holiday hired Mingus as a sideman. He claimed she also advised him on becoming a pimp: "Billie Holiday. Charles remembered when he had written a song for her—'Eclipse'—and, how did it happen?—she'd given him a madam's phone number" (210). I would venture to say Mingus meant the story as a compliment. Dissonant and octave-stretching, "Eclipse" is a modern take on the idea of the blues for a singer often associated with the blues, though they were not her métier. Although Holiday never recorded "Eclipse," she figured in Mingus's pantheon as one of the great jazzmen. As he said of another composition written as a portrait of someone he admired, perhaps "Eclipse" represented not a desire to actually write a song that person would sing, but one which would show how he liked "feeling about her."[46]

Black feminist scholars and new jazz historians such as Angela Davis, Farah Jasmine Griffin, and Eric Porter have steadily reexamined Billie Holiday's image, seeking to understand Holiday as an intellectual, an artist concerned with politics and protest, and as a woman making choices about her career and personal life. These scholars do not claim to speak for her; indeed, Farah Jasmine Griffin's work is an explicit refusal to assume Holiday's voice. Instead, they are concerned with interrogating the contexts she lived in, the contexts in which she was racialized and gendered. Rather than the victimized singer of torch songs, Holiday emerges in their work as a complex individual negotiating a number of discourses and social constraints, with "Strange Fruit" marking a creative crossroads. In choosing to sing an elegiac about a burned black body, lynched in the South, Holiday draws upon a tradition of protest within black musical practice and effects a new "stylization" in her performances, revealing the extent to which jazz singing requires as much "thought" and "art" as does the music created by male instrumentalists.[47]

Both Mingus's appreciation of Holiday and Holiday's own approach to her work offer us entry into how women were navigating jazz as performers with ambition, provide critical perspectives on the conditions of their work and the environment it occurred in, and shed light on the personal relationships formed and shaped by their music. Holiday's experiences reflect the varieties of the (black) masculine enacted in jazz culture, performance, and discourse. Like other women in jazz, Holiday assumes characteristics of jazzmasculinity as a creatively empowering source for self-expression and political engagement. She shows, as Judith Halberstam's theory of female masculinity suggests, that jazzmasculinity is a habitable space both theoretically and experientially for women. Instead of presuming that only men can perform masculinity, Halberstam demands, "Rather, why not ask whether . . . anyone can do it better? Why not detail the forms of masculinity that emerge from the project of disentangling maleness, manhood, and masculinity."[48]

Holiday's example illustrates the trouble women present to the neat categories of genre, genius, and authenticity that have so dominated various disciplinary approaches to jazz history. In the experiences of women like Holiday, we also gain another vantage on the sway of black jazzmasculinity on those who found in jazz a vehicle for self-expression and political engagement. As I will demonstrate in chapter 4, women such as Hazel Scott adopted a fluid conception of what it meant to be both race women and jazzmen. Much like Mingus's fractured self, women who were jazzmen embraced the conflicting demands of racial authenticity and loyalty, emotion and genius, and masculinity and femininity as essential to their identities as artists.

Mary Lou Williams offers just one example of how a woman can choose to perform masculinity in better ways than some men, and how that choice neither diminishes nor negates her identity as a black woman. Williams modeled herself on Lovie Austin, whose performance of jazzmasculinity inspired her at a critical creative juncture. Williams recalled her "surprise and thrill to see a woman sitting in the pit with four or five other male musicians, with her legs crossed, cigarette in her mouth, playing the show with her left hand and writing music with her right hand for the next act to come on the stage."[49] Williams acknowledged the gendering discourses of jazz culture and subverted them by describing her own style as a performer and composer as masculine. She embraced "masculine characteristics" such as discipline, strength, experimentation, and endurance as fundamental to her identity as a composer and instrumentalist.[50] In her self-conception, Mary Lou Williams seems to embody jazzmasculinity in that she "refuses the authentication of masculinity through maleness and maleness alone, and . . . names a deliberately counterfeit masculinity that undermines the currency of masculinity."[51] In other words, Williams's jazzmasculinity depends not on a desire to be seen as male, but on a desire to embody the characteristics of masculinity that are valued within her chosen community. Even as she embraces the unavoidable fact of masculinity's privilege within jazz, she values and commits to the terms of creativity, skill, and respect demanded of jazzmen.

Halberstam notes that heteronormative masculinity "exhibits some anxiety about the status of its own realness: male masculinity as an identity seems to demand authentication: Am I real? Is my masculinity real? The fact that male masculinities of all kinds seem to require recognition of some kind also has the counterintuitive effect of marking their instability and their distance from the real."[52] The emotional realness of male jazzmen can seem directly proportional to the "realness" of their masculinity—their virility, their aggressiveness, their sexuality, and their class roots. A female jazzman's emotionality challenges that certainty by steering the language of authenticity away from the persistent association with men's experience and performance. Masculinity, suggests Halberstam, does not describe behaviors that only "real" men can do, but rather identifies the traits associated with it, which are performable regardless of gender, sexual orientation, or biology. In exploring what Halberstam calls "minority forms of masculinity," I will show how musicians like Hazel Scott do jazzmasculinity better than other critics admit. Despite the studied femininity of her appearance, Scott's performance technique was aggressive and muscular; her attitude toward the music was to dominate it, to control and shape it into her own image. This insistence on nonconformity was a rejection of attempts to pigeonhole her into the limited frameworks of sexuality and desire available to female performers. When we understand that what is prized about male jazzmen often are their specific ways of representing social ideals or performance techniques or marginalized voices, we recognize how well, if not better, some women do jazzmasculinity.

Jazzmen like Scott composed their experiences as women through negotiating the expectations of jazz culture, on stage and off. They were politically conscious individuals who understood competing narratives—embracing some, rejecting others—about femininity, emotional truth, masculine authority, and authenticity in definitions of jazz genius. By exploring the power structures[53] in their conditions of performance—including the ways in which women related to one another through their work as musicians, generating gender-specific narratives centered on youth and sophistication, protection and vulnerability, radicalism and racism—we enrich our understanding of how women's genius is represented and defined.[54] Representations of female musicians, as Susan McClary argues, expose the conflict between their musical personas and competing political agendas about racial and gender propriety (in other words their race womanhood).[55] Their experiences illustrate how discourses around music are "where the ongoing work of social formation occurs."[56] Parsing the application of the language of emotion and affect by and on female musicians, underscores how embodied experiences shape the imaginative structures we all use to make sense of the world and our place within it.[57]

Often the route into female jazzmen's experiences is through their marginalization by male jazzmen, from musicians to critics to fans, who may have embraced the "exceptional" performer like Mary Lou Williams, but on the whole preferred consigning women to the role of bit players.[58] This marginalization reveals how difference shapes the contours of the jazz world. Difference gives meaning to who is included and excluded, to who is and is not capable of expressing feeling. Authenticity and sincerity are the provenance of men, while women are relegated to adornment and mimicry. Women are the defining Other in the homosocial jazz world, a notion striking for "the ambiguity of men reproducing men without women," as Hazel Carby observed.[59] Eric Porter notes the irony of the culture's historical roots among female blues singers, explaining that against those roots an "ethos of male camaraderie provided refuge from the outside world, a model for behavior on the bandstand, and an ethos for artistic growth in a friendly yet competitive atmosphere."[60]

Homosociality is the competitive context for ethical behavior as well as the gendered aesthetic shaping the artist's creative choices and growth. In the postwar period, the racialization of that context intensified. As Ruth Feldstein writes, "African American musical virtuosity . . . implicitly equated cultural creativity with masculinity. . . . White audiences especially regarded this as a countercultural or oppositional masculinity. Gendered meanings of jazz infused the music with an avant-garde radicalism *and* with associations to a modernist universal high culture in ways that seemed to preclude women."[61] Racial and gender difference are politicized cultural markers affecting who is heard and how they are listened to. Some female jazzmen thrived in this homosocial culture by embracing the aggression, competition, arrogance, discipline, and creativity associated with men—and, at times, "doing" it better than men.

An explicitly gendered study of jazz that appreciates women's experiences alongside those of men, also asks, "What is it . . . that the listener is being invited to desire and why?"[62] To understand how the listener characterizes what she comprehends from the performance, we have to understand how artists negotiated the expectations for their performances as musicians and as women. We find answers to these concerns in seemingly unlikely places, those that appear tangential to the core concerns of the jazz public. Sherrie Tucker explains that, to understand the relevance of those experiences, we must link them to those of women not in jazz culture, discuss how women saw themselves at the center of jazz culture, and look to the conditions of work women encounter as they seek to make a livelihood in a culture that limits their opportunities.[63] Accordingly, I devote significant attention to exploring the role Celia Mingus played in managing their independent label, Debut, in the 1950s. For both Celia and Charles Mingus, the label was a claim for independence, security, and opportunity. The conditions of work she encountered as label owner (like those Hazel Scott experienced as a musician) were framed by real-world politics, including the movements for Civil Rights and integration, anticommunism, and changes in postwar beliefs about dissent, difference, and equality. Female jazzmen negotiated all of these contexts as they shaped the sounds that drew listeners in and represented their experiences. How did they succeed in that creative world? What sexual and gender politics are troubled or reinscribed when a woman is a leader on the jazz scene?[64] These questions shape my reading of Hazel Scott's and Celia Mingus's significance for identifying female jazzmasculinity as key to the postwar experience of racialized masculinity in jazz culture.

Jazz is a narrative, a performance in word and text representing layers of sound, emotion, and reason. Often jazz writing is about polemic and mythology. But it should be about the way we make meaning out of jazz as a site of identification and creativity. The way we talk about jazz tells us about much more than the music. That talk reveals the values we draw as communities tied together by an art whose emotional compass ranges from hot to cool, groovy to cerebral, traditional to the avant-garde. Mingus's story pushes us to consider the stories not often told about representations of masculinity, beauty, and artistic mastery. Mingus creates an opening for female jazzmen—like myself, like Hazel Scott, like Celia Mingus—to acknowledge why we continue to love jazz and jazzmen even when our experiences are often marginalized. By telling part of Hazel Scott's and Celia Mingus's story alongside that of Mingus, I show how both men and women were struggling to retain their integrity as they aspired to the heights of music.

ONE

"Self-Portrait in Three Colors"

Emotional Life in *Beneath the Underdog*

Dear Charles,

Actually, I don't know how to start these few lines but its for sure I hopes that you are well, and doing fine! . . . I got a message from Vivian through Phillip that you have quit working! (that is with your music) going around with something in your hair to make it much nappy and saying that you are an African! I told Vivian Phillip is a big Lie! He lies period! Please tell me it isn't so!!! No! I'm not just writing because of this I heard somehow I just had to mention it. However he also told her about the autobiography that you are writing of your life which I think is wonderful! Because I really don't think anyone could tell about our life as well as you. . . .

Love your sis Grace

"In other words, I am three. One man stands forever
in the middle, unconcerned, unmoved, watching, waiting to be
allowed to express what he sees to the other two. The second man is like
a frightened animal that attacks for fear of being attacked. Then there's an
over-loving gentle person who lets people into the uttermost sacred temple
of his being and he'll take insults and be trusting and sign contracts without
reading them and get talked down to working cheap or for nothing, and
when he realizes what's been done to him he feels like killing and destroying
everything around him including himself for being so stupid.
But he can't—he goes back inside himself."
"Which one is real?"
"They're all real."
Charles Mingus Jr.

In 1971, the year he won his first Guggenheim fellowship for musical composition, Charles Mingus Jr. released his much anticipated (at least by him) autobiography, *Beneath the Underdog*. He started writing it in the late fifties, reportedly inspired by the publication of Billie Holiday's *Lady Sings the Blues* (1956). Holiday was one of Mingus's favorites; he composed "Eclipse" (1953) for her and recorded it with singer Janet Thurlow on his Debut record label and with Honey Gordon on the live recording, *Charles Mingus and Friends*.

Holiday's book had been crafted from conversations between Holiday and William Dufty, a reporter for the *New York Post* who was married to her good friend Maely Dufty, herself a jazz booster.[1] The opening lines of *Lady Sings the Blues* are a lie: "Mom and Pop were just a couple of kids when they got married. He was eighteen, she was sixteen, and I was three."[2] In truth, Holiday's mother was the elder of the two and the pair never married. The conviction with which Holiday casts these "facts" as the origins of her narrative whets our appetite for reading between the lines as she details her life with blues-inflected emotionality, including stories of prostitution, sexual molestation, heroin addiction, love affairs, Jim Crow, and the music.

Norman Granz used *Lady Sings the Blues* to stage Holiday's 1956 comeback at Carnegie Hall, blending text and song in an expertly produced show of emotion. He later released a live recording of the concert in which Gilbert Millstein, who wrote for the *New York Times*, reads excerpts from the book while Holiday sings standards like "Good Morning Heartache" and "Fine and Mellow." Audiences and critics applauded the performance as her most riveting in recent memory, leading many to hope that she had turned a corner in her personal life. But Holiday died in 1959, claiming never to have read the book. Despite her disavowal, the book nevertheless persists as a testament to her "real"-life "blues."

David Ritz, ghostwriter of autobiographies for artists such as Ray Charles and Marvin Gaye, characterizes the veracity of Holiday's *Blues* as, "in the mythopoetic sense . . . as true and poignant as any tune she ever sang. If her music was autobiographically true, her autobiography was musically true."[3] For Farah Jasmine Griffin, *Lady Sings the Blues* "is not a song, but a series of them; it is a carefully constructed performance of a life. A realist (not realistic) portrait of the 'jazz artist.'"[4] Both Ritz and Griffin allude to the importance of performance in transforming a jazzman into a subject for writing.[5] Whether assisted by an amanuensis or not, jazzmen script stories of their life experiences through layered enactments of gender and racial knowledge, troubling perceptions of truth in jazz culture, and documenting the work of making music. In composing autobiography, jazzmen integrate the emotional sources of their creativity, an understanding of their audiences, and a desire to tell a story.

Mingus's *Beneath the Underdog* is the paradigmatic realist self-portrait of the black jazzman. It is also the rare example of a jazz autobiography written by the musician alone.[6] Through a full-throated improvisation of narrative authority, revealing "slipperiness, mobility, and inventive flexibility," Mingus navigates the restrictions of authenticity marking him as a black jazzman.[7] Composing the memoir over the course of more than a decade, Mingus expands the boundaries of feeling in jazz autobiography by embracing uncertainty, multiplicity, and vulnerability. He portrays himself as always in a state of becoming. He opens the story in the middle of a session with his therapist, deluging us with images of a subject irreparably split. To tell his story, he embraces those multiple selves, unconcerned with one identity dominating the others. The book's continual shifting between subject positions shapes the narrative as both a critique of the autobiographical form and a challenge to the jazz public to acknowledge its role in the music's performance. Mingus explores racialized masculinity through stories about becoming a musician and the relative failure of jazz to transcend race.

In this chapter I begin by discussing how *Beneath the Underdog* is structured, paying particular attention to how Mingus uses the narrative frame of talk therapy, allowing him to shift back and forth in time as he scrutinizes his experience. Despite the criticisms leveled at *Beneath the Underdog* as embracing an "emasculating masculinity,"[8] one that is sexually aggressive and vengeful, I see Mingus as offering a nuanced composition of his emotional landscape using chords of racial alienation, creativity, and individuality to write a discourse on love: fraternal, familial, and sexual; jealous and obscene; faithful and adoring; disappointing and dreamy. In his excesses, ribald humor, and confessions, Mingus walks the line between what is real and what is imagined, what is documentable and what is laughable. In his book, Mingus discloses the conflicting demands associated with pursuing a career as a musician, the personal relationships built and lost, as well as the toll of racism. *Beneath the Underdog* insists that the reader be a witness to the real in Mingus's experience of being a black male jazz musician, and his upending of signifiers of racial authenticity extends to those about masculinity.

Mingus's preoccupation with sexuality was a frequent target of critics who reviewed the book. I pay particular attention to these critics' narrow construction of black masculinity and their reluctance to view themselves as part of the performance that Mingus constructs. *Beneath the Underdog* reminds us that we must complete the musical event by remodeling social behaviors and imagining new ways of being in the world.

Mingus envisioned his autobiography as a composition, a representation of his world; to read *Beneath the Underdog* is to witness a performance of race, masculinity, and music. Not content to put on a standard performance, Mingus interprets the "reticences, repressions and distortions"—as W. E. B. DuBois advocated in *Dusk of Dawn*—that constituted his life.[9] Mingus digs deep into the telling: "What do I care what the world sees, I'm trying to find out how I should feel about myself" (3). In his effort to understand his experience, he rejects the idea that he must conform to expectations of how that story should be told. Mingus's clarity about his objective in writing *Beneath the Underdog*, a wildly imaginative, borderless, multivocal composition, embodies what Elizabeth Alexander defines as the black interior: "what . . . we learn when we pause at sites of contradiction where black creativity complicates and resists what blackness is 'supposed' to be." The black interior is a profoundly self-reflective and therapeutic space, a radical site for affirming black personhood, genius, and emotion. As Alexander explains, it is the "one place where we go to make sense" of "the world's ills."[10]

To tell his musical story, Mingus writes his emotional story, one that derives from the experiences of three selves embodying, respectively, ambivalence, fear, and gentleness. He depicts his journey into manhood as an often-thwarted search for avenues of honest expression, beset by racism. Emotionality not only grounds his musical compositions and performances, but also informs his performance of jazzmasculinity. With his gender and racial identity in constant tension, the tumultuousness of his private world provides a source of creativity. Through the artifice of these multiple selves, Mingus details how he negotiates public perceptions of black masculinity while trying to achieve mastery over himself and his instrument. These elements of *Beneath the Underdog* improvise on conventional ideas about jazz as an expression of masculine and racial authenticity, as well as on our notions of emotional truth and truth-telling in jazz composition and performance.

"BACKGROUND FOR THOUGHT"

An involved bit of writing, far too confusing to be digested at one hearing,
and even intricate enough to call for a halt by Mingus and then a fresh start.

George T. Simon

Don Juan Mingus . . . , Mingus as lightweight Iceberg Slim . . . ,
Mingus the son, Mingus the husband, Mingus the father, Mingus the comic
sufferer on the psychiatrist's couch, ranting about the Jews who buy and sell
black musicians, pouring out his soul to his Jewish analyst.

Al Young

The Negro is not. Anymore than the white man.

Frantz Fanon[11]

Loosely structured as a dialogue with a fictionalized psychologist named "Dr. Wallach," Mingus's published memoir is an abridged version of a manuscript he had been writing for nearly twenty years, chronicling his life from 1924 to some undefined point in the late 1950s to the mid-1960s. Unconcerned with providing either a linear narrative or the standard revelations about a musician's life, Mingus blends memories, thoughts, people, music, and politics into a seamless though chaotic concert. The fantastic events that characterize the memoir's excesses—libidinal, musical, spiritual, and gastronomical—mark Mingus's individuality.[12] Through these excesses, Mingus defines desire (musical, sexual, emotional) as central to his own experience.

By alternating between three writing selves, which he asserts "are all real," Mingus manipulates tropes of black masculinity to interrogate his limited privilege as a black man and to document the instability of black masculinity as an identity. He imagines black men not just as desired objects of mimicry and spectatorship,[13] but as desiring subjects. He asserts an identity that is self-determining and self-reflective, conscious of how social relationships are lived, negotiated, and transformed, and cognizant of the intersections between "power, identity, and social subjectivity."[14] My reading of Mingus's "most involved bit of writing" looks closely at how this representative jazzman negotiated the structures of feeling that shaped postwar jazz culture.

Mingus the master time-keeper conducts *Beneath the Underdog* along multiple time registers, each with a different beginning, each challenging the role the jazzman plays in discourses about jazz and racial authenticity, criticism, the music business, and gender. Though Mingus is looking back on his life, he uses the different registers as ways to be present in the telling. The first register finds Mingus in a therapy session with Wallach. (We eavesdrop on this particular session throughout the book.) Mingus's "strategic performance of confession"[15] reveals him to be vulnerable, manipulative, and defensive. Though Mingus is being "analyzed," he steers the analysis, pulling Wallach along in a tumultuous story of redemption, excess, and music. Toward the end of the book, Wallach interrupts Mingus, asking questions that break his stream of consciousness and reminding us that Mingus's search for answers is mediated by the doctor-patient relationship.

In alternate registers, Mingus explores how race, spirituality, and sexuality shaped his family life, musical relationships, and ideas about masculinity. He recounts the story of his childhood and youth in Watts, where he falls in love with girls and with music, makes friends, and learns to fight. In one long register, we encounter Mingus coming into his own as a musician, becoming a father, and searching for a father figure—a search that represents the enduring conflict he experiences among the paternal, spiritual, and religious. He shifts registers to document the events leading to his arrival on the New York jazz scene—where he endures such doubt and insecurity that he commits himself for psychiatric observation at Bellevue. This stay in the hospital reveals that the greater danger facing Mingus was not a society fixated on repressing the expression of a free black consciousness, but his own acceptance of society's limitations.

Beneath the Underdog is as much an exhumation of the self as it is a representation. Tracing his birth, death, and rebirth as a black jazzman, Mingus explores questions of fidelity to God, to spouse, and to band members. He begins at the moment of his first resurrection, stating emphatically that, in this place, "1621 East One Hundred and Eighth Street in the City of Watts in Los Angeles County in the State of California," a child who hovered between life and death was saved. Mingus's birth had been cause for celebration, he "was the boy they'd longed for in the family" (9). Like Duke Ellington and Jelly Roll Morton, musicians from whom he felt descended, he is the darling for whom "the whole world, the whole world is waiting to sing (his) song."[16] As Mingus's sister Vivian recalled, "Charles was it. . . . Mama was crazy about Charles. . . . Charles would carry the Mingus name."[17]

And yet, despite the reverence with which his family greeted his birth, they refuse to see him clearly: "[T]hey loved him like a puppy. He was becoming a person and no one took notice" (10). Mingus gradually becomes aware that despite his privileged status in the family, he is nevertheless burdened by their needs and hopes. They expect him to perform masculinity in a way that ill suits him. Chafing against those expectations, the young Mingus cracks. He becomes conscious of himself as split, caught between experience and emotion, thought and performance. At this juncture, Mingus relays the story of his two-year-old self's near fatal injury. While playing with his sister, "Baby" falls, "his head split wide open on the corner of a Goodwill-store old-fashioned second-hand-me-down white-folks' bedroom-set dresser" (8).

As Baby lies unconscious, blood gushing from his wound, Mingus levitates out of Baby's body and surveys the small family drama, coming to realize "how important the little fellow was. Everybody got so upset" (8). Baby is rushed to the hospital in Daddy's Chevrolet sedan, his parents and sisters crying and praying all the way.

> But though they had so much faith in this guy named God, Baby wouldn't respond. I decided to go back inside and take over until he could get himself together. No one seemed to notice as I climbed up on the white table where Baby was laid out and materialized myself into the big hole over his left eye. Just to console everybody, I breathed deep and exhaled and Baby let out his first scream since early that morning when Grace had tickled his stomach till it hurt. . . . I started to leave again when the family did but Baby had hold of me now and was hanging on for dear life, so I stayed with him and I've been with him ever since. (9)

Mingus resurrects Baby, breathing into his lungs, comforting and protecting him throughout his life. He describes similar mystic powers later in the book as well ("He felt he was able to touch people, to contact certain souls in the next room or miles away or even those who had died"), and notes that he and artist Farwell Taylor "often experienced a mysterious awareness of each other while in different parts of the world" (57). This Mingus exercises godlike powers, prescient enough to know he will have to mediate between the spirit and the body as Baby heals and matures. That body will remain a source of pain and recovery, a site of both injury and the self-knowledge that arises from its healing. Recognizing how little his life's external expectations jibe with his selfhood, as undefined as it was at that young age, he associates that selfhood with divinity. As he grows older, he questions the idea of "God" even as he embraces spirituality, morality, and love as guiding principles. Music becomes the ultimate articulation of selfhood and creativity.

Mingus claimed that his book was really a religious work. While he was certain that divinity existed, he was skeptical of his family's fervent religiosity. In the narrative, their convictions impede their ability to recognize "Mingus" as an individual. Nevertheless, he yearns to discover where he fits in the spectrum from good to evil: "He figures he must be somewhere in between Jesus and the Devil—closer to the Devil but unable to perform a perfectly evil act" (55).

Musician Jack Kelso remembers encountering a Mingus who was "searching and looking, desperately looking," when Kelso returned from World War II. "He was talking about the big questions of life—religion, God, philosophy."[18] Kelso and Mingus shared an impulse to explore "their personal understanding of themselves in relation to creation" (119). Mingus developed bonds with men like Kelso and Taylor because of their mutual desire for a life of creative expression. They nurtured one another even as their ambitions put them in competition for recording and performance opportunities. Their compassion provided Mingus with a sense of safety and encouragement when he doubted himself and the path he had taken. "So my boy worked, studied and meditated, and though it seemed this was the lowest ebb of his life it was a time of development" (183).

Mingus's persistent striving to achieve a better, more mastered self provides the ethical core of *Beneath the Underdog*. The book is a statement about his struggles to overcome his own moral failings. Reviewing the impact of his actions on himself and others remained a steady source of anxiety and contemplation for Mingus. According to Nat Hentoff, this makes the book resemble his music "not only in its explosive honesty but in its insistent focus on trying to find a personal morality."[19] Mingus depicts the jazz scene as a spiritual minefield, rife with economic and racial challenges to an individual's integrity. He questions whether a career in music is advisable for jazzmen who are sensitive to racial injustice, especially considering the case of trumpeter Theodore "Fats" Navarro, with whom he felt particularly close. "He was the one who deep down understood me most clearly, I now believe, and I dug him too. We didn't see too much of each other during his lifetime but every time we talked it counted and it may be he was the closest friend I ever had" (355).

The depiction of Fats Navarro, like other portraits in the book, is both based on a real person and a construction of what was real about him. Navarro is revealed as a kindred spirit, someone willing to fight for respect, a key tactic for surviving as a spiritually whole jazzman. He and Mingus meet while play-ing in the Lionel Hampton Orchestra. Echoing the circumstances of Mingus's own firing from Duke Ellington's band, when he chased Juan Tizol around the bandstand with a fire extinguisher, Navarro, Mingus tells us, draws a switch-blade against a musician who doubted his facility with sight-reading (185–87). His knife-wielding stands in stark contrast to the feminizing terms with which he has been described by other musicians; nicknamed "Fat Girl" because of his weight and his "strange wispy voice, like that of a querulous girl," Navarro was a "sort of a cherub, big fat jaws and a big stomach, and he was so young." Dizzy Gillespie thought of him as "sweet. He was like a little baby." Other musicians remarked upon his "almost feminine concern for the welfare of his friends."[20] Like Mingus, his contradictions make him attractive.

In his conversation with Dr. Wallach, Mingus uses Navarro to show how comparatively well-adjusted he is in the jazz world. Mingus sees Navarro as trapped by the "death wish" common to black jazzmen who despaired of "the whole American scene [which] seemed like hell" (120). Navarro intimates that he turns to heroin to cope with despair and, because the addiction provides no relief, has purposely contracted tuberculosis to end his misery. Like Mingus, Navarro believes that the white men who own "the magazines, agencies, record companies and all the joints that sell jazz to the public" are determined to silence him. "If you won't sell out and you try to fight they won't hire you and they give a bad picture of you with that false publicity" (188). Death is preferable to the silencing he is experiencing in (and because of) jazz. Mingus identifies with the depression Navarro feels, but believes that through faith in the self and the music, one can resist falling into a bottomless pit of despair and anxiety. This faith has helped him escape the death wish many times (119–23).

Mingus urges Navarro to embrace spirituality. When Navarro asks who is God, Mingus replies, "Bird without wings, motherfucker! Bird!" (362). In Mingus's theology, God is manifest in the passionate creation of music. In Charlie Parker, he perceives the continual striving toward that perfect note as faith in its even-tual expression. This saving grace of the music, Bird's commitment to working toward creative expression, provides a balm to despair and manifests his divinity.

Mingus warns Navarro that his attempt at suicide will create more damage than it prevents. "If you know there's no God then you have the power of God. There's no need to kill yourself—*think* yourself to death." He believes he can save Navarro just as he saved Baby. "But it's lucky for you *I* believe, 'cause you come here with a suicide complex like that's original and you weigh one hundred and ten pounds and I could oblige your wish in seconds. But I know that's wrong, I know I was born an extension of life itself" (361). Mingus offers Navarro a vision of faith defined by an ethic of love and support between men, and an understanding of the music as a reflection of a higher sense of self and duty. Though Mingus persuades Navarro that love is "where it is" (366), Navarro is too far gone to turn the death wish around. This inability to save Navarro reinforces Mingus's desire to see his music as more than a way to make a living. Jazz is soul-sustaining; spirituality—and its reflection in music—ground Mingus as an individual.

Though he nurtures an inner belief in the power of his spirituality to guide him as a black jazzman, Mingus knows he must confront the soul-murdering effects of racism by delving into the lessons imparted by his father about being a black man. Charles Mingus Sr. left an indelible impression on his son's ideas about race, sexuality, and masculinity. Though Mingus Sr.'s imposing personality seems to have left little room for a close relationship (Mingus describes being regularly beaten by his father), he supported his son's musical ambitions and helped him navigate the terrain of growing up as a black male child in a segregated city. From his father, Mingus develops tactics for respecting himself and challenging racism even as he discovers that his father's staunch sense of self didn't preclude him expressing racial biases.

Working through his feelings toward his father, Mingus adds nuance to his emotionally complex definition of black masculinity and his ideas about racial belonging. To be a black man was to be marked as sexually threatening to white people, regardless of age, color, or class. Virility was to be prized, but its expression would always be judged against stereotypes imposed on black men. White people would punish any transgression, real or not. Black communities were no different. They embraced distinctions of color and class, reflecting white biases. Nevertheless, Mingus Sr. did not intend his son to be diminished by the limitations levied by those stereotypes. *Beneath the Underdog* shows the scars obtained in navigating those psychological and emotional land mines. And as the healing takes place in smaller, subtler phases, the stories of injury become increasingly fantastic.

Mingus Sr. retired from the U.S. Army after twenty-seven years of service, and spent the rest of his working life at the post office, entrenching the Mingus family in the black middle class. An unrepentant race man of a certain genus, Mingus Sr. expresses contempt for those blacks who pass for white for economic security (23) even as he acknowledges that he passed "whenever it seemed like a good idea" (129). He understood light skin as a marker of privilege, and passing (in limited circumstances) meant he was in control of the racial dynamics. Grace recalls that many people at the post office thought her father was white, which allowed him to advocate for the black workers. "I think he was an activist," she says; "he didn't like to see the black misused."[21] Even so, "He taught race prejudice to his children—said they were better than others because they were lighter in color. Grace was hurt when Daddy said this and she cried and complained that by his teaching she was the lowest one in the family because she was the darkest" (26). The impact on Grace was so great that she spent years not believing she was her father's child. She also remembers not being allowed to play with the other children in the neighborhood. "We had to sit on the porch and watch them. Charles too. Daddy didn't allow it. . . . Daddy didn't want us to play with the little black niggers down the street." According to Vivian, their father felt that their own company was sufficient.[22]

While the Mingus children were playing "blackest one in the family," Mingus's stepmother, sometimes taken for Mexican and, according to Mingus, believing herself to be part Indian appears to have been alternately loved and reviled, her beauty diminished by her country manners and her dark skin. Grace describes her as an attractive woman who would "fix herself up"; Vivian remembers her as having lots of moles, with a "high nose" as evidence of her Indian heritage. She was good to the children and they loved her, despite her snuff-dipping.[23] Nevertheless, Mamie is recognized as Other, both in the family and in the neighborhood. "The kids all laughed as they passed and [Mingus] didn't know if it was at him or his mother, who had taken off her work clothes and put on her Sunday go-to-meetin's for this occasion. He had overheard Daddy saying, 'Take that damned snuff out of your mouth! And don't dress so damn sloppy. You ain't fit for a pig to come home to!' It had to be true, Daddy was next to God and even sometimes told God what to do: 'God *damn* it!' he'd say when he got good and angry" (11).

Though severe, Mingus Sr. was a fiercely protective father. He understood that despite their youth, his children would be viewed through the lens of racial and gender stereotypes. Mingus describes his first awareness of himself as a sexual threat when four-year-old Baby is caught "pouring nice hot sand down inside his pants because it felt so good," and he is called a "SEX PERVERT." He's also called "a nasty thing" after "sitting on a bench at lunchtime, peeking around a corner of the schoolhouse, watching the girls and making eyes" (12–13). Later, after accusing him of looking up a little girl's dress, school officials rough him up. Unsure of what he has done wrong, Baby waits anxiously for his father, who has been called to the principal's office. When he arrives, Mingus Sr. challenges the official account and demands that the principal and truant officer recreate the playground incident, with himself in the role of Mingus Jr. With the alleged crime scene reconstructed and the maltreatment of his son exposed, Mingus Sr. rages at the other adults. "Now, you red-necked son-of-a-bitch. . . . You low trash, wasting my time bringing me down here! Lay a hand on my son again and I'll kick your ass all over this county of Watts!" (16). Mingus Sr., the real angry man in Mingus's life story, refuses to let his son be a victim. Because of his father's efforts to protect him, though, Mingus's innocence is shattered. The anxiety with which he will later cast sex and sexuality seem rooted in experiences like this.

Mingus attributes his father's rage to thwarted ambition. He was a "sick (man), frustrated at a life spent in the post office when he'd trained to be an architect and confused in many ways" (26). Mingus sees this frustration as grounded in the legacy of slavery. He recalls Mingus Sr.'s relish in recounting a fantastic tale, marking the family as "authentically" black. Their surname, according to Mingus Sr., was "one of the few real African names" (128) in the country and his own father had been in love with "Abe [Lincoln's] cousin and she with him. No one knew about this and they were never caught" (128). Although he had benefited from the whiteness of his skin (he felt "just like a Southern white man, the way I was raised!"), Mingus Sr. claimed "it don't make no difference to me any more. It took all these seventy-six years to find out it's all so much hogwash. Isn't that the way I told it to you, son, when you was little? 'Cause that's the truth" (129). Mingus understands these stories as the boastings of an elderly man who looks on his life not just with regret, but also with pleasure. Eventually, he will come to his own conclusions about why race is "all so much hogwash."

Steering through the multiethnic community of Watts, the young Mingus searches for allies and guardians. Feeling emotionally distant from his father, Mingus finds other father figures, among them his friend Buddy Collette's father, who taught him how to train women to give him money.[24] He discovered that a willingness to fight bonded him to the other young men who liked to box and lift weights on neighborhood playgrounds. The pianist Coney Woodman recalled being a member of a youth gang, called the Tarzans, who were all musicians, loved sports, and liked to fight. "Everybody liked us, and we socialized with everybody. . . . Mingus, he liked to try to fight all the time. He wanted to fight everybody, man. We'd just look at him and laugh, because we could whoop him."[25] Fighting was about posturing, preening for other guys, and attracting women. Fighting masked self-doubt, the desire for revenge, and efforts to control the expression of both feelings.

Mingus took up fighting because bullies targeted him relentlessly. As another friend recalls, "Kids used to make fun of him. They used to take his lunch from him; they used to tease him."[26] At first, the unskilled Mingus preferred running away. Then the sons of the neighborhood Japanese grocer took pity on him and began teaching him judo. When his usual tormentor, Teddy, next challenged him, Mingus thrashed him, but restrained himself from beating "the life out of the punk" (55). Caught between worrying about the salvation of his soul and feeling shame at the inordinate pleasure he took in demonstrating his physical prowess, he holds back. But Mingus would not always suppress his desire to trounce his opponent. The desire to fight back—"one coordinate of [his] identity that exists in a constant dialectical relation with other coordinates"[27]—wards off the shame of being seen as less than a man in the eyes of other men and women. Although "That fear is almost gone" (55), Mingus's struggle to overcome humiliation persists in the stories of his rage against the limitations placed on him because of race.

According to Mingus, part of the challenge of bringing people together, of encouraging them to express their higher nature in regard to one another, was the problem of race as a signifier for belonging and a measure of individual character. The inability to overcome those deeply ingrained social concepts would vex and exasperate him throughout his life. "Charles," the figure in *Beneath the Underdog* who represents Mingus in early adulthood, believes his blackness lacks racial integrity; it is of everything and nothing, devalued and segregated, celebrated and maligned, of his body and not. "Whenever he looked in the mirror and asked 'What am I?' he thought he could see a number of strains—Indian, African, Mexican, Asian and a certain amount of white from a source his father had boasted of. He wanted to be one or the other but he was a little of everything, wholly nothing, of no race, country, flag or friend" (66). Mingus desired inclusion within the black community, even though intraracial color politics positioned him as "the underdog because, well, he was kind of a mongrel, lighter than some but not light enough to belong to the almost-white elite and not dark enough to belong with the beautiful elegant blacks, the kind that make a man like Bud Powell say to Miles Davis, 'I wish I was blacker than you'" (65). Despite his efforts to fit in—from "burning his hair with his mother's hot-comb hair straightener to wetting it to make it kink up for the real beautiful natural dignified wiry and woolly look" (65)—he gained no traction. "The black hate in the air for Whitey was turned on him, a schitt-colored halfass yella phony" (65). Contrary to his father's experiences, his color provides him neither privilege nor security.

The rejection he experienced by white and black people led to his "running" with the other mongrels, "the few Japanese, Mexicans, Jews and Greeks at Jordan High." Their acceptance led Charles to seek a new way of being a black man: "He fell in love with himself." In doing so, Charles renounced "race" as a barometer of character—"I dig minds, inside and out. No race, no color, no sex. Don't show me no kind of skin 'cause I can see right through to the hate in your little undeveloped souls" (66). "I don't dig badges, skin colors, blood lines. I'm not using any of the rules" (131). Skin color does not correlate to an ability to nurture love, the trait so necessary for creating community, family, and music. Mingus, having witnessed Charles's travails, sympathizes with his decision to reject racial categories even as he laments the fact that Charles was too innocent to grasp the futility of such a strategy. "I understood what he was trying to do. I've met a few other people who live on that colorless island" (66).

Although "that colorless island" might have provided a temporary refuge from the emotional trauma imposed by racialized thinking, Mingus knows his body as a site of difference, violence, and *radical otherness.* According to philosopher Charles Johnson, radical otherness is the feeling that "I *am* my body while I am also *not* my body . . . I am conscious of the world through the medium of my body."[28] Mingus sees himself by looking through the eyes of others. The looking is a violent breach of his subjectivity, stripping him of the ability to give the experience of his body his own meaning. He experiences this breach as *epidermalization.* Johnson explains that as an individual responds to epidermalization, his sense of self "is violently emptied of content: one, in fact, draws a 'blank,' though clearly for the white Other my interiority is, if not invisible, a space filled with sensuality, crime, or childlike simplicity." Mingus rejects the denial of his self-defined interiority. He realizes "that this dark and light routine was all the bunk. Because if there's any 'Negro' in your ancestry you're a nigger to all greasers, redneck peckerwoods and like-minded folks whether you're coal black or yella like my boy or gray as the palest Caucasian with hazel eyes and sandy hair like Daddy and you better get to know it" (30).

The physiological feeling of epidermalization is of a subjective disorientation that is at times conflated with the expression of sexual desire. According to Johnson, the feeling "spreads throughout the body like an odor, like an echoing sound. This feeling differs little from that of sexuality: a sudden dizziness and disorientation, an acute awareness of my outside, of its being for others, a tight swell at my temples."[29] Discovering that sex and sexuality have been emptied of their substantive expression of racialized gender experience, Johnson suggests that black men seek other ways to cast those terms. Black men, he writes, fill those absences by assuming one or more of several roles, including the Trickster who "craftily use[s] this invisibility of [his] interior to deceive, and thus to win survival," the Cosmopolitan who "pretends that [he is] not Afro-American at all, but part Indian, Jamaican, or an African—a flight from the historical experience of American antebellum slavery in which epidermalization reaches its acme," or the Cultural Nationalist who is "radical, and seize(s) the situation at its root by reversing the negative meaning of the body" but, nevertheless relies upon meaning that "still issues from the white Other."[30] Despite these strategies, however, "the black body remains an ambiguous object . . . still susceptible to whatever meanings the white gaze assigns to it."[31] Mingus's distress over the ambiguity of his blackness finds him representing himself as all three figures—Trickster, Cosmopolitan, and Cultural Nationalist—because all three are real articulations of his experience.

Mingus depicts his early adolescent love affairs as the sources of his desire for a true, everlasting, romantic love. As he grows older and becomes more curious about sex, he relates stories about his sexual awakening. His experience of racialized masculinity is defined by his sexual relationships with women. Mingus's stories about his sexual escapades illustrate his understanding of how the white gaze has shaped black self-perception and the ways his body is marked by its radical otherness. As poet Elizabeth Alexander writes, "There is no escaping our bodies, even if we—or as we—transcend the limitations and drawbacks of racialized thinking."[32] Mingus chafed against the internalized colorism fostered by his father and within the black community, turning instead to the "mongrel" community of Watts. But the relationships Mingus built with other young men across race and ethnic lines did not preclude them from policing his sexual access to their female relatives. He realizes that his racial difference, the fact of his blackness, makes prohibitions against interracial sex inviolable. Ever the romantic, he "makes eyes" at an Irish girl, then fights with two Mexican boys to be her guy; the shame of his beating pales beside his realization that his sexual desire and his racial identity are in contention: "Losing his girl and becoming a nigger all in one day was too much" (27–28). Unable to bridge racial lines through the pursuit of a white girl, Mingus experiences his most deeply felt moment of belonging in the black community when he is with Rita, a "pure" and "pretty black." Rita pleases him by noting the size of his penis and favorably comparing the color of his "Taurus sacs" to her own complexion. "For the first time Charles felt completely accepted by a black Negro" (92). She sees him.

Mingus shares juvenile, ribald ramblings about his sexual prowess and the power he wields, sometimes viciously, sometimes reluctantly, because of it. His narrative preoccupation with sex and his awareness of the privileges afforded him intensifies as the book continues, provoking critic Hollie I. West to write, "The pornography keeps piling up until it becomes an inconsequential bore. Mingus is acting out a role, looking at the world from a phallic point of view. But inevitably he must face the problems of race."[33] Here West ignores Mingus's insistent focus on showing how sex and race are inextricably intertwined. Without proscriptions around sex, a "mongrel" like him would not suffer from racial exclusion; without racial bias, a man like him wouldn't be a mongrel.

After Mingus marries, the depth of his feeling for his wife Barbara provides an insufficient counter to his ambitious musical desires and sexual appetites. Mingus connects the problems in his first marriage with his admitted infidelities, with his musicking, and with the demands of nightclub owners. Over the course of several pages, he describes the events that lead to an epic scene of sexual excess. During the night of the Mexican whores (a scene that draws comment from most reviewers of the book), Mingus has sex with dozens of prostitutes over the course of two hours and remains willing and capable of going on. This testosterone-driven expression of control arose out of the vulnerability he felt working for a Southern white woman: Nesa Morgan, the owner of the nightclub where his trio was then performing.

When Morgan orders Mingus to come to her office, everybody knows what's on offer. "Watch out, Mingus. Her husband won't be in tonight and she's got on a tight red dress cut down to the titties, hanging just right to make a man think wrong and no drawers on showing pure ass. She said send *you* in and tell anyone else she's busy. Careful, friend" (163, emphasis in text). Mingus recounts the experience by evoking the cultural mythology of the black stud and the eager white woman. Masking the terror he felt behind sexual bravado, Mingus succumbs to Morgan's sexual demands. His decision affects his marriage, his security (both at work and physically), and his art.

Through dialogue, Mingus captures a scenario that would have resonated for black men and women living in a period when even a hint of interracial attraction could result in death. Mingus emphasizes black male vulnerability through a preoccupation with hypersexuality. To be afraid to be alone with a white woman, particularly one who paid him and his band members, is to reveal oneself as unmanly. Better to be sexually dominant and wrest financial and dialogical control away in representing the experience. As Nesa attempts to seduce him, he cries out, "Oh, Lord! I never thought I'd die this way, this far from the South. I'm married. I got sons." She responds, "That's why I want you. You ain't about to talk" (165). But he does talk: through his resentment of her calling him "nigger" and "boy"; his choice of lubricant ("flax seed" from the "waveset on the desk" [166]); his teasing performance designed to extend their pleasure; his growing awareness of how a pimp is born ("If you want a man and got to hide with him, something's got to compensate. This [taking money from her purse] will remind you you have to give up something too, dig? You play, you pay" (168); his admission that he is falling in love (again). He talks her to awareness that she has "pulled a dirty Southern thing" on him (169).

In the aftermath, Barbara announces that she is leaving him and taking their two sons. Unable to convince her to stay, Mingus despairs, asking his father to teach his boys the manly arts while he makes money to send back to them. Mingus takes a trip to Mexico with Nesa Morgan and two others. The infamous drunken, marijuana-filled orgy ensues. We next find him in San Francisco, where he "just had to get away. . . . in search of he didn't know what. . . . He wanted to make it alone without help from women or anyone else and he didn't want to have to go back to work for Nesa" (180–81). At this juncture, Mingus grapples with the demands of commitment and fidelity required by marriage. Despite his desire to be a family man, he is not prepared for it, due both to poor financial prospects and to immaturity. He admits to the attraction of some aspects of the nightlife scene, but is not ready to succumb completely. "Even if [Nesa's husband] looked the other way, to work in his clubs and take care of his household chores too just didn't appeal" (181).

Burdened by doubt in his ability to express himself through music, Mingus assumes the figure of the pimp to explore his competing motivations as a young man in search of love and a young musician seeking the fullest expression of his voice. The pimp is a foil for Mingus's insecurities, a mask for his deeply conservative desires. He yearns for respectability (as a musician, as a man, and for the women he loves); craves security (he wants to be tied to someone he can trust with the knowledge of his multiple selves, he wants a wife and family, he wants fellowship with other musicians); and above all he desires community (the fulfillment of the democratic promise of jazz). He believes that performing the pimp role makes it possible to expose the stereotype that black men are solely motivated by rapacious sexual appetites. It's not just because he's a man that he can become a pimp,[34] it is because he's a "Black Man" that he does. And it's because he's a "fat-ass half yella schitt-colored nigger!" (52) that he must.

Young Mingus is enthralled by Billie Bones, "The Black Prince of Pimps," who "said he was from the West Indies, spoke with some kind of accent, and looked like a dark-skinned Latin actor playing Gary Cooper playing a swinging bullfighter" (235). Mingus would love to be like Bones, sexually assertive, beautifully black, wealthy, self-confident. But Bones is also a deadened version of himself, a man who ignores his black interior, embracing white men's beliefs about what his body represents. When asked what he would do if he could live his life all over again, Mingus responds that he would become a bigger pimp than Billy Bones. "I wouldn't get involved with music or women at all, other than what they could do for me. My main motive for living would be getting money to buy my way out of a decaying society that's destroying itself while it tries to figure out what to do with the new kind of 'black' it produced. . . . I wouldn't believe in any bullschitt like 'love' and I wouldn't get involved with any woman who talked it. . . . I'd study bass for kicks, I wouldn't get involved in commercial competition" (353–54).

The pimp's alienation is the only way to be successful in a culture that devalues traits associated with the expression of love. To be a pimp would be to renounce community. No ties of family, creativity, or society would bind him. Art would be nothing more than a hobby. But this vision of life is unacceptable. Mingus abandons the vision of life as a pimp because he sees Bones as corrupt, bereft of emotion. Love is what's needed in a rotting, increasingly consumerist society failing to live up to its principles. If his readers were not themselves caught up in the fantasy of a "new kind of black," they could recognize his performance. Mingus understands masculinity as a performance, both denigrated black masculinity and yearning black manhood. A "true" pimp, like Billy Bones, is soulless, while Mingus retains his humanity.

As published, *Beneath the Underdog* is an abridged version of a much longer manuscript, resulting, as Eric Porter explains, in a somewhat disjointed narrative—the memoir is told in a manner Mingus intended, but perhaps not exactly or completely so. He divulges the history of his life during one marathon session with his therapist, the stories unfolding in a chronological manner but recounted during a single event. Once characterized as a book "full of profane machismo,"[35] it recounts through multiple narrative arcs the conflicts Mingus negotiated on his journey to manhood and in his growth as an artist, including his relationship with his father, the impact of racial experiences on his sexuality, and his efforts to grapple with the presence of "Jesus and the Devil" in himself and others. *Beneath the Underdog* embodies in narrative form Mingus's own description of himself as juggling a fractured subjectivity, one that vacillates among ambivalence, fear, and naiveté. Caught between transcending his faults and being consumed by them, Mingus makes judgments about the culture of jazz, its fetishization of blackness generally, and of black men specifically. He exposes his black interior, the source of his creativity as an artist. In this black interior there lies vulnerability alongside aggression, anger alongside love, outsized sexuality alongside conventional values. Mingus tells us of his experience as a jazz musician by telling us of his experiences as a black man.

"ALL THE THINGS YOU COULD BE BY NOW IF SIGMUND FREUD'S WIFE WAS YOUR MOTHER"

This extension of psychiatry to Harlem must not be confused with philanthropy, charity, or missionary work; it is the extension of the very concept of psychiatry into a new realm, the application of psychiatry to the masses, the turning of Freud upside down.

Richard Wright

Today with the emphasis on psychiatry, the hidden recesses of the mind and their connection with the body and the scientific research being done to test the possibility of mind over matter . . . , I feel that this new field of development also has a place for expression in music.

Charles Mingus Jr.

In *Beneath the Underdog*, Mingus confesses to his therapist his desire that his music say something about who he is and strives to be. Mingus works through his anxiety about being a jazz musician by embracing psychotherapy and psychiatry as narrative strategies in music and memoir.[36] His desire to make music is fundamentally a desire to be heard, and he agonizes over the possibility that he never will be. Mingus damns the insanity of the music industry for wreaking havoc on his sense of self, his ability to make his own music, and his reputation as a jazzman. The pull of psychiatry, he intimates, is the opportunity it provides to "integrate" fully into society.

Mingus's understanding of the recording industry and the music business shaped his demands for working with the label owners, festival organizers, and nightclub entrepreneurs who employed him. Certain that nearly everyone in the music industry (including record producers, promoters, nightclub owners, and even other musicians) was capable of silencing him, he once lamented that he could not "presently even afford to die with the comfort of knowing that I have beaten the jackals who prey on dead musicians."[37] Likening jazz to sharecropping,

Mingus drew attention to inequality and racism in jazz culture by performing a radicalized jazzmasculinity. His critiques harmonize with those of other black jazzmen who recognized that their identities as jazzmen, the acclaim or infamy that greeted them because of their talent, did not benefit them financially. Jazz was a hustle—and if they were not out making deals or getting gigs, then they would only have crumbs handed to them. Keeping time with them were white jazzmen who, sometimes in harmony and sometimes in dissonance, expressed their own emotional investment in Mingus and jazz. Despite his insistent demands for respect, however, Mingus was not without his own anxieties over what it meant to be a black jazzman, how to make music that reflected that experience, and how those fears influenced his actions when recording on jazz labels.

In *Beneath the Underdog*, Mingus, desperate for sleep, committed himself for observation at Bellevue. His insomnia was the result of feeling "sped up, tired out, I couldn't think who I was, I wanted to lay down and sleep. I was like a child lost with people milling all around me and no one to love me" (329). He chose Bellevue over his private analyst partly because the two were estranged, partly because he did not want friends to think he was looking for sympathy, and partly because, drawing on popular culture, he thought it was where the best people could be found to help him get some rest.

> Anyway, I kept walking east on Fifty-first Street and turned down on First Avenue, I guess I knew where I was going. . . . I kept on till I saw the gates of Bellevue Hospital. There was a guy in a sort of booth or sentry-box and I went to him and asked him how to get in. I said, "Look, man, I haven't slept in three weeks," and he said, "This is no rest home, this place is for the mentally disturbed." "Look, man," I said, "I *am* mentally disturbed. I'm a musician, I need help, and I once saw a film that said if you need help the first and most difficult work is to ask for it, so help me, man!" The gatekeeper said, ". . . Ain't crazy or nothing, are you?"
>
> I said, "Maybe I am, maybe I'm not." (330–331)

Mingus's mental disturbances derived from his uncertainty about being able to make a living at his music, with the attending depression causing insomnia and mania. Once Mingus is let into Bellevue, he recognizes the gap between how he sees what brings him there, and how the hospital sets the terms for acceptance. Like a musician entering the music business, a hospital patient rarely gets to call the shots, much less define his experience the way he chooses.

As soon as he had walked through the gates, Mingus wanted to walk right back out. He had discovered himself to be far from insane, just as the gatekeeper had forewarned. After walking through Bellevue's door, he was swaddled in a straitjacket and sent off to a cellblock before he could even get his bearings. "Right that second I knew Bellevue wasn't the right place to go and cry help, 'cause their ideas was to *scare* people back to normal" (332, emphasis in original). Trapped, he contacted everyone he could think of to spring him, including critic Nat Hentoff, his lawyer, and his analyst. Mingus plays on perceptions of himself as an angry, impulsively violent man by representing Bellevue as run by psychotic, self-hating doctors who are set on wreaking social havoc. Mingus cries for help, insisting, "There's a Nazi-thinking Jew called Dr. Bonk or something down here saying all Negroes are paranoid and he knows just the treatment for them, which is frontal lobotomy. He's a prejudiced white cocksucker so high on white supremacy that he's blowing the whole U.S.A. scene on integration singlehanded" (328). Mingus may have envisioned Bellevue as a sanitarium, but the clinic was neither an artist's retreat nor a health spa offering vitamin supplements and a quiet room to rejuvenate one's spirits. Bellevue was an institution with its own rules that operated without regard for the comfort or politics of its patients.

Launching his path to recovery, Mingus the narrator comes clean to Wallach, confessing his regard for him as a model of a successfully integrated subject. "Doctor, you're everything I could be myself if I could just find my hang-out, my notch on the stick, my crowd of people" (329). By flattering Wallach, Mingus primes him to empathize with his experience of the horrors of Bellevue and, in particular, Dr. Bonk. Bonk is a "short dumpy man, built like Winston Churchill, with a round, shiny bald head," who apprises Mingus within minutes of meeting him that "Negroes are paranoiac, unrealistic people who believe the whole world is against them." Mingus asks, "'[I]s this paranoia we all have curable?' And he said, 'Yes, this is what I am so happy to tell you. I can cure this disease with a simple operation on the frontal lobe, called a lobotomy, and then you'll be all right'" (333). Bonk's diagnosis distresses Mingus. "[N]obody knows where I am," he cries; "here I am on my first day at Bellevue . . . and before lunch I'm told Negroes are paranoiac and threatened with a lobotomy" (333). When Wallach interrupts to ask if he knows what a lobotomy is, Mingus replies, "Yeah, that's why I was so scared. I read a piece about it in *Life* Magazine a long time back and I thought 'Now I know what Bud Powell meant by his tune "Glass Enclosure"—they didn't have to cut the front of *his* head off to teach him to shield himself from the devils.'[38] Oh I was definitely afraid of Dr. Bonk, he was too eager to pounce on me and carve out a piece of my mental unrest"[39] (331–334).

Mingus is then led to his own glass enclosure, where "The lights were all on and through the glass [he] could see hundreds of people in there asleep." When he asks for a quiet room, he learns he has no other choice but a padded cell (332).

When Mingus asks to be released, so he can return to analysis with his own private doctor, the Bellevue doctors insist that he has not been there long enough to see any results, and suggest that he make a list of reasons as to why he should be treated privately. Titling the list "Why this is not as good as being treated privately by my own psychologist or Hellview of Bellevue," Mingus presents seven criticisms of the facilities and care he has received. Straddling the line between complaint and paranoia—"Some kind of bugs are leaving marks all over me. They itch" (338)—the list reveals glimpses of the anxiety and helplessness Mingus feels in the hands of those doctors. He writes, "I felt hopeless. The gateman was so polite and proper so long as I was outside but now I was in the looney bin and I saw I'd been fooled so I went quiet and didn't offer any counter-moves" (332). Remorseful, he concedes culpability. "I know now the reason I came was a childish protest against my doctor because when I missed two weeks in a row he wrote and said he could hold no more time open for me," and "I have learned my lesson. Let me have my freedom" (338).

His experience of negligence and discomfort while under observation—"The attendants were cold and standoffish and kept their distance like they thought craziness was a contagious disease" (333)—proved to Mingus the hospital had no interest in comprehending his specific mental disturbances. Dr. Bonk had no more than two minutes at a time to listen to him talk, and even then Bonk did all the talking. Others charged with providing treatment had their own agendas, and the hospital imposed routines on patients that differed sharply from the rhythms of their regular lives. "The time schedule alone is enough to destroy a night worker like me," Mingus reports. "They shout in my ear to get up before I even get to sleep" (338). To Mingus, the regimentation of Bellevue is as destructive as the individual circumstances that brought each patient there. He attempts to practice his own form of occupational therapy by organizing the other patients—a mathematician, a chess champion, a linguist, and a dancer—to teach classes in their areas of expertise. But the clinic breaks up the classes. Bonk finds that Mingus's plan substantiates his initial diagnosis of paranoia, defined by an obsessive need to organize (342–43). But, as Mingus and most other musicians would admit, the composer's goal is to organize.[40] The insults Mingus endures from Bonk reflect Bonk's own grandiose image of himself as an analyst. Mingus writes, "Dr. Bonk keeps saying I am a failure. I did not come here to discuss my career or I would have brought a press agent" (338). Unlike Mingus's fictionalized analyst, Bonk does not possess a fully developed ability to listen; furthermore, he is no jazz expert. Bonk thinks he knows Mingus but refuses to hear what Mingus is telling him, just as he refuses to listen to Mingus's music.

Once released into the custody of a relative, Mingus ruminates on his experience and concludes, "You know, I believe Bellevue did me some good. How could anybody outside bug me when I remember those closed-in helpless people? Everywhere I go I'll take those bars with me in my mind. . . . Those bars stand for power over others, the power to make you hold still and take it. Is that why I feel so much better out here where the real insanity is?" (347).

While Bellevue may represent a problematic space for achieving sanity, the working environments that pushed Mingus to the hospital are equally problematic. Mingus juxtaposes the two in this passage: "The toilets are a drag. Men vomit and stand or stoop over the seats during bowel movements and miss their aim when they urinate. I have long been removed from filth, dirt, homosexuals and criminals. I am a composer" (338). (Here, Mingus's denunciation of homosexuality as akin to filth and criminality is framed by his preoccupation with mental disturbances and his rejection of performing an "act" to attract audiences.) As Bill Whitworth reported in 1964, "Mingus says he is about to become an authentic loony because of the conditions under which he has to perform, because he is being denied his rightful earnings, and because gangsters have threatened his life." Without some fleet footwork on his part, the outcome is, potentially, an irrevocable descent into madness. "He believes he may be killed at any time, and he claims to be giving consideration to leaving the country to escape premature death and the other problems facing him here." Mingus defends himself against "the dangers he sees around him [with] a program of dieting and exercise that has brought his weight down from 287 to 190 pounds. He is getting in shape for something, he doesn't know just what."[41]

Mingus would tell anyone who listened that while jazz drove him to the "nut house," negotiating the nuthouse of jazz culture strengthened his resolve to be an effective communicator—despite the demands of postwar audiences for static personalities. Mingus wrote, "After going (to Bellevue) on my own, and the news got out, I drew more people. In fact, I even used to bounce people out of the clubs to get a little more attention, because I used to think that if you didn't get a write up, you wouldn't attract as many people as you would with a lot of publicity. But now I see what harm that kind of write-up has done to me, and I'm trying to undo it." The layers of alienation between the jazzman and his music imposed by jazz culture—involving the construction of a personality, the development of an audience, the clamor of that audience for the continued performance of that personality, and the jazzman's investment in being that personality—blurred the line between real and feigned mental disturbances and shaped any performance of jazz, race, and masculinity. Mingus illuminated this tension in his own documentation of his struggle to make music with feeling.

Throughout *Beneath the Underdog*, Mingus considers leaving music to become a full-time pimp. As some critics have noted, the figure of the pimp functions as one example of Mingus's condemnation of the music business. Young men like him embraced the pimp as an idealized representation of racialized masculinity: being a pimp meant proving that you were a man. When Wallach asks Mingus what he wants once he's proven that, Mingus replies, "Just to play music, that's all" (6). Mingus discovers that he doesn't have the heart to pimp, especially with Donnalee, the corporate name he gives to two women—"sweet-and-hot marshmallow-and-chocolate" (341)—who loved him. Donna is a white woman; Lee-Marie is a black woman and his childhood sweetheart. When Mingus pleads with Lee-Marie to stop, she demurs, saying she sells sex because she knows he won't be able to make music if he has to take on a job. Mingus insists his creative drive is stronger than that, stronger even than her own commitment to the music. He leaves after she calls him a hypocrite for condemning her for his own sins, for putting the music above people. "You think I've lost my soul and yours has just begun to grow" (300).

When Mingus is in Bellevue, he begs Hentoff to contact the two women. They visit him at the hospital, which "stopped existing in the presence of their beauty." His emotions shift from a lingering resentment to pride and awe that these women had loved him enough to willingly prostitute themselves for him. Wallach asks if he still loves them. Mingus responds, "More than ever. Actually, I guess I left because I was jealous, I couldn't stand the phone ringing and hearing them make dates and watching them get dressed to go meet their johns. I wanted them for myself, I couldn't stand sharecropping" (310). When Wallach challenges him on his sudden change of heart, Mingus responds, "[W]hat Lee-Marie and Donna did was for real and I could never do it. . . . It was easy to be proud and feel contempt and say to those beautiful women 'I don't want your dirty money!' I never knew how it felt and never had to do it that way for the rent man or anybody else. So that was one good thing that happened in Bellevue, having a feeling of love and respect for them again and being glad they found good lives for themselves" (342). In one sense, Donna and Lee-Marie live a life that Mingus can't because of the pull of music and his dependency on it. "The truth is doctor, I'm insecure and I'm black and I'm scared to death of poverty and especially poverty alone. I'm helpless without a woman, afraid of tomorrow" (341–42).

Mingus claims that playing music proves his masculinity in a way that being a pimp never could. His music can make him cry and he glories in that. A refusal to "sharecrop," whether as a lover or a musician, helped defined his identity as a black man in jazz. In his individual struggle to be successful, financially and emotionally secure, and creatively vibrant, Mingus asks us to accept his failures as a man, his vulnerabilities to the traps of madness and exploitation.

The Mingus of *Beneath the Underdog* sees his multiple subjectivity as evidence of his "real" self, which is always reorienting itself, considering the effects of its actions on others, determining how to negotiate extant models for being a man, and desiring sexual and spiritual intimacy. Mingus tracks the impact of the larger social world on his ever-evolving experience of self through a nuanced, multilayered story about his experiences as a musician and his ideas about music. Music expressed his sexual, spiritual, and intellectual aspirations and his social consciousness. "My music is evidence of my soul's will to live beyond my sperm's grave, my metathesis or eternal soul's new encasement" (343). It is his "living epitaph." Music *orientated* Mingus to the world, in specific locations, within specific cultural and political contexts, and in relation to other people negotiating similarly shifting subject positions.[42]

Beneath the Underdog exemplifies how one "textualizes a life" to realize individual self-discovery through literary invention. Mingus's representations of his sexuality as excess, his desire to love and be loved, his experiences of inclusion and exclusion, color and class, lead some critics to yearn for more lascivious details and others to understand the book as a critique of the music business. Through the framing device of the master narrative of psychoanalysis, Mingus rejects the idea that a memoir should serve primarily as a biographical record and embraces the form as "the act of self-inscription." According to Thomas Carmichael, Mingus explores his lived experience as a black man and his "excess and lack" as a musician, by "connect[ing] the trials of the subject in the text with the cultural practices of jazz itself," and with "the rejection of the cultural industry of jazz as a racist institution." His feelings of "profound ambivalence"[43] are mediated through the psychoanalytic confession. Analysis dredges up Mingus's "Oedipal terror," while recounting his adolescent romances enables him to work through his racial and sexual anxieties—"all of it singularly energized by the transgression of a founding taboo: miscegenation," knowledge beat into him literally and figuratively by his father.[44] His "frenetic, copious confessions" simultaneously embrace and reject psychoanalysis as a tool for liberating himself from the boot of the insane music industry and the white men who control it.[45] He turns the act of confession inside out, proposing it as an antidote to the silences produced by racism and as a self-interrogation of sexuality in jazz.[46] "I play and write me," Mingus emphasized in an interview with Nat Hentoff, "the way I feel. And I'm changing all the time. As long as I can remember, I've never been satisfied with the ways in which people and things seem to be. I've got to go inside, especially as far inside myself as I can."[47] In fact, Mingus explains, "We create our own slavery, but I'm going to get through and find out the kind of man I am—or die."[48]

If the resolution of Oedipal terror is about finding one's place in the social order, Mingus's confessions are part of the process of knowing himself as a creative individual and incorporating what he's learned into his music. In his "Hellview of Bellevue," the declaration "I am a composer" is an assertion of status in the world, of a right to property in the self. Even the writing itself is composition, the practice of ordering knowledge derived from experience of being in the world and observation of beings in the world. The confessional form allows for his embrace of "self-revision"[49] as a creative project and a deconstruction of personality, as recognition of the inchoate desires expressed in his ambivalent embrace of "being in jazz," as acknowledgment of the labor involved in producing jazz music and living in jazz culture. Like Hortense Spillers' "inadequate fictions" and Sherrie Tucker's "unstable categories," Mingus's confessions challenge the jazz public (a self-identifying community grounded in a commitment to liberal ideas about race) for its unwillingness to communicate truthfully about the lived experiences of "race." Mingus speaks through his "own garbled, private language"[50] to voice his self-knowledge. Traversing "the realm of the ludic and the ludicrous,"[51] Mingus sees his music as prescriptive and as providing a site for negotiating constricting definitions of race, gender, and sexuality. He knows himself as subject of and to representations of black jazzmasculinity, of black masculinity, of the black man. He is concerned with how he feels, not as the object of the gaze that figures him as a problem, but as an author of a gaze that names, values, and is a being in the world.

Claudia Tate defines desire as "not simply . . . sexual longings but all kinds of wanting, wishing, yearning, longing, and striving—conscious and partially conscious."[52] Mingus signals that the confession required in therapy inadequately expresses his desires as a black subject. The confession (his talk therapy with Wallach and the writing of his memoir) fails to release Mingus from the anxieties produced by his desires; they remain, even as he promiscuously confesses a yearning for intimacy in sexual and musical relationships. Music vividly expresses his yearnings for a truly integrated society.

Mingus is among those black creative individuals who turn to psychiatry to explore the silences that race imposes on their ability to speak about their desires, their authentic selves, and their emotional experiences. Quite reasonably they also disclaim the psychiatric cure as a model of self because of its inability to imagine their experience. But why use it to condemn the predominantly white audience to whom you're tied by artistic labor? (By "white," I refer to Marlon Ross's definition: "being white, as a structure of feeling within the self and within history—a structure of felt experience that motivates and is motivated by other denials."[53]) Mingus's confessions are not in service to exhibitionism or an embrace of celebrity, but are a rejection of invisibility. He confesses in order to name who plays here. The confession is a practice of truth-telling, the truth of being a black, gendered subject with a sexual identity, who pursues creative intellectual projects. His truth-telling exposes how ideas about race constrain dialogue even in the most integrated and intimate relationships. Mingus explores how his sexuality is a "synecdochic characteristic defining [his] blackness."[54]

Though silences around race and sexuality are articulated in different registers, fears about being silenced nevertheless speak volumes about a racial subject's ability to represent difference. As Ross notes, "No matter how articulate an oppressed group may be, they cannot explain what it feels like to inhabit a society that represses their desire, not only because feelings are notoriously internal but also because expression is notoriously decided." Indeed, "The more desire is unarticulated, the more motivation there is for talking about it, the more there is to say about it."[55] Poet Audre Lorde and novelist Samuel Delany both use autobiography to explore their creative desires through the lenses of psychoanalysis and confession, to interrogate their sense of self as racialized and sexualized subjects, as well as to expose the difficulties of talking about race as a lived experience in liberal circles. Lorde, attempting to find her poetic voice, recognized that the disconnect she felt between discourse and experience stemmed as much from the postwar period's dominant racial politics as it did from the public invisibility of any black women loving other black women. Lorde writes, "it seemed that loving women was something that other Black women just did not do. And if they did, then it was in some fashion and in some place that was totally inaccessible to us, because we could never find them."[56]

As Delany writes of his stay in the Mount Sinai Day/Night psychiatric program, the focus was "firmly oriented toward the present, rather than toward the histori-cal retrieval of psychic minutiae," which is probably why he "spent so much time when [he] was not in session hunting through [his] past on [his] own." In his experiences as a developing writer, as the son of black middle-class parents from the South who had migrated to the North, as a black homosexual married to a white woman poet, Delany sought the critical tools needed to make the language of race and sexuality as lived categories comprehensible to a public that had no immediate concern about these intersections. In the process of recouping these memories and exposing them to public view, he discovered that "when you talk about something openly for the first time . . . for better or for worse, you use the public language you've been given. It's only later, alone in the night, that maybe, if you're a writer, you ask yourself how closely that language reflects your experi-ence. And that night I realized that language had done nothing but betray me . . . [s]peaking the language I had, I now knew, was tantamount to silence."[57]

Silence is death. But in performance, in the composition of music that chron-icles feelings and experience, that provides the opportunity to express emotional truth from the knowledge gained through self-interrogation, there is life. "[M]y need is to express my thoughts and feelings as fully as is humanly possible all the time," writes Mingus. "I have worked and I have produced music that has not been played and I have written words that have not been read" (335). Mingus, like Lorde and Delany, most fears the silence that comes from not being emotionally truthful. He rages because "Anger is an emotion that has some hope in it" (332). But when he feels hopeless, his thoughts turn dark and suicidal. Feeling hopeless brings him to Bellevue's door. Music provides a way out.

MINGUS MINGUS MINGUS MINGUS MINGUS

Some names in this work have been changed and some
of the characters and incidents are fictitious.

Charles Mingus Jr.

But truth, like beauty, is in the eye and the experience of the beholder.

Ann DuCille

Reviews of *Beneath the Underdog* tend to focus on Mingus's use of the figure of the pimp to tell his story. The reviewers are typically condescending, some leaning toward pity, others toward contempt in reaction to the wrongheadedness of the memoir. The book is, in many respects, of a time and place when depictions of sex and sexuality were becoming acceptable themes in American popular culture. Coupled with this openness was the increasingly vocal expression of radical black cultural politics and their often regressive gender politics, particularly the embrace of the pimp as "a heroic figure." The pimp operated as both an assertion of control and a reinscription of white beliefs about black deviancy. But as Eric Porter and Scott Saul argue, Mingus recasts the figure of the pimp as a critique of the increasing commodification of jazz and the corruption of the music business, as an embrace of the homosocial ties binding together the jazz community, and as a meditation on maintaining artistic integrity.[58] Mingus adopts the narrative of the pimp as a way to fill the void left by the absence of other models of successful black manhood. He attempts to subvert that narrative by framing the pimp as a confessor figure, challenging him on his journey toward self-knowledge.[59] Mingus rejects the pimp's inability to feel love or genuine human compassion and connection. The emotional distress he feels when he finds himself pimping makes him realize that being a pimp is succumbing to soul murder. "There was a sad, tight, crying feeling deep inside him but he had not tears to let go. He feared that he was now a full-fledged devil waiting to be cast into hell-fire" (210). Here, Mingus's representation of the pimp becomes more than a metaphor of exploitation in the music business—Mingus uses the pimp as a performance tactic to reject soulless subjectivity.[60]

Contemporary reviews of *Beneath the Underdog* expose critics' investment in conventional narratives of subjectivity, music, and race. Charles Fox writes that "Black Americans incline to whole-hearted male chauvinism, and none more so than Charles Mingus."[61] For Jonathan Yardley, "[Mingus's] sexual trumpeting is an attempt not merely to conform to the myth of black sexuality but to embroider upon and ultimately personify it."[62] Some who reviewed *Beneath the Underdog* concluded that, with another draft or two, Mingus might have sifted through the stories of his fantastic orgies and heroic posturing to find those anecdotes that best edified readers about the "truth" of what it meant to be a black musician. "It would have been preferable," Burt Korall writes, "if Mingus had concentrated on music, its makers and the business—about which he has a depth of specialized knowledge."[63] For Korall, Mingus reduces the jazz canon by not telling a verifiably true story about his experiences working with other musicians and in different venues.

Others critics find Mingus's character failings reflected in the narrative, using ridicule in an attempt to reclaim the sole authority of white men to represent universal truths from their experience. "Predictably, it's like the man himself," observes Philip Larkin, "muddled, violent, sophomore-sophisticated, suffering from elephantiasis of the ego, stylistically of the school of [James] Baldwin and [William S.] Burroughs, politically somewhere near LeRoi Jones. . . . Is this *really* original? Wouldn't it be *much* better cut by two-thirds? It's doubtful, in sum, if this book has a place in jazz literature. Put it among the literature of the American Negro, mid-century, X-certificate protest."[64] Larkin criticizes Mingus for not being more sexually explicit, then describes him as failing to be original and relying on juvenile antics to tell his story.

Peter Davies first praises Mingus's cinematic writing style, particularly the vividness with which he crafts images of youthful exuberance and adult crises of confidence. "The raw power of the writing, the range of experience it covers, from youth's lyrical ecstasy to the wilful [*sic*] self-debasement and degradation of the grown man, have the impact of dramatic script rather than prose narrative." But having gorged on the narrative, Davies is repulsed by the pleasure he took in the indulgence. Out of shame he complains that Mingus "cheat(s) us—and himself" by "overloading his account with the lurid side of his activities. Sated with debauch, I began to feel another kind of craving increasingly asserting itself after the halfway mark."[65] Though appreciative of Mingus's facility with language, Jerry DeMuth bemoans the fact that "His book reads well but gives no insights into the jazz world, musicians or even the numerous girls and women with whom he has affairs. Concentrating on his love and sex life, he gives a lot of surface detail but little more."[66] Other critics, echoing DeMuth's demand for more detail, opined that if Mingus could have been less circumspect with the details of his sexual conquests, he could have devoted more attention to recounting his experiences as a musician. They imagined his sexual adventures as embodying his musical experiences.

The critical responses to *Beneath the Underdog* labored under an inability to conceptualize a musician questioning his blackness as an authoritative inter-rogation of jazz culture.[67] The critics substituted their self-professed "expert" knowledge of jazz and jazz autobiography as a literary form for Mingus's expert knowledge about his own experiences. His insistence on two seemingly mutually exclusive subject positions—a defiantly black jazzman who doesn't care about race when it comes to the music or his personal relationships—confounded the critics and made them defensive about the "truth" he articulated. Jonathan Yard-ley reads Mingus's story as a form of reverse racism; according to him, Mingus ignores the vital contributions of white jazzmen to the music and culture even as he is inspired by "white" music. He writes that Mingus's "music is determinedly black, and only on the rarest occasions does he acknowledge the competence, not to mention the 'soul,' of a white jazz performer. . . . The Mingus who flaunts the blackness of jazz is constantly drawn to the white-composed classical music he first encountered as a youth."[68]

These reviewers depict Mingus as a histrionic black apologist of racial chauvinism. Neil Tesser, for example, prefaced his review by recounting a conversation he once had with Mingus about why only portions of his score for a Joffrey ballet choreographed by Alvin Ailey had been performed. When Mingus responded, "Because I'm black," Tesser feigned the shock of the colorblind. "[S]uddenly [Mingus's] blackness rose up in his massive frame. . . . Mingus's blackness had never drawn my attention—even as a major part of his music, which is paradoxically black but universally colorless at the same time." Only after reading his "autobiographical novel" could Tesser recognize "the size of the trauma [years of prejudice] produced."[69] Like Tesser, Clive James sees Mingus as a tragic jazzman, laid flat by the world's racism, instead of as a self-determining black man who, as a writing subject, can create a story of himself that affirms his subjectivity and individuality. James likens *Beneath the Underdog* to Eldridge Cleaver's *Soul on Ice*, arguing that although Mingus is not as good a writer as Cleaver, Mingus's book "has a stronger core. The central, desperately defended vulnerability is not just love, but the creative spirit in its entirety; and although the book is full of contempt for Whitey, the author's fundamental alliance with white artists and writers lends humanity to the hymn of hate." James pities Mingus because his sensitivity leaves him vulnerable to racism, evidenced by his inability to integrate his fractured selves into a whole subject. "Mingus takes the impact of Jim Crow full on the nerve-ends . . . he is incapable of building a stable private world. Mingus builds an unstable private world in which the horrors are compensated for by wild excesses of lust. . . . Art is not enough to balance out the world's hostility. A great pity, but true for him."[70]

These reactions to Mingus's memoir reveal the difficulties contemporary readers had in appreciating his efforts to reformulate the jazzman's narrative, and also highlight some white men's investment in black masculinity as Other. The narrow readings offered by Larkin, James, Davies, and others reduce a complicated portrait of individuality, race, masculinity, and music into a minor attempt at writing pornography. They reflect anxiety about the expression of a self-determined black masculinity, evident especially within jazz critical circles that were (and continue to be) dominated by white men. These reviewers exposed the book to the gaze Charles Johnson describes as emptying black men's experiences of their "content." Their reviews are evidence of the "psychodrama of white masculinity" that insists on thinking that black men only see themselves as reflections of white constructions of black masculinity.[71] They take Mingus's narrative as a literal performance instead of as a farce. Kobena Mercer explains that "identity only becomes an issue when it is in crisis, when something assumed to be fixed, coherent and stable, is displaced by the experience of doubt and uncertainty."[72] This anxiety intersects with the rise of competing representations of authority in jazz. Black men were depicting their own varied experiences without concern for how white men might *feel* about that expression.

Mingus's disinterest in writing a strictly biographical narrative shakes up expectations. His book challenges us to rethink how we discuss his music and his development as a musician.[73] The traditional music biography primarily concerns itself, as Jed Rasula argues, with tracing the musician's life from performance to performance, album to album, to create an evolutionary paradigm for understanding the growth of the artist and the music. Early efforts to legitimize jazz as a historical, critical, and aesthetic form resulted in narratives that take the form of a coherent story of progress, peopled by a "canonical hierarchy of 'major figures'" such as Duke Ellington, John Coltrane, and Louis Armstrong.[74] These histories struggle to articulate "the continual improvements of the medium without at the same time implying that these evolutionary ancestors were disposable."[75] The continual reevaluation of these facts enabled white jazz critics and fans to pride themselves on looking past the race of black musicians into the depths of their creative genius. As William Kenney argues, racial blindness, or obfuscation of the "conflict between surface appearances and underlying reality," was, and continues to be, a fundamental component of hip awareness in writing about jazz.[76]

Mingus practices "identity as performative impersonation." In fact, when Associate Editor David Solomon pitched *Beneath the Underdog* to his colleagues at *Playboy*, he described the memoir as "the compleat Mingus . . . You can not believe it all because much of it is obscene and hateful and therefore absurd. But, then the idea isn't so much to believe it, but to feel it (as in jazz) and that's where this diamond-in-the-rough really comes off."[77] Solomon is on to something when he suggests that, in his moments of absurdity and obscenity, Mingus is struggling with presenting both a damning and redemptive narrative about himself. Solomon gets to the complex negotiation of "feeling" that the jazzman faces when he tells his story, whether in text or in music, and the reactions of the audiences for whom it is performed. The truth that the book's critics sought had little to do with the deeply engaged negotiation of dominant categories of masculinity that so obsessed Mingus. "Charles Mingus is a great and historic jazz bass player—but if you didn't know it before, he doesn't strain himself to tell you."[78] Such criticism revealed anxiety about explicitly articulated, multifaceted black manhood.

Beneath the Underdog is a schema for embodying subjectivity. Mingus desires to act with pure motives rather than labor under those corrupted by the deadening weight of racism. The autobiographical Mingus thrives as a composite of three real, complete, and interacting selves. He writes a realist text that is full of excesses: fear, shame, love. No amanuensis mediates the relationship between musician and biographer. Mingus constructs a model of masculinity out of his own lived and self-contradictory gender experience. His body betrays him in numerous ways: it marks him as Other both intra- and interracially, it undermines him as a performer even as he masters his bass, and it renders him vulnerable and aggressive. His black body is under constant pressure, a strain that leads him to voluntarily commit himself to a hospital for psychological help. Once there, however, he realizes that what he once thought of as self-imposed problems undermining his mental stability are actually broader cultural problems. He affirms the truth of his own experience in defining himself as a black jazzman. He abandons the pimp lifestyle and commits to music and a new love.

While Mingus does not feel "obliged" to write his story through a typical narrative structure, he is nonetheless compelled to tell a story that sets the record straight. He questions his own assumptions about black masculinity by judging and assessing his experiences as a black jazzman. He insists that there can be no single representation of himself because a single representation cannot contain the complexity, multiplicity, and intimacy of his black interior. Throughout Beneath the Underdog, Mingus interrogates the power of race—be it framed through skin color, sex, identity, or culture—by examining his experience of racial belonging and racial authenticity. Mingus's representation of masculinity shows an unrelenting struggle between self-hate and anger, between passivity and aggression, between self-love and disgust. These conflicting coordinates of embodiment shape his fragmented private world and his sense of what it means to be a man. He is wracked by self-consciousness, by his experience of embodiment and epidermalization. His warring selves are racialized and gendered, and his understanding of them ultimately realized in the composition of his music.

Mingus is concerned in the autobiography with the dynamics of his private world, his black interior, because it is the source of his creative energies. His self-consciousness emerged from intense scrutiny and the negotiation of competing narratives of masculinity and manhood. In trying to distance himself from stereotypical images of black masculinity, he faces self-betrayal. He strategizes, sometimes successfully, sometimes not, to articulate an identity that resists expectations of racialized gender experience. Autobiography provides Mingus with the tools for exploring the disjunction between who he is and what he hopes to be. His jazz autobiography reveals black masculinity as an unstable category; it is an "active term"[79] within a series of performances. Black masculinity is the expression of a situated knowledge and the articulation of emotion as embodied experience. By recognizing that ideas about masculinity are constructed in relationship to other identities that cohere along lines of class, race, and sexuality, we understand how Mingus negotiated race as a social and cultural construct.

In *Beneath the Underdog*, we have a complex portrait of the jazzman executing his role as a writing subject in an autobiography. Mingus's self-analysis illustrates his struggles in navigating the competing emotional and psychological demands—freedom or control, fear or despair, love or hate—he encounters between the white gaze of contempt and pity, and the black (collective) resistance to that gaze. Postwar jazz audiences often expected to witness a welling up of the musician's authentic or true self, channeled through his chosen instrument. This was especially true for performances of compositions with suggestive titles, such as Mingus's own "Myself When I Am Real."[80] Nat Hentoff, the usually insightful critic of jazz performance and the material experiences of jazzmen, fans those flames when he suggests, "The title means that it is on these spontaneous, trance-like occasions that Mingus feels his real, his most inner musical personality emerges."[81] While Hentoff writes specifically about a "musical personality," many readers might assume he was describing Mingus's actual self. Yet why do audiences expect a jazzman's "real" self to be revealed anyway?

Anticipating the perennial demand from fans and critics to explain what he was feeling when performing, Mingus frames performance, artistic intent, and the everyday (i.e., why I perform the way I do at any given moment) as a feeling that interprets converging moments of time: the real-time "mood" of the performance occurring at that moment, the archive of feeling represented by the already composed music about to be played, and the memory of a state of mind during performance and its physical effects. In the liner notes to *Mingus Plays Piano*, Mingus writes, "Depending on the mood I'm in, this sort of thing comes out differently every time I play it. I go into a kind of trance when I'm playing this kind of number. I remember that when we were recording this one, I noticed suddenly I didn't seem to be breathing."[82] While engaged in the work of recording, Mingus vacillates between the boredom of banal routine and feeling so consumed by the music that his breath is literally taken away. Mingus, like other jazzmen, is performing feeling even as he looks from a distance at the context of his sound. His performance style ties together his judgments and assessments of feeling with how he is situated at a particular time. He demands we hear his music as expressing his dissonant experiences of everyday life, not as the unmediated welling up of emotion exposing a true self.

If musicians' autobiographies tell the truth about anything, we hope they tell the truth about what their experience of living with music has been. We look to these stories as evidence of shared recognition between what the musician has performed and what we have understood them as expressing. We look askance at any narrative that seems to skirt the truth.[83] But *Beneath the Underdog* does not hew to a conventional representation of a musician's life. As a result, it is continually misread as failing to tell the truth, where truth-telling is a contested signifier for authenticity, representativeness, and creativity. As Guthrie Ramsey observes of Kellie Jones's work on the connection between the art object and "history's truth claim," a book like *Beneath the Underdog* "teaches us that the [personal content contained in the art] object may be the only reliable index of 'truth' between the 'what happened' and 'the what is said to have happened.'"[84]

TWO

"West Coast Ghost"

Composing Jazzmasculinity, Music, and Community

I can't change the fact that they're all against me—that they don't want
me to be a success. . . . Agents and businessmen with big offices who tell me,
a black man, that I'm abnormal for thinking we should have our share of the
crop we produce. Musicians are as Jim-Crowed as any black motherfucker
on the street and the . . . the . . . well, they want to keep it that way.

Charles Mingus Jr.

And from Charles Mingus's severest critic ****** "This album is so perfect a
fulfillment of what I mean in my music that I cry when I hear it."

Charles Mingus Jr.

I'm living in New York and everybody considers me "east coast,"
but I'm "west coast" in that it was my home since I was three months old
and I did a lot of my learning there.

Charles Mingus Jr.

Mingus . . . courts only himself and his own genius. A one-man clique,
he invents his own fashions and discards them when they are discovered
by others. The content of his compositions—most jazz compositions
have no content at all—is often repellent; it can be ornery, sarcastic, and
bad-tempered. His own overbearing, high-tension playing pinions its
listeners, often demanding more than they can give.

Whitney Balliett

Charles Mingus's volatile temper and propensity for lashing out verbally and physically led one reporter to dub him "the Muhammad Ali of Jazz." Another critic proposed creating a "Charles Mingus Wind-Up Doll. You wind it up, put it on the table, and it gets mad at you."[1] Indeed, Mingus's jazz legend revolves around stories of his temper. He cursed and he scrapped, his huge fists and corpulent frame seemingly ever ready to battle.[2] There was the time Mingus smashed the embouchure of a loyal trombonist; when he chased another with a fire ax in front of his idol; when he wrenched the strings of a piano out with his bare hands; when he destroyed his own basses because audiences were making conversation while he performed.[3] Everyone, it seemed, had a story to tell about Mingus's ferocity.

Mingus's rage was not the mechanical anger of a wind-up doll engineered to amuse, but an often-natural response to emotional risk-taking in musical and personal situations. Underlying the "punch first, apologize later" personality of tabloid fodder was his struggle to overcome fears about being silenced, a state he often likened to that of madness. Mingus believed he couldn't make music worth saying something about without being emotionally honest or invested in the idea that music matters in everyday life. Even though the postwar jazz scene imagined itself as a liberal, integrated culture, black musicians still experienced bias in their freedom of movement, their ability to exert control over what they created, and in their relationships across the color line. "Saying something" in jazz demanded unvarnished depictions of musicians' experiences. Believing that music was a language of emotion, Mingus wrestled with the grammar of its expression, sometimes disastrously and at others with compelling authority.

The composition of Mingus's anger joined a litany of miseries, connecting unresolved childhood pain to the desire for technical perfection, to a racial animosity that shrouded him in a veil of victimhood even as he rejected the mantle, to the righteous indignation of a man throwing off the shackles of a business that exploited him. His antagonistic acts of self-preservation, a volatile mix of creative frustration and high expectations, confounded critics who often mistook his passion for inarticulateness. Musicians whom he knew from adolescence speculated that Mingus's brutishness reflected the competing demands of a strident and over-inflated ego and an emotionally vulnerable psyche. His most fervent advocates believed that despite his rages, he had a pure heart. Yet, while often enrobed in the mantle of "Jazz's Angry Man," Mingus understood it as a performance, a thumb in the eye of the poseurs, rubberneckers, and frauds that saw in the jazzman's art a spectacle for their enjoyment. Jazz culture had always invited affected exhibitions of emotion, masculinity, and race by its participants, and none reveled in those dramas or exposed their pretenses more than Mingus.

Shortly after Mingus's death in 1979, Nat Hentoff recounted a public instance (perhaps apocryphal) of the toll taken by such demonstrations. Some years earlier, when Mingus had been performing with Thelonious Monk, Charlie Parker, and Bud Powell (all of whom had been or would be at some point hospitalized for psychiatric observation), Powell and Bird got into an intense argument that ended only when Powell left the stage. For what seemed like forever, Bird called Powell's name. Mingus took the microphone and said, "Ladies and gentlemen, please don't associate me with any of this. This is not jazz. These are sick people." Mingus told Hentoff that after everyone had left, Monk approached Bird and Powell and said, "I told you guys to act crazy, but I did not tell you to fall in love with the act. You're really crazy now." Hentoff asked their response; "Nothing," said Mingus. "They just stood there, limp. There was truth to what Monk was saying, you know. Some musicians were putting on an act in those years to get attention. Bird did that sometimes. And Bud. And Lester Young, with his homosexual mannerisms. There was a bass player, he's dead now, who started acting like a junky. He wasn't. Not then. But he'd sit and nod to get people talking about him. Sure, it's a kind of sickness, and it can become real. Like with Bud. But I had my act going on, too."[4] Mingus would go on to explain that though he had engaged in similar behavior to draw in audiences, he eventually concluded that the added attention wasn't worth it. Undoubtedly Mingus understood that these musicians had dealt with serious emotional and mental setbacks as he had himself over the course of his career. As was his wont however, he characterized his point in language that favored hyperbole over accuracy to elicit a reaction. Nevertheless, Mingus's reported interpretation of the incident suggests that jazz musicians understood their work as blurring the lines between performance persona and the self, an emotional leapfrogging between cultural expectations of jazzmasculinity and their experiences of masculinity in jazz culture. In the music they performed, musicians created auditory "paintings" of those experiences.

Because Mingus understood himself foremost as a composer, in this chapter I explore his evolving ideas about what it meant to him to write music capable of eliciting his own tears. I begin by returning to *Beneath the Underdog*. Contrary to what some reviewers have written, it is manifestly about the music—what it meant emotionally to Mingus, how it bound him to other people, how it shaped his choices as a husband, father, and bassist. *Beneath the Underdog* distills Mingus's various early jazz experiences into representative moments, capturing his struggle to learn how to play, to make a living in music, and to have a life beyond the performance. In the book, Mingus opens up about the insecurities involved in creating in jazz, showing us that they are rooted just as much in doubts about one's ability to effectively articulate musical ideas as they are in the effort to live a life undiminished by segregation and racism. Mingus reveals his struggles to live in the world in ways that don't undermine his self-confidence and ability to create. *Beneath the Underdog*—when considered as Mingus intended, a composition of his life—depicts in almost operatic terms the emotional highs and lows of black masculinity, creativity, and community-making in jazz.

Mingus's development as a bassist and composer was tied inextricably to the "simple west coast colored no-name music" of his youth, where he learned to value essential traits of jazzmasculinity such as an ability to nurture, to be disciplined, to approach music with an understanding of theory and tradition, and with racial pride. In his own bands, Mingus hoped to reproduce the creative freedom, the feeling of belonging and control, that defined the behaviors of his boyhood music culture, learned in Watts alongside the friends who journeyed with him into manhood. To further explore the "west coast" community Mingus was so fond of, I incorporate perspectives from musicians with whom Mingus built relationships on the playground, in the orchestra, and in the jam session. Like the crowd of young jazzmen from Watts making their way to Central Avenue and beyond, Mingus cultivated a worldview that favored emotional honesty, an ethic of care and encouragement, and the provision of musical safe spaces, where experimentation, professionalism, discipline, and dreams were nurtured.

By 1953, having permanently relocated to New York, Mingus understood himself as having "come to the point musically and personally, where I have to play the way I want to. I just can not compromise anymore."[5] In the final section of the chapter, I delve into just how Mingus came to that point by highlighting particular moments in his growing belief in himself as a composer. As he asserted his musical authority, Mingus encountered both self-imposed and external challenges. He realized he needed to step out from under the shadow of his idol, Duke Ellington, and to serve as a mentor to other musicians and fans. Leaving the role of sideman to become a leader brought economic and creative trials. Foremost among them was facing the reality that race had an impact on one's ability to make a living in jazz, a world that mirrored the larger dynamics of postwar American society.

Mingus was angry. Mingus was a fighter. But foremost, he was a man who believed he could build a loving community through the music that had nurtured him from adolescence through manhood. The musically thriving but racially stratified cities Mingus worked in shaped how he conceptualized his music and his interactions with the people who both performed with him and were his audiences. His jazz personality reflected his journey toward self-understanding and creative expression and the crossing of boundaries of genre, instrument, neighborhood, and race. Mingus seethed with passion, frustration, and hope. His anger fueled his great expectations. Love fueled his anger.

"MINGUS FINGERS"

Wood heavy with tenderness,
Mingus fingers the loom
gone on Segovia,
dogging the raw strings
unwaxed with rosin.
Hyperbolic bass line. Oh, no!
Hard love, it's hard love.

Yusef Komunyakaa

The bass was Mingus's third instrument. In *Beneath the Underdog*, the relatively straightforward biographical story of how Mingus found his way to the bass—including how he was influenced to change from one instrument to the next, how he gained musical literacy, how he thought about the connections between jazz and classical music—is rerouted through fantastic detours depicting episodes of insecurity, anxiety, disloyalty, and ego. As a young artist, Mingus is beset by numerous creative and social threats. There are the "itinerant" music teachers who, "not always skillful or well-educated in music themselves—traveled from door to door persuading colored families to buy lessons for their children" (25). These lessons fall far short of expectations. The vulnerable Mingus struggles to assert his musical vision as he interacts with unscrupulous musicians who have little regard for him. He occasionally happens upon fellow travelers who share with him a desire to make music in a modern way and who look out for him as they stumble toward their goal. Mingus also encounters bullies who stalk him, a pigeon-toed, awkward, and timid boy who can't help falling deeply in love on a regular basis. The musical, physical, and emotional threats and triumphs catalogued in *Beneath the Underdog* give shape to Mingus's expectations about how jazzmen should express themselves through music. His account bares the stakes of living a life in music.

Mingus began on the trombone—a Christmas gift he received at age eight, ordered by his father from the Sears Roebuck catalogue. The trombone was "the only interesting looking musical instrument he'd seen up to that time" (24). According to Grace Mingus, there was no doubt that all of the children would play an instrument. Despite not playing an instrument himself, "Daddy had music in him. He was determined his three kids would play instruments."[6] Each child had to practice at least one hour a day. (Vivian played the piano and Grace the violin.) Vivian taught Charles the treble clef, unaware that the trombone was played on the bass clef. So armed, Mingus played for Mr. Young, the choirmaster of Watt's largest black church. Young, himself a trombonist, ridiculed him. Mingus attempted to teach himself to play the ungainly but "beautiful horn" by ear. Despite his enthusiasm for the instrument, the younger Mingus was far from mastering it. His father grew so "disgusted" that he traded the trombone for a cello.

His new teacher, Mr. Arson, faced demands similar to those of other Watts music teachers: "His short weekly sessions had to result in satisfying sounds that proved to parents their children were really learning something in a status-building, money-making field" (25). Although Mingus had begun to develop some facility with reading, Arson did little to help him build his knowledge. "Without bothering to name the notes, he showed him where to put his fingers on the cello to make that sound. It was as if a bright child who could easily and rapidly pronounce syllables was never taught how syllables fit into words and words into syntax . . . . [C]ount[ing] as he bowed his muted, sloppy, gypsy-sounding violin with its resin-caked surface," Arson used "simple scales and familiar tunes." Mingus followed "as best he could by ear, knowing only how it sounded and having no conception of the technical processes he should have been learning at that time" (25–26). According to Mingus, Arson "cheated his pupils . . . he took no time to give the fundamental principles of a good musical education . . . and the parents, as usual, were paying for something their children were not getting" (25). Arson's "shortcut method," Mingus claimed, shaped his approach to improvisation, such that he would listen "to the sounds he's producing rather than making an intellectual transference from the score paper to the fingering process" (25). Here lay the roots of what he would later describe as his preference for composing on "mental" score paper.

Despite his early inability to read music fluently, Mingus became skilled enough to join the cello section of the Los Angeles Junior Philharmonic. During this experience, Mingus realized that playing music and being a lover were intimately connected. It's while sitting out a recital that he falls for his first great love, Lee-Marie, who was at that time the first cello. "How could a little girl be that good at music and so beautiful too?" (32). His youthful efforts to court her, like showing her around Simon Rhodia's Watts Towers or calling her nightly with the excuse of needing her music teacher's number, continued by fits and starts through his teenage years. To the young Mingus, Lee-Marie represented black middle-class stability, innocence, and racial pride. Throughout *Beneath the Underdog*, Lee-Marie functions as a reminder of "west coast" values and their fragility in the face of debauched "east coast" influences. As Mingus grows older, the connection between music and love (and love-making) persists; he succumbs to his worst impulses at times, despite a desire to be good. Lee-Marie is one casualty.

With his reputation preceding him, Mingus joined the Jordan High Symphony Orchestra, which "lacking a cello, had been waiting for my boy Charles, the child prodigy from One Hundred and Eleventh Street Grade School." His sister Grace was the second violin. Despite the initial welcome, Mingus often locked horns with the orchestra's conductor, Mr. Lippi,[7] who humiliated the still struggling sight-reader before the whole orchestra by announcing he had "noticed that most Negroes can't read" (63). David Bryant recalled how "Lippi clashed with a lot of people. [He and Mingus] couldn't get along."[8] Despite Lippi's opprobrium, Mingus continued to play music. He switched from the cello to the bass at the suggestion of classmate William Marcell "Buddy" Collette. Collette, described by Mingus as "an exceptionally good musician, already classically trained," laughed "at Charles' despair" about the cello, assessing Mingus "a funny kid." Collette had learned of Mingus from other musicians in their Watts neighborhood. Collette recalled, "one day I'm walking on ninety-eight and Compton and I see this bow legged kid. His hair's kind of shaved and he had a shoeshine box on his shoulder, but it was a most unusual shoeshine box—about three feet tall. So I said 'You've got to be Mingus right.'"[9]

Mingus's eccentricities made him an easily recognizable figure around Watts. Coney Woodman remembers meeting Mingus when "he was learning to play music. He was just carrying that cello, walking by the house from school. I guess it got old; he got codgers that would laugh at him carrying that cello. But he sure could play. That's how he learned to play so fast. That cello put him in that position to play bass, because cello you execute more than you would on bass."[10] Mingus was dedicated to the music. Vivian commented that she knew he was serious about music when he began, uncomplainingly, to carry his bass on his back during the four-mile walk to and from Jordan High School: "he wouldn't leave it at school."[11] His struggle to find an instrument through which he could voice the stream of musical ideas dammed up in his head reflected a dogged determination for creative expression, mastery over his instrument, and recognition that he deserved more than he was getting. From trombone to cello to bass, the search for an ideal musical voice was shaped by his experiences as a young black man, for whom race frequently marked his opportunities. He responded to the challenges with anger as much as he did with music.

William "Brother" Woodman and Britt Woodman recollected their teenage years performing with Mingus in the Jordan High Senior Orchestra, wrestling and boxing on playgrounds in Watts, and romancing girls. Though the siblings describe themselves as best friends with Mingus at the time, Brother Woodman, a tenor saxophonist, believed Mingus "thought himself above other musicians, which was a very bad attitude that he had taken. He had a very mean temper."[12] Trombonist Britt Woodman, looking back on Mingus's career after his death, thought his rages resulted from the confluence of experiencing racism and having anxiety about entrusting the performance of his music to others: "most of the time, when he'd strike a person, it had a background to it. The person to him was prejudiced, or the person, one of the musicians, claimed to be great but didn't play his music right. So the person would say something to make him angry, then he'd want to hit him." He thought black musicians just didn't understand Mingus, who felt like a racial outsider his entire life. "He never had too many black friends, just his musicians that were with him: Eric Dolphy and Ted Curson and his drummer, Dannie Richmond. But lots of the other black musicians, they didn't really know him, his heart, how beautiful a person he was." He remarked that Mingus spared neither black nor white people when he exploded. "So he didn't hate white people, he hated prejudice. And that's when he'd get angry."[13]

According to Buddy Collette, "there was another side to him, a very quiet and very nice side that he didn't show very much unless he was in a comfortable setting. And I would help him find that. Nothing that I did particularly. I was some person that he could be comfortable with and he believed what I said."[14] Their relationship remained a lodestar for Mingus during periods of stress; when troubled, he knew he could call on Collette. Like a younger brother, Mingus admired the worldlier Collette. Their shared musical and personal histories allowed him to trust Collette's counsel when it came to making the music that shaped both their lives. "That was Buddy, who later got him onto bass and helped brighten up his musical talent and finally his soul" (65).

Collette describes Mingus as always thinking about music and developing his skills. He remembers Mingus exercising his hands with rubber balls to increase their flexibility and strength, and his dedication to eight hours a day of practice. "We'd practice all the time, going from house to house with bass and saxophone. He'd walk from 108th to Ninety-Sixth Street with a bass on his back to jam before breakfast."[15] Technique and a natural tendency toward showmanship pushed Mingus to be more than a "supporting bass player." "Mingus was a very creative, very inventive guy who loved a lot of fanfare. As a young man he would always be doing something to sort of attract the crowd or have people look at him. . . . [He] could do things like that without feeling self-conscious."[16] Collette and Mingus would "get on the Red Car at 103rd and Grandee, near the Watts Towers, and ride into Los Angeles for the half hour it took us to get there. As soon as we got on board, Mingus would unzip his bass cover and say, 'C'mon, let's jam.'"[17] (Saxophonist Pepper Adams once called Mingus a "pathological exhibitionist."[18]) Their history allowed Collette to see Mingus as an individual with a shared sense of values and ideals. Their relationship suggests how much trust, mentorship, and the embrace of eccentricity and difference were prized by jazzmen.

Mingus remembers Collette telling him he'd "never make it in classical music no matter how good you are. You want to play, you gotta play a *Negro* instrument. You can't slap a cello, so you gotta learn to *slap that bass*, Charlie!" (69). Collette also hinted that if Mingus stopped dressing like a hobo, he could "make bread and wear the sharpest clothes in the latest styles," as well as "have the finest chicks in town" (68). If he became a professional and joined Local 47, then Mingus could join his band.[19] Mingus welcomed Collette's invitation to join the band, both for the chance to perform and for its affirmation of his musical ability. He also characterized the local as a front for criminal activity; the members had branched out into music to deflect attention from their other activities. (Mingus would have us believe the mob infiltrated all aspects of society.)

With his parents' permission ("as usual not really knowing but hoping for the best") and financial help, Mingus exchanged his cello "for a brand-new German-made double bass and Daddy forked over one hundred and thirty dollars in addition" (69). But how to play it? "Not even knowing the names of the strings or how to tune his instrument, Charles began practicing hour after hour standing by the RCA Victor console radio in the living room. After a few weeks, he began to get the feel of it. He could follow what he heard, using cello fingering" (69). Mingus's first bass instructor, Joe Comfort, sung him the notes to correctly tune his bass and advised him to keep playing along with the radio. Comfort, then the bassist with the Woodman Brothers band, explained that playing along with the radio was how he got started. Mingus, admiringly, believed that Comfort "never even tried to read. He'd hear the parts and go on to the right notes. Britt [Woodman] said Joe could hear a note before it started to vibrate." But as a caution, Woodman added, "anybody who isn't as fast as Joe, better learn to read a little." And regardless, he added, "don't worry Charlie, because mainly all bass players do is keep time" (70). The assumption that the bass was not a solo instrument would frustrate Mingus as his proficiency increased and his musical ideas broadened in scope.

Collette's advice, to embrace a jazz technique, "to practice and . . . to stay in tune . . . to be a good musician,"[20] led Mingus to study with bassist George "Red" Callender and trumpeter Lloyd Reese. Callender epitomized the black masculine ideal for young jazzmen like Mingus. He was "a tall redhead with light brown skin and a freckled face and the physique and build of an athlete. He was super-cool, his movements were slow, and in everything he did he seemed at ease." He was a bass player who "sounded like a horn" (75). Callender bowed "up high in the harmonic positions" (76), inspiring Mingus to focus on both high and low registers on the bass. "[W]hen I start really learning to play people will see me big, with a big bass, but when I want it they'll hear a viola, my magic viola that plays high as a violin and low as a bass and gets rid of all the muddling under-tones and produces a pizzicato sound with the clarity of [Andrés] Segovia" (76). Red's generosity—Mingus would pay him two dollars for each lesson and Red would spend it taking him to the movies—allowed them to build "a brotherly friendship and lifetime relationship" (76). Callender, he writes, was also doing him the solid of "setting [him] up for some record dates" (133).

Callender recollected of that period, "What I taught him primarily was how to get a sound from the instrument. However, even then, he knew exactly what he aspired to be—the world's greatest bass player. That was his all-consuming passion. . . . That's the secret of his greatness: the hours he put into it." While at Jordan High School, Mingus was also devoting time to writing his own compositions. Callender was himself dividing his time between writing music and playing tuba and bass. Their main difference as composers, Callender would say, was that he took a simpler approach to writing music than did Mingus.

Because a note happens to be playable on an instrument, it doesn't make it always practical to write it. . . . And it took me a long time to realize that, hey, a cupped instrument cannot be played as long as a saxophone. . . . So during [Mingus's] earlier writings, everything was almost impossible to play, because he didn't think of the difficulty of a wind instrument. Like, a string player can play forever, you know; they don't have to breathe. But when you play a brass instrument, you must breathe and have time to rest and get some blood back in your chops.[21]

Buddy Collette advised Mingus to take lessons with Lloyd Reese, who instructed local musicians on piano and theory. Reese was "considered the greatest all-around teacher and a fine instrumentalist himself. He was said to be able to hang a trumpet on a string from the ceiling and play a high G by use of the buzz system—blowing into the mouthpiece without touching the horn with his hands" (76). His students (including Buddy Collette, Eric Dolphy, and Dexter Gordon) were easily identifiable, Collette recalled, because "it wasn't just that they could play the instrument well. They had to be able to meet with people, conduct themselves, properly. They knew how to make time. They were concerned about the whole orchestra. . . . Everybody had to play piano. [Most] could write, most could conduct. . . . He was opening our minds. . . . This guy was preparing you to be a giant."[22] Mingus attributed his approach to the bass and to composing and arranging to his practice at the piano. "I never really understood the bass until I started working out harmonies and other things on the piano. Then I came to regard the fingerboard of the bass like a piano keyboard."[23] Embodying these characteristics of black jazzmasculinity—generosity, cool, discipline, mastery, professionalism, musical versatility—enhanced Reese's ability to nurture not only his own career, but those of others as well. These were the values that Mingus associated with the "west coast colored no-name music" he preferred playing over "jazz."

The relationship Mingus had with Herman Reinschagen, former principal bassist with the New York Philharmonic, then teaching at the University of California, Los Angeles, was like his relationship with Lippi: combative. Callender pushed Mingus to work with Reinschagen. "Charles Mingus would argue with him," recalled David Bryant, who became Reinschagen's student after Mingus introduced them. Mingus studied with Reinschagen for five years. According to Bryant, Reinschagen would tell Mingus, "'You're supposed to do it this way.' And Mingus would say, 'Well man, you can do it this way, too.' Yeah, he'd argue with the teacher. That's why he was what he was. He took what you told him, but then he expanded on that. But that's what you're supposed to do."[24] Bryant admired the self-imposed high expectations Mingus labored under to master his instrument and the theory behind the music. Mingus admitted wanting to prove something to Reinschagen. "I'll stay him out, then I'll do what [Pablo] Casals and Segovia did—work out my own fingering system" (133). Segovia, the Spanish virtuoso, transcribed scores and, using his own fingering system, transformed classical music by making a place in it for the guitar, influencing generations of musicians. Mingus planned to develop such a facility with the bass that any who listened to him would imagine him slinging his bass around his neck and strumming it as easily as a guitar, radically changing the role of the instrument. Mingus also concentrated on developing speed as a technique after admiring bassist Jimmy Blanton, who had achieved a national reputation while working with Duke Ellington.[25] The love of the trombone remained. Describing his own intricate, emerging style, Mingus explained it as "thinking *notes*, sounds you hear, same as a horn" (162).

As he transitioned from an amateur high school player into a professional, Mingus benefited from the opportunities that Los Angeles afforded to musicians. California had beckoned black people since the nineteenth century. They were drawn there for economic opportunities and a reprieve from the racism in the South and Southwest. The Mingus family had moved to Watts from Arizona in the early 1920s, joining another wave of black migrants to the Golden State. At the time, Los Angeles had an established black middle class that sustained an economically and culturally rich community centered on Central Avenue, the "Black belt of the city,"[26] born out of the civil rights activism of black Angelenos. Central Avenue was a "little Harlem," surrounded by ethnically and racially diverse enclaves. Jazz music swung from a number of nightclubs catering to white audiences, like the Cadillac Café and the Apex, as well as the black-owned Lincoln Theater. Budding musicians developed into seasoned performers who imparted to even younger cats musical knowledge and lessons on the art of "making it" in jazz. While the idea of a discernible West Coast sound didn't arise until the fifties with Cool Jazz, the Los Angeles scene was notable for showcasing a range of music styles from Jelly Roll Morton's "hot jazz" to the more conservative aesthetics of local, formally trained, musicians.[27] Buddy Collette remembers Central Avenue in the late-thirties as exciting, "the after hours-spots and the drugstores and things that had malts and food and stuff late at night where people could meet after whatever job they have."[28] Bassist Billy Hadnott recalled, "There was no air conditioning then and every bar and restaurant had a juke box. You could hear music coming from every doorway or open window."[29]

Segregation in Los Angeles limited opportunities for black musicians hoping to perform anywhere other than Central Avenue; many Los Angeles clubs instituted a "white bands only" policy that was not widely repealed until after World War II.[30] Work on Central Avenue and in Hollywood made, by the late-thirties, the black musicians' Los Angeles local of the American Federation of Musicians second only to Chicago's in terms of membership. With the amalgamation of the city's black and white locals in 1953, black musicians in Los Angeles began to see an opening up of opportunity.[31] In the decade prior to amalgamation, only New York and Detroit had integrated locals, while Chicago, Philadelphia, Los Angeles, and San Francisco were segregated. Black locals accounted for only thirty-two of the nearly seven hundred locals across the country. But Mingus was in New York by then. Of that time, Collette recalled mischievously, "The actual beginning of the amalgamation, I'll give Mingus credit for that. He was always fighting the battle of the racial thing. He got a job with Billy Eckstine at the Million Dollar Theatre on Broadway. Mingus was the only nonwhite or black in the band. Since Billy Eckstine was a black leader, he figured, 'Why couldn't there be a few blacks in there?' Mingus was the only one, and he let them know that he didn't like it. And he could be tough on you. Everybody in the band had to hear it every day."[32]

Mingus aspired to be a soloist and a leader and he didn't believe he should be held back by his race. He was both outraged and devastated by racism. Mingus's insistence on exposing the subtleties of racism was a demand for acknowledgment about the pervasive inequality black jazzmen had to navigate in a supposedly open and accepting cultural environment. He was not alone in thinking about the hypocrisies manifest in the jazz scene. Brother Woodman remembered, "All of us felt that segregation was a terrible thing. We're all here as human beings and musicians. And particularly musicians, we're supposed to be like brothers and sisters. They say music is the greatest language in the world, so why are we separated? It doesn't make sense. We knew white musicians, and they used to say the same thing. And [amalgamation] came about."[33] In the meanwhile, black jazzmen had to find ways to succeed in the limited spaces available to them.

One way of making a living was to take advantage of the recording opportunities presented by the numerous small independent labels operating in California during the 1940s. Mingus recorded as a leader, under the name "Baron Mingus," for Excelsior, 4 Star, Dolphin's of Hollywood, Fentone, and Rex Hollywood. Mingus assumed the moniker during the forties, bonding him to jazz royalty like Duke Ellington and Count Basie. As Baron Mingus, he recorded many of his own compositions, including "Weird Nightmare," "Shuffle-Bass Boogie," "This Subdues My Passion," and "Story of Love." Working with him were musicians from the neighborhood like Buddy Collette, Britt Woodman, and Lee Young, as well as musicians popular on Central Avenue like pianist Lady Will Carr, singer Claude Trenier, and Jimmy Bunn, along with a few from San Francisco like Jean Hansen and Herb Caro.[34]

Just as in New York, Chicago, and Kansas City, a jam session in Los Angeles enabled musicians to create ties that facilitated musical experimentation and community. Mingus learned early that the bandstand was a place of contest, with the musician pushing the boundaries established by the leader, showing himself exceeding expectations of his skill. But jam sessions weren't a way to financially sustain a career. He "was allowed to sit in free just about anywhere. There was no law against giving it away, it was just that Class A jobs, the only kind that paid good money, were reserved for a special breed called whites" (182). Mingus's aspirations to be a soloist were not a priority for the bandleaders from whom he sought work, just as his friend Britt Woodman had forewarned. The experience was demoralizing.

David Bryant remembered how "One night I was practicing at home late at night. I heard a knock at the door. . . . [Mingus] came in and he was crying. 'They won't hire me. They won't give me any work.' And we sat down and talked. They wouldn't hire him because Charles Mingus felt like the bass should be able to solo too. He wanted to be on the front line."[35] Pianist Gerald Wiggins recalled going "to a jam session and—Mingus and I used to walk out on them, because they'd get up there, each one of them would play twenty or thirty choruses, and we're back there sweating you know. And they never thought about giving us a solo. If they give a piano player a solo, maybe one chorus, and they were back in on him again." In the jam session, where musicians competed to show their skill, sometimes skill was not enough to be noticed—or to avoid being taken advantage of. Wiggins continued, recalling how "One night, Mingus said, 'Wig, come on. Let's get out of here.' And he picked up his bass, I left the piano, we left, and they didn't stop. . . . Didn't miss us at all. Oh, they'd work you to death. Yeah, that's why I don't go to jam sessions anymore."[36]

Even though Mingus seemed to be doing many of the right things to advance his career, there was little certainty of success. Plenty of musicians were brilliant talents and many spent their careers unrecognized. To reach the audiences that a musician like Mingus imagined were his due required an entrepreneurial perspective. Working with a group of musicians to showcase their talents in the context of a group, thinking seriously about their music as art, and sharing collectively in the success of their efforts were attractive goals for Mingus and the other musicians with whom he'd grown up, those like Buddy Collette and Britt Woodman who wanted "to play for more than money" (133).

Mingus and Collette, who had recently returned from military service, put together a group with "a corporate idea in mind" called the Stars of Swing. They did not want to name a leader, preferring to work as a cooperative, envisioning it as a platform for their talents. Among them were saxophonist Lucky Thompson (who had worked with Charlie Parker and Dizzy Gillespie when they performed the first West Coast "bebop" show at Billy Berg's in Los Angeles), trumpeter John Anderson, Britt Woodman (who would go on to work for Duke Ellington), drummer Oscar Bradley, and pianist Spaulding Givens (with whom Mingus would later record on Debut and who Mingus credits with turning him on to Strauss, Debussy, and Stravinsky). Woodman remembered that "Each musician in it was leader conscious but at the same time maintained his feeling of individuality as a sideman. As a result, each idea that a musician put forward was treated with respect by the others and made use of." The group encouraged each musician to experiment and explore. Of Mingus, Woodman notes, "Often [he] would introduce a composition requiring a different approach to jazz playing."[37] Mingus described Givens's music as "the most difficult compositions and good ones."[38] Givens recalled, "it was born of writer's frustration. Every one in the group was a writer and no one could get anything played. So we formed into a band and within two weeks we had a complete book."[39] Collette remembered how they "started rehearsing at Mingus's house, every day for about three or four weeks with dynamics. We'd go have a sandwich for lunch together, come back and blow another two or three hours. Just everyday. Nobody was going anywhere," except, Collette notes, if it was to go to something related to music, like a lesson.[40] Collette's vivid remembrance focuses on how the interpersonal ties nurtured in their community of musicians—imagination and enthusiasm for the music ("with dynamics"), the breaking of bread, their commitment to their musical vision ("Just everyday")—were forged not only by their desire to making a living by making music, but also by growing up together and engaging in various activities marking the transition from boyhood to manhood. The music was rooted in the trust developed between them from their experiences as young black jazzmen.

After developing a repertoire of about fifteen songs, the Stars of Swing invited the management of the Downbeat, "the hot spot right on the avenue," to a rehearsal. Having rehearsed daily for over a month, they had developed a cohesive sound that reflected each member's musical ideas. They were hired immediately. The first sign announcing their engagement was made with each individual name in a star—equal billing for a group of equals. That was on a Monday, says Collette. "'Tuesday,' we said, 'we won't rehearse we'll just show on the job that night and we'll play.' We come to the thing all happy, we walked up—the sign has been changed."[41] Thompson had convinced the club management to change the billing to feature him and "his" all-stars. Thompson's betrayal of the group's values was reflected not only in his playing but also in the group's ability to sustain its momentum. What they had created grew out of the collective work from their rehearsals, in which they subsumed ego for a different approach to the jazz band. "You know, we just were outdone. The people are waiting; we're in the back of the thing arguing about this. It took all of the fight out of us, I mean, what we had. . . . [Thompson] still played his can off that night, but he wasn't a team player anymore, because now he knew he had blown it. And we left the sign up, which hurt us, because we were thinking of that instead of with the music."[42] Though the band managed to continue performing together for about six weeks, Thompson stopped showing up, leading Collette to bring him before the local AFM trial board.[43] They were able to recruit Teddy Edwards as a substitute, but the music was not the same. Edwards had not been there with them while they were developing and conceptualizing the music, causing him to miss "some shadings" they had realized because of their emotional ties. This experience began to sour Mingus on a scene he had once regarded with great enthusiasm.

Mingus began considering other opportunities, including moving to the East Coast. According to Miles Davis, "Mingus could play the bass and everybody knew when they heard him that he would become as bad as he became. We also knew that he would have to come to New York, which he did."[44] David Bryant concurred, stating, "a lot of people had to go to New York to make it because of the attitudes out here." Also, people "just didn't like Charles Mingus," according to Bryant, "So he had to go to New York to make it."[45] Mingus needed a ticket out and found it with Lionel Hampton's orchestra. In *Beneath the Underdog*, Mingus recollects his excitement when Hampton invited him to join the band. "Mingus went home and scored 'Mingus Fingers' for big band and twelve other tunes as well. Hamp used 'Fingers' at every performance after that, and to my boy's surprise, at his first recording session with the band for Decca, Hamp called the tune. It was his first original composition and arrangement recorded by a major band" (183–84). Hampton crowed, "I brought Mingus from California when nobody wanted him to play. I brought him to New York."[46] During his year with Hampton, Mingus placed on the *Metronome* reader's poll for best bassist.[47] After touring with Hampton, Mingus returned to Los Angeles before making the move east final. There was still the possibility that he could make it in his hometown.

Mingus's growing dissatisfaction with the Los Angeles music scene had coincided with the demise of his first marriage and his search for a sustaining gig. He lived for a time in San Francisco and Oakland, trying to establish a six-month residency there to qualify for a local AFM membership, performing in nightclubs, composing and, some say, hoping to earn a chair in the San Francisco Symphony. In *Beneath the Underdog*, Mingus dramatizes his experiences in San Francisco as another emotional turning point in his burgeoning despair at his chances of having a lasting career in music.

> Luckily, he met a great piano player named Harry Zone who asked him to join his all-white band and got him in the union. . . . Local Twelve [was] for whites and the Jim Crow union for Negroes and Chinese. Harry Zone went to Local Twelve headquarters with him, and they thought my boy was Mexican, therefore "white," and let him in. One of his own race turned him out. A delegate in the black union walked in on the job and said Charles didn't belong there. He lost his tiddy, his first good gig in Frisco. But Harry Zone's attitude gave his faith in the humanity of some white-skinned people a little boost, to about the same extent as the black delegate's Tomism filled him with scorn. (181–82)

Mingus admires Harry Zone's willingness to transgress racial proscriptions in segregated nightclubs. But he is both embarrassed and angry that a local delegate rats him out; he sees it as a betrayal of unspoken rules. While the black delegate might have thought he was protecting the interests of black musicians, Mingus saw his actions as capitulating to an internalized form of slavery. The "Tom" sold out both Mingus and the race while protecting his own interests. The self-professed rabble-rouser fumed: "They cancelled his Local Twelve membership and gave him an ex-slave's card good only for the few clubs in the colored section of town and for the all-black bands that sometimes got together to play ballroom dates, though the union officials liked to hold out these jobs for themselves" (182). In a sense, the black union officials were sharecropping the sharecroppers. Mingus acknowledges that his decision to pass was ultimately self-defeating. But, ever willing to bring the racial dynamics within jazz into broader perspective, he doubles down on the imagery of sharecropping and Jim Crow to emphasize the structural impediments circumscribing black possibility. Not only did Jim Crow make jazz performers into sharecroppers who could not get out from under the boot of the record industry, it denied their authority to speak the truth of their experience or to ground the music in distinctly black structures of feeling.

Mingus played on racial stereotypes in ways that were confrontational, subversive, and often funny. His willingness to thumb his finger at conventional racial proprieties confused people who were close to him and alarmed those who already felt threatened by the assertion of a black jazzmasculinity refusing to shrink before supposed racial betters. At times his actions seemed to betray the race. Buddy Collette remembered going to see Mingus when he was working with Red Norvo and Tal Farlow. He went with an interracial, mixed-gender group to a club on La Cienega Boulevard to hear the trio. "We go to the restaurant and we sit down and we're trying to order, and all of a sudden the waiter comes and says, 'We can't serve this table.' So all of a sudden [Jerry] Fielding says, 'What do you mean you can't serve this table?' 'Well, it's mixed company.' So right away, I'm knowing that the band is too. They probably don't know that Mingus, with his light complexion and wavy hair, is black. I didn't want to blow the whistle. But it was weird. We got angry." Red Norvo came up to the table, perhaps to prevent any further disturbance. Collette recalled feeling "surprised at Mingus. But I guess they needed money. They just took that way out. So we backed off that one."[48] Despite excoriating segregation and its impact on black musicians, Mingus took advantage of the ambiguity his complexion provided. He was performing, acting out a role in order to fulfill his own ambition and to make a living. In acknowledging the performance, Mingus highlighted the stress it placed on musicians and the compromises they had to make. In *Beneath the Underdog*, he wonders, "How many jazz musicians would stay in the clubs if they could even make a *living* playing in parks and simple places without the big build-up that's now an absolute necessity for survival? Tote that Down Beat, win that poll, hope I get a mention before I'm too old!" (340).

In his memoir, Mingus depicts his life as a musician, including how he became part of many communities of musicians, including his youth orchestra, the small bands he formed with friends, the bands he was hired to play in, and those he led. Through ties of musical discipline and experimentation, musicians built relationships that were marked by emotional bonds, gendered experiences, and racial histories. Mingus raged against the "everyday madness" he confronted while negotiating the business of making music. Rather than provide proof of an ungovernable, disorderly personality defined by anger, his choices reflect the insecurities he struggled to master over the course of his career. They were evidence of the exacting standards he maintained as a composer, performer, and leader. Mingus demanded dignity and respect. He insisted that record labels, club owners, the federal government, and various unnamed gangsters all were compelled to cheat him because there were no restraints placed upon them and no public outcry about the plight of musicians.[49]

EAST COASTING

What if we all gave up on fame and fortune and played 'cause we love to,
like the jazzmen before us—at private sessions for people that listened
and respected the players? Then people would know
that jazz musicians play for love.

Charles Mingus Jr.

Once you respect a musician, he in turn respects you. Dealing
with a creative person is a little bit different to dealing with somebody
in the assembly line. The average musician has a self-built in pride, because
it's the only occupation where the individual is aware of his limitations
without anyone telling him. It's the only craft where you don't have
to be told what you can and what you can't do because
you're aware of that before anyone else.

Eddie "Lockjaw" Davis

"Everywhere musicians are wondering 'who is this guy Mingus?,'" applauded Ralph Gleason, a columnist for the *San Francisco Chronicle* and *Down Beat*, in his review of vibraphonist Red Norvo's breathtaking trio featuring Mingus and guitarist Tal Farlow.[50] Before joining the trio in 1950, steady music work on the West Coast had eluded Mingus. He made his living as a mailman, a job his father, a longtime postal employee, had urged him to take. Musically he managed by working as a sideman for people like Billie Holiday, touring with Louis Armstrong and Lionel Hampton, or gigging occasionally on Central Avenue with Buddy Collette, Britt Woodman, and others. Long a Mingus fan, Gleason felt it was "double gratifying to see him coming back [to the Bay Area] as a star with the hottest thing in music at the moment."[51]

Norvo had first used a trio of vibes, guitar, and bass in 1949, with guitarist Mundell Lowe and bassist Red Kelly. Regarding Mingus's contribution to the newest incarnation of the group, Norvo enthused, "The great thing about Mingus was that he had a point on the note, which you'd need if you didn't have drums."[52] On another occasion, he recalled that, "During 1950 and 1951, while this edition of the trio was performing, the musicianship was there. And the emotional quality was very, very, high. Once Tal and Mingus were with me and everything started to work, I had few doubts about the trio. . . . After awhile, we really were together and had a distinct personality of our own."[53] Tal Farlow, who joined the trio after Lowe left and before Mingus joined, remembered that, "Mingus got such a distinct sound. Each note would 'ting' with great clarity, no matter what the tempo. Unlike so many other bass players, he could separate one note from the other, no matter how fast we played. And he was so relaxed. I was always amazed, just watching his right hand. He played as if it were no effort at all, as if the bass were a guitar."[54]

Mingus's skill at pushing the tempo of the group while expressing his own melodic lines fundamentally shaped how the trio made music. According to Farlow, "a lot of the tunes we did were built around things that only Mingus could play."[55] Mingus described his virtuosity as the perfection of discipline, a desire to overwhelm the competition, and the expression of unadulterated self-confidence. He made it a point to "try the hardest things incessantly," like using his third finger "all the time." As he improved, he "concentrated on speed and technique as ends in themselves. I aimed at scaring all the other bass players. . . . There seemed no problem I couldn't solve."[56] The trio's palpable closeness fostered the affective connection between them necessary to create innovatively. Norvo once kidded a reporter that the group had only had two rehearsals, and in the second they just sat around and talked.[57] The combination of emotionally connected musicians and their commitment to improvisation made the group a unique voice contributing to the modern music of the postwar period.

Critics, showering the group with positive press, agreed that with Mingus's presence the trio had finally hit its stride. In 1950, *Down Beat* featured the inter-racial trio on one of its covers, and in 1951 named them one of two top small groups. To *Metronome's* George T. Simon, Norvo's trio exemplified "at last . . . [a] classic example of a modern trio that really swings, that exhibits impeccable taste, that has a cohesive feel and perfect performing integration, and which . . . proves that jazz can be both polite and completely convincing." Burt Korall described Mingus as the "spine" of the trio: "Mingus provided the kind of rhythmic security that permitted his colleagues to give of themselves, freely, unstintingly."[58] Jack Kenney wrote that Mingus "came in on bass to weld [the group] together and add the impressive cohesiveness which came to be its characteristic."[59] Extending the metaphor, Jack Tracy found that Mingus's skill "welds the two other instruments together with a never flagging beat and a choice of notes that makes one wonder where he's been hiding for the last few years."[60]

Norvo had picked him up when he was struggling to make a living solely through music. Though he'd slipped under the radar, musicians hadn't forgotten about him. Norvo sought Mingus out when his previous bassist, Red Kelly, decided to leave the group just after they had opened at The Haig in Los Angeles. Pianist Jimmy Rowles reminded Norvo "about this bassist who had worked with a group [Norvo] had used to back Billie Holiday in San Francisco . . . And we started looking for Charles Mingus. We couldn't find him anywhere in San Francisco. Finally we located him in Los Angeles. He wasn't playing. I think he was delivering mail."[61] Mingus, then divorced, the father of two boys, and about to remarry, had taken a job at the post office to go "into hiding," as he described it, from the music scene. Though creatively stultifying, the post office job paid the bills; nevertheless, when Norvo came looking for him in 1950, Mingus was ready to go. He eagerly seized the chance to reshoulder what he called his "aesthetic responsibilities." He left "the Blue-Cross security" of his job for the roller-coaster life of the musician.[62] According to Norvo, it wasn't an easy decision for Mingus to live with. He remembered Mingus as being so insecure about his playing that he was afraid to perform for at least nine months of their time together. Norvo attributed some of this fear to the fact that the twenty-eight-year-old had not had a steady gig for a while before he joined the trio. "I said, 'Don't worry about it. Come on, take a chance.' Every night, every night for a month he'd cry. 'Oh no, I can't do it. I can't play with you and Tal. It's too much.'"[63]

The trio toured the West Coast for a year and a half, debuting at the Embers in New York in July 1951. Despite their success in the jazz press, what could have been a major breakthrough for the trio, and for Mingus in particular, ultimately proved disastrous for all involved. Booked to back singer Mel Tormé on his weekly CBS television program, the trio seemed on the verge of mainstream success. Before they appeared, however, Norvo substituted a white bassist for Mingus, who did not yet have a Local 802 union card. No one disputed the assumption that an integrated trio would have offended the network's predominantly white audience.[64] While small integrated combos drawn from big bands had been appearing intermittently since the mid-thirties, they did not frequently headline nightclubs and concert halls, especially in areas less cosmopolitan than

Los Angeles and New York. Those catering to predominantly white audiences continued the practice of racial segregation on stage, radio, and television.

Television offered an opportunity for work during a period when musicians' unemployment on radio was rising. Acclimating to television required musicians to adapt their performing styles to the medium, sometimes effecting a noticeable change in their stage performances.[65] Musicians who performed modern jazz had an even more difficult row to hoe if they hoped to perform on camera. Television hosts, advertisers, and program directors rarely broadcast jazz, insisting that the music had to be explained to audiences in order for them to really "get it." Jazz, particularly modern jazz, seemed too esoteric. Most network executives, who didn't believe it was their responsibility to educate the audience, or even to care if they were educated, would have agreed with this rationalization by CBS's Garry Moore: "We make a mistake getting sore about it. People either like jazz or they don't. I don't like classical music, but I won't oppose it. After all, television is basically an entertainment medium." Even the jazz press cautioned against viewing television as a bulwark against the parochial interests of the public. Critic George T. Simon advised musicians to accept that the medium was not suited for "some crazy sounds [that] might entertain a musician's loving friends and admirers . . . [but] be pure death to the rest of the world." Programs hosted by popular white singers "backed by a jazz beat" were more the norm. One exception was NBC's *Tonight*, the late-night show hosted by Steve Allen. Despite his affinity for jazz, however, Allen attributed his success to knowing that his audience would only appreciate the music if they were briefed beforehand. "I just like to give them a little background—you might call it sort of a reason for our presenting jazz." It was not until 1956 that television stations regularly programmed jazz-oriented specials and shows.[66]

Though excluded from the television gig, Mingus continued to work with Norvo at the Embers. But his frustration with the hypocrisy of being allowed to work the integrated stage of the nightclub but not that of television led him to quit the trio. In *Beneath the Underdog* Mingus describes the emotional roller coaster he rode: "How does it feel when the Redhead's trio is asked to do an important, special television show in *color*? It feels great," until you're dropped without explanation (322). "You never get a chance to discuss it with him. Schitt, he can't talk anyway—can't talk about anything real, only about what chick you're going with and like that. You can't talk to the guitarist about it either, he never says anything. Two dumb white boys that can't talk to you. So you quit the trio. How can you play with guys you can't talk to?" (323). Mingus is crushed by awareness that what he believed was an emotionally honest connection turned on his willingness to perform a stereotype of racial hypersexuality for white jazzmen. The Mingus of *Beneath the Underdog* felt his ability to make music with the trio had been irreparably damaged by their inability to talk. In "real" life, there was nothing he could say to change their minds.

Not long after Mingus's break with Norvo, the trio was dropped entirely from Tormé's show. Tormé's off-hand explanation for the exclusion was tinged with ageism, perhaps the only prejudice Norvo was susceptible to, foretelling the increasingly youth-oriented culture that would transform the entertainment industry over the course of the decade. Tormé told an interviewer from *Down Beat*, "Look, Pappy, I fought to get Red's trio on the color TV show. But when we went over to black and white, CBS wanted a younger-looking show. I told Red he couldn't help it that he was born 20 years before we were, or that Clyde Lombardi, who's a great bass player, happens to be bald." (Defense mobilizer Charles E. Wilson had requested the network-wide switch from color to black and white "in order to conserve critical materials for the national emergency.") Though Tormé suggests that veteran musicians were anathema to viewing audiences, television programmers often preferred them as less risky options for the emerging industry to attract an audience.[67] Though Tormé's glib explanation undoubtedly rankled Norvo, he had more options than Mingus. A relative newcomer in New York, Mingus needed to find some way to secure both financial and artistic independence so that, in the future, he would not have to compromise his aesthetic integrity as had Norvo and Tormé.

According to Celia Mingus, Mingus had also chafed at Norvo's reluctance to play his compositions—Mingus "really wanted to play his [own] music."[68] He was, after all, a composer, and he wanted an audience. While launching both a record label, Debut, and a publishing company, Chazz-Mar Inc., Mingus continued gigging with musicians up and down the East Coast—Billy Taylor, Bud Powell, Charlie Parker, Max Roach, Art Tatum, and his idol, Duke Ellington.[69] Debut released *Jazz at Massey Hall* (1953), a live recording of the Toronto concert featuring bebop's greatest musicians; Mingus also recorded as a sideman for Ellington, Powell, and Miles Davis, among others, on labels such as Savoy and Prestige. He began attracting attention from other labels, like Atlantic, which signed him as a leader. Just as he was building his reputation, the jazz scene was changing, and Mingus hoped to influence it in his favor.

Jazz tastes varied regionally, according to one deejay, who claimed, "in the Northwest we have a much different listening and buying population than . . .

in the East."[70] Many radio stations resisted programming "real" or "undiluted" jazz shows because sponsors could be reluctant to offend their listeners' sense of propriety. One writer noted that because radio executives "run their stations for advertising or good will . . . as soon as any one looks at them cross-eyed their knees shake."[71] Deejays converted audiences to jazz from popular music through various methods, including niche programming or devoting an hour to jazz out of a six-hour programming block. Jazz-oriented performance venues were becoming harder to come by. On LA's Central Avenue and New York's 52nd Street, blocks of jazz clubs that once streamed with talents like Charlie Parker, Billie Holiday, and Art Tatum were practically nonexistent by the early 50s.[72] Instead of in clubs, jazz fans discovered new music in magazines such as *Down Beat*, *Metronome*, and *HiFi*, and relied on a network of fans, deejays, musicians, and critics to promote the cultural legitimacy of the music.[73] Liner notes introduced listeners to the music and showed buyers how to be fans by dispensing historical and musicological information about the style in which a particular artist performed or providing impressions about the particular contexts in which the albums had been produced—in a studio, for example, or live at a festival, nightclub, or concert hall.[74]

Mingus wrote indignant rebuttals to reviews of his music, intervening in the critical discourse around jazz by explaining what his music represented aesthetically and emotionally, as well as by opining on the cultural work of the black jazzman as composer. He also responded to queries from fans who felt the jazz press inadequately reported on his music.[75] Because he had friends like Nat Hentoff and Bill Coss, Mingus understood what critics were after. Nevertheless, he believed, as his hero Duke Ellington once wrote, that surely "critics have their purpose, and they're supposed to do what they do, but sometimes they get a little carried away with what they think someone should have done, rather than concerning themselves with what he did."[76] Mingus often wrote his own liner notes, envisioning them as a critical complement to the recording. For *Autobiography in Jazz*, listeners were told that the "selections were placed . . . so that the listener can easily follow the changes of mood and pace and also to produce the best effect for high fidelity play back," rather than, as one would expect, in terms of chronological release.[77] In the liner notes to *Jazzical Moods*, Mingus explains the structure of the compositions and offers commentary on their extra-musical significance as well. In those for *The Black Saint and the Sinner Lady*, he muses on the meaning and tempo of time and offers his analyst's assessment of his personality as revealed in the music. In *Charles Mingus Presents Charles Mingus*,

Blues & Roots, and *Let My Children Hear Music,* he delves into the question of how well contemporary musicians performed their knowledge of jazz history.[78]

If a fan somehow piqued his interest, Mingus was willing to go even deeper to explain his motivations as a composer and performer. Gary Soucie, a young cadet enrolled in the U.S. Air Force Academy in Denver, wrote to Mingus in early 1956 to compliment him on the recent release of the Debut sampler *Autobiography in Jazz.* The album was described as Debut's "own story as told by many of the recording artists, large and small" who had made it "a name to be reckoned with among major and independent labels wherever good jazz is sought." It featured sides by, among others, clarinetist Sam Most, bassists Percy Heath and Milt Hinton, pianists Billy Taylor and Paul Bley, drummers Arthur Taylor and Max Roach, and trombonists J. J. Johnson and Kai Winding.[79] Gary Soucie purchased the album through a special $5.00 package that the label offered in the jazz press. Although he knew it was a "sad, sad story," he inquired about the possibility of receiving another order blank, because cadets did not have a lot of money to buy things outside of their monthly necessities.[80] Taken by his enthusiasm for their music, Celia Mingus sent him two more order forms.[81]

In the late fall, Soucie again wrote Mingus, praising the newly released albums and volunteering to write liner notes. Soucie felt "quite confident that [he] would be capable of doing a fair job, for [his] greatest 'talent' [lay] in the fields of writing and in jazz appreciation." Shortly after first writing Mingus, he had won "first place in the Metronome-RCA Victor contest which netted him twenty-five Victor LPs" on the basis of "writing liner notes of a sort," and *Metronome*'s editor, Bill Coss, had given him some "slight encouragement."[82] Mingus responded that while they presently had no releases needing liner notes, he was willing to read samples of Soucie's work in case they could use him in the future.[83]

When Soucie submitted his sample, he admitted to some weaknesses in the short story he had written about a musician. He now felt that he "could much easier work in a more definite and pronounced jazz feeling than [he] did a year ago." His desire to write for Mingus stemmed not just from his love of Mingus's music, but also from the decision that he and two other friends had recently made to resign from the Academy and go "to a civilian college and study English, psychology, and law." Writing about jazz would have to support him, as he would be totally independent once he left the Academy. An assignment from Mingus would give him the recognition he needed "to boost the salability of articles and short stories on jazz [he intended] to write to sell to various and sundry magazines."[84] Soucie made sure to tell Mingus that he had been able to "convert two classical addicts to jazz" by having them listen to Mingus's *Pithecanthropus Erectus* and the Modern Jazz Quartet's *Django*. He further divulged that he and his friends had "formed a jazz trio (piano, bass, drums) to play at intermissions of [their] formal dances. . . . [They had also done] their interpretation of the Mingus sound . . . [which had] left the people a little breathless and astonished, but . . . now [they] got requests for it."[85]

Some months passed before Mingus provided Soucie with feedback. Soucie's request for an evaluation of his writing represented an ideal opportunity to give meaning to the feeling of jazz. Here was the chance to attune a potential critic to what it is that musicians think about when they are creating their music and how they think critics should approach their interpretations. Mingus found that while Soucie had a talent for writing, he seemed to lack the insight that could be gained by experiencing life as a musician or interacting with musicians. Soucie, importantly, seemed to understand jazz, but he could benefit from listening more to Lester Young, Charlie Parker, Miles Davis, Billie Holiday and others.[86] Mingus believed that a musician needed a thorough grounding in the history of the music to find his unique voice.[87]

With his resignation from the Academy looming, Soucie intensified his efforts to interest more people in jazz and provide a welcoming space for it on campus. He believed the public needed to be "educated towards jazz," and he aimed "to bring the people and the musicians closer together."[88] Soucie wanted to write a lot of things—such as an "accurate jazz novel" he planned to complete "after quite a bit of assimilating the jazz tradition"—and he needed "experience." Soucie's appreciation for jazz fed his interest in "studying and writing about the race problem in the U.S." He was concerned however, that he might find it "impossible to accomplish" "this last task" since he was a "caucasian." He hoped that Mingus would be able to offer him some advice about achieving these goals.[89]

Since the school year was nearly over when Soucie sent his last letter to Mingus, he requested that Mingus forward his response to an address in Kankakee, Illinois. Mingus's last letter to Soucie vividly explains the lessons Mingus thought could be learned from his experiences and how one might avoid romanticizing the jazz life. Mingus's sympathetic response to Soucie acknowledged the anxiety he felt about expressing feeling from his position of racial difference. Mingus did not think that his race provided him with any privilege when it came to interpreting what he had experienced, nor did he think Soucie's whiteness precluded him from exploring more deeply. The only thing that would limit Soucie's growth as an individual (and as such affect his writing about jazz) would be his reluctance to interrogate his own experience and to shy away from new experiences. Mingus wrote expansively about the tasks and responsibilities of a composer. He considered the composer as able to speak to all layers of human experience because of his openness to emotional complexity. The heterogeneity of urban life and its continual confrontations with new ideas, places, and people, force individuals to come to terms with difference, to question the assumptions they have held dear.[90]

Perfecting one's craft was a way both to pay dues and to develop emotional literacy. Mingus practiced incessantly to master his primary instrument, the bass, as well as his secondary instrument, the piano. Andrew Homzy believes that Mingus could have been an important pianist because "his conception is original and his technique is formidable," with his album *Mingus Plays Piano: Spontaneous Compositions and Improvisations*, comparable to the work of Earl Hines, Bud Powell, and Art Tatum.[91] Because of his mastery of technique and understanding of the structures of composition across classical music, jazz, the popular songbook, and Latin-based forms, Mingus recommends that Soucie do the work of learning how to write. He also advises him that dues are paid when the artist puts himself in situations that are out of his comfort zone, as Mingus himself had done when he moved from Los Angeles to New York. Mingus counsels that learning about racial difference and its impact on experience is going to be of particular concern for Soucie. Although Soucie feels a connection to the music, according to Mingus, that connection would only be strengthened after he experienced living with racial difference. For Mingus, living with music was living with the fact of race. Drawing on the film *Gentleman's Agreement* as an example, Mingus underscores his belief that an appreciation of jazz demands empathy, rejection of privilege, and honesty.

During this period, Mingus was developing his own theories about composition. He called his approach to writing and improvisation "spontaneous composition." The musician was saying, "Listen, I am going to give you a new complete idea with a new set of chord changes. I am going to give you a new melodic conception on a tune you are familiar with; I am a composer."[92] He had particular ideas about how this would be accomplished. The improviser should not aim for slavish replication, but for a considered effort at reimagining what had been composed before. The improviser should be able to relate his music both to other compositions and to the solos of the other musicians with whom he is performing. Mingus understood his performances as structured to frame his priorities as a jazzman.

My music is as varied as my feelings are, or the world is, and one composition or one kind of composition expresses only part of the total world of my music. . . . At a concert or night club I call tunes in an order that I feel is right for the particular situation. Each composition builds from the previous one, and the succession of compositions creates the statement I'm trying to make at that moment. The greatness of jazz is that it is an art of the moment, it is so particularly through improvisation, but also, in my music, through the successive relation of one composition to another.[93]

In other words, the "spontaneous composer" presents his audience with emotional knowledge gleaned from practice, thought, and experience.

Mingus further refined his approach by developing "rotary perception" as a technique for managing the tension between composition and improvisation. As he describes it in Beneath the Underdog, "If you get a mental picture of the beat existing within a circle you're more free to improvise" (350). Later he notes, "When I first introduced the name to the press, I admit it was only a gimmick like 'Third Stream.' I was tired of going hungry and I wanted to catch the public ear but, although the word was a gimmick, the music wasn't. . . . With Rotary Perception you may imagine a circle around the beat. . . . The notes can fall at any point within the circle so that the original feeling for the beat is not disturbed. If anyone in the group loses confidence, one of the quartet can hit the beat again."[94] According to Dannie Richmond, he and Mingus would "feel each other out as we go; but always, when the time comes to get back into the original beat, we're both always there. The best way I can explain is that we find a beat that's in the air, and just take it out of the air when we want it." Nat Hentoff explains that Mingus and Richmond used rotary perception in the version of "All the Things You Could Be by Now If Sigmund Freud's Wife Was Your Mother" that appears on Charles Mingus Presents Charles Mingus. Hentoff, the album's producer and owner of Candid, the label for which they recorded it, writes, "The musicians keep the original structure of 'All the Things You Are' in their minds but do not even play the tune's chord structure. The piece in general is based on A flat. Again, the rhythms change. There is no set beat, and yet there's an implicit rhythmic flow, up and down, throughout the work."[95] Musicologist Stefano Zenni describes the effect of rotary perception as "a manipulation of time perception" leading to "increased changes of tempo and meter."[96]

As a composer, Mingus felt himself entitled to a respectful audience willing to engage with him in the music-making. Mingus believed he should have such cultural status that he could demand deference, even from paying customers at a typical nightclub gig. Even as he was, as Hortense Spillers explains, "playing around" in "the realm of the ludic and the ludicrous," creating "*no thing* we know," Mingus himself felt he had "something to offer in jazz a little more worthwhile than the same old worn-out cliché's of Bird and Dizzie, that you hear over and over again."[97] He "didn't mind the drinking, but the night-club environment is such that it doesn't call for a musician to even care whether he's communicating. . . . [T]he environment in a night club is not conducive to good creation. It's conducive to *re*-creation, to the playing of what they're used to."[98]

Focused on shaping how the music might best be understood, Mingus tried to create a responsive audience, believing that jazz is a percussive dialogue between musician and audience. According to Duke Ellington, jazz swings because it "hits home to the people who hear it. It speaks their language and tells their story. It's the musician and his audience talking things over."[99] By this standard, a jazz composer's skill should be measured in terms of his effectiveness in communicating. Mingus thought the musical innovators had relinquished control to those who owned the business of making music, transforming innovation from a matter of creative control to one of economic interest. "Tastes are *created* by the business interests. . . . But it's the musicians' fault for having allowed the booking agents to get this power. It's the musicians' fault for having allowed themselves to be discriminated against."[100]

Mingus began moving away from providing musicians with fully written compositions because he was trying to solve a musical problem—how to get musicians to play the music he could hear in his mind. Precise notation failed to elicit the feeling he desired, consequently, he wrote compositions "but only on mental score paper—then [he would] lay out the composition part by part to the musicians." As Mingus explained, "I play them the 'framework' on piano so that they are familiar with my interpretation and feeling and with the scale and chord progressions to be used. Each man's own particular style is taken into consideration, both in ensemble and in solos." By providing the musicians with "different rows of notes against each chord," they are given freedom within a structure to improvise, "except where a particular mood is indicated." Such an approach enabled Mingus to keep his "own compositional flavor in the pieces and yet to allow the musicians more individual freedom in the creation of their group lines and solos."[101] The added benefit, he told Diane Dorr-Dorynek, was that musicians would "learn the music so it would be in their ears, rather than on paper, so they'd play the compositional parts with as much spontaneity and soul as they'd play a solo."[102] Mingus also thought that by not providing a traditional score on paper, he might avoid complaints from some musicians that his music was unplayable. He "had been accused of being 'way out' compositionally. True or false [his] ideas had not changed—only [his] method of producing them."[103]

But "mental score paper" also could create unforeseen problems, as Mingus would realize in 1962 while preparing for a concert at New York's Town Hall. The concert may have been doomed from conception, with problems mounting as the date was pushed further back. Mingus intended to perform with a newly formed orchestra for which he was composing new music and arranging some of his previous work. Ever interested in radically transforming the practice of jazz, he envisioned the concert as an open workshop for the orchestra. While in the throes of writing, Mingus continued to tour with his smaller ensembles and also recorded *Money Jungle* with Max Roach and Duke Ellington. There was no rehearsal space, and neither George Wein, who'd contracted with Mingus for United Artists to record the event, nor United Artists itself paid the musicians for attending rehearsals. Because the musicians had other individual gigs, they could only meet during the early hours of the morning to practice the music that Mingus was still writing and Jimmy Knepper, Melba Liston, and others were helping to arrange. Mingus and Knepper had been performing together for years. Knepper took on most of the arranging, working "Almost daily for . . . six weeks . . . shuttl[ing] by bus, ferry, and train two hours each way between his new Staten Island house and Mingus's Uptown apartment to pick up and drop off sheet music. He worked on his new dining room table, on the ferry, and on the subway using a clipboard."[104]

At one practice session, Mingus swung Knepper's trombone at him, hitting him in the mouth. Knepper lost several front teeth, and his sound was never quite the same again. He began wearing dentures, enabling him "to push notes out though he [had] trouble with slurs" and the plunger mute. Mingus claimed the altercation had been an accident and that he had intended Knepper no harm. "I didn't really hit Jimmy, but Jimmy was leaving the door, and I opened the door in his face, and it bumped his teeth out. I didn't hit him. He claims I hit him."[105] Knepper explained that the fight had started because Mingus wanted him to do more than copy the music. He "also wanted me to write background figures, but I told him it was his music and he should do it, it should be his composition. Suddenly he called me a white faggot and punched me. I thought I better fall down in case he decided to hit me again, and I did." Brushing off the insult, Knepper continued to like Mingus and believed he "talked a lot of nonsense about whites. . . . [H]e married three white women, and he had a great respect for white musicians."[106] Knepper understood Mingus's racial statements as performances aimed at hiding emotional vulnerability. Despite their blowup, preparations for the Town Hall concert went on, with Knepper committed to seeing the music performed. Buddy Collette remembers their rapprochement. "At rehearsal Jimmy Knepper came, missing one tooth, and they were again like lovers, man they were so close. He couldn't play the trombone but he still brought his music in. He was dedicated to him."[107]

These appearances notwithstanding, Knepper later hauled Mingus into court. During the sentencing hearing for his conviction on third-degree assault, Mingus's lawyer offered mitigating evidence of Mingus's contributions as a "great jazz musician." Though the judge suspended the sentence, an indignant Mingus turned to his lawyer and said, "Don't call me a *jazz* musician. To me the word 'jazz' means nigger, discrimination, second-class citizenship, the whole back of the bus bit." His lawyer (Manfred Ohrenstein, a former New York State senator) was flabbergasted. "What shall I call you," Ohrenstein asked. Mingus replied, "I'm just a *musician* man. A composer."[108]

As Stanley Crouch explains, Mingus didn't set much store in looking at jazz as a "calendar" of styles. "If it was good then, then it's good now."[109] And he had complicated ideas about what his music could be. Though he worked in the jazz idiom and sought recognition as a leader among his contemporaries, Mingus claimed the shorthand of "jazz" inadequately defined his musical ambition. "I've always been a musician. I studied music in school and played where I could get a job—a job playing any kind of music. But I had one kind of music in mind as a goal, and that's ALL music. I'm working in jazz, and I play in that medium. But my goal is much higher."[110] Acknowledging his ambivalence toward jazz as a creative label he explained: "[T]he word jazz bothers me. It bothers me because, as long as I've been publicly identified with it, I've made less money and had more trouble than when I wasn't."[111] In his eyes, the diminution of his music into "jazz" reflected the artistic, economic, and racial policing of black men.

That Mingus was concerned with how he was categorized artistically—in the midst of a hearing which could have resulted in his being jailed—underscores his belief that status and renown as a jazzman was no protection against the insidiousness of racism. He understood that the identification of jazz with black cultural experience exposed the expectation that jazz musicians would articulate a limited range of emotional expressivity. Black jazzmen were burdened by expectations that their music would fulfill the emotional needs of their audiences. They could experience this burden as a form of silencing, which they could resist in a number of ways, including snubbing the term "jazz" to categorize their music, rejecting traditional ideas of composition and performance, and challenging racism and prejudice on the music scene and in the social contexts in which they lived. Mingus consistently raged against even the threat of being silenced while, at the same time, he cultivated the tools and techniques of a performer and composer who could express his feelings.

George Wein was willing to put up with Mingus's tantrums for the Town Hall concert. He admired "Mingus's basic musical talent . . . [a]s an organizer of music. He can present." As he told writer John Goodman, "The thing about Charlie is he basically has more love than hate. He may spew hate, but hate is bullshit with him. Charlie is not antiwhite . . . In fact, the beauty about Charlie is that he responds to love and that's a very important thing in the man."[112] Knepper's and Wein's characterizations of Mingus as someone whose words belied his feelings and beliefs echo the sentiments of many musicians who worked with him. They recognized his temper as *performance*.

Mingus expected United Artists to "tape [their] final rehearsal so the musicians could hear what [he] was trying to do. This was stopped when the engineer said he couldn't get into the hall and didn't have speakers but would have them there for the concert."[113] Mingus's plan ran completely aground on the night of the concert. As Buddy Collette recalled, "George Wein wanted a concert; Mingus wanted an open recording session, where you could play a tune, then you could stop it if you didn't like it and do it again."[114] Collette was in town to provide "moral support." According to him, "There were times when [Mingus] definitely needed me, because the people didn't understand him, a lot of people. But when I came around he was like a kitten—he was a nice, nice man all the time. . . . He just had all the faith in the world in me."[115] Collette recalls that the rest of the musicians were dressed in suits on the evening of the concert, while Mingus came dressed in dungarees, looking like a farmer. The show started late. Adding to the confusion, according to Mingus biographer Brian Priestley, the musicians could not hear themselves during the concert and, because of the configuration of the hall, the engineers could not see them. The engineers "would open the stage door to the right wing, peer out . . . , whistle and wave their arms and then shout, 'From the top again, Charlie,' or 'You weren't on-mike Charlie; do it again.'"[116] Mingus repeatedly suggested that members of the audience demand refunds. Nearly one hundred received them. The promoter, Joe Glaser, was furious. (As Dan Morgenstern opined, "If there were ever two people who were destined not to get along, it was Mingus and Joe Glaser.")[117] As the union-mandated closing time grew nearer, the curtains closed, and the crew began turning off the lights. A few musicians began to jam and the audience crowded the stage.

Later, United Artists allegedly ordered Wein into the studio, without consulting Mingus, to cut and edit the concert. The resulting album earned a five-star rating in *Down Beat*. Nevertheless, many critics believed Mingus had overextended himself compositionally. Some critics marked the concert as a flop, suggesting that it was perhaps the lowest point in his career as a composer and a leader. Even the usually sympathetic Bill Coss concluded, "Mingus . . . lost an opportunity that he has long wanted and deserved. It was not, in any sense, taken away from him."[118] Added Buddy Collette, "It was a marvelous concert, which [Mingus] spoiled because he was fighting with George Wein."[119]

According to Mingus, "That whole thing was a farce. They knew I was doing a recording and writing music, and they called me to do an Ellington date which slowed me down. I would have been ready but for that Ellington date." He insisted that it was not meant to be a concert but an open rehearsal. "I got the idea from watching Ellington record the same way in California, with his first record that he did for Columbia in California. He had the copiers on the stage. He used a theatre, and people who knew about it got to come through the door in the back, the few people that heard about it got to come to the recording session."[120] Mingus had long measured his ambition and its roots by his admiration for Duke Ellington. He loved to tell of his ecstatic response to hearing Ellington live for the first time. "When I first heard Duke Ellington in person, I almost jumped out of the balcony," he said. "One piece excited me so much that I screamed."[121] Ellington's music epitomized the possibilities of jazz as a form capable of rendering the complexity of black life into sound.

As previously noted, Mingus had joined Ellington and Max Roach on the 1962 album of Ellington compositions, *Money Jungle*. (Mingus also had worked with Ellington earlier, but had been fired in 1953 after an altercation with Juan Tizol.) Critic Don DeMichael observed, "I've never heard Ellington play as he does on this album [*Money Jungle*]; Mingus and Roach, especially Mingus, push him so strongly that one can almost hear Ellington show them who's boss—and he dominates both of them which is no mean accomplishment."[122] Roach later said, "I believe that a musician must continue to work on his craft and address the most valid music of the younger players if he can do so without losing his own direction. Duke Ellington did it: he recorded with both John Coltrane and with Mingus and myself—and he sounded like Duke at every note." This willingness to be challenged by other musical ideas was key to Ellington's lengthy, brilliant, and ever-modern career. He was not what trumpeter Clark Terry called an "old-fogeyism type cat."[123]

The serendipity of being called for a recording date with Ellington while Mingus was attempting to compose his biggest musical statement to date cast the scope of Mingus's musical aspirations in sharp relief. In order to truly be a composer—and his own man—Mingus had to separate himself from Ellington, even as he crafted music that spoke to his love for him. He had advised the musicians who followed after Charlie Parker to do more than simply copy him—they had to play themselves. In one sense, that is what kept Mingus composing: while struggling in Ellington's shadow, he worked to create a body of music that reflected his own experiences and consciousness.

Music critic Peter Goddard recognized both a physical and aesthetic resemblance between Mingus and Ellington. He writes, "A neatly trimmed beard framed his handsome face and set off eyes which strangely enough resembled Duke Ellington's. . . . And in the history of jazz there is a parallel between the two men. For Mingus is the Brahms to Ellington's Beethoven; the one who dominates the later period of jazz as Ellington did its beginnings."[124] Other critics picked up on this connection as well. "Mingus stands in relation to this period as Ellington did to an earlier one; summing a great deal of it up and influencing it less by provoking imitations than by providing it with an example of the very fullest and most devoted kind of artistry."[125] Others used similar terms to commend Mingus as a bandleader: "When Mr. Mingus hits the mark . . . he makes it evident that he is an ensemble creator who deserves to be ranked in that special jazz category that has been occupied almost exclusively by Duke Ellington ever since jazz moved beyond simple New Orleans polyphony in the Twenties."[126]

Beyond his aspirations to emulate Ellington's creative successes, Mingus desired to bend his musicians' sound to his service just as Ellington had done with his. Mingus challenged his musicians, wresting ungrudging respect from them. To work with Mingus required a complete break with past musical habits. "Mr. Mingus is in the middle of getting a 'new' band together. It is new in the sense that he is trying to get them to try to play what he wants now—not what they think he should keep playing."[127] "Mingus," recalls Gene Shaw, "made extraordinary demands on the musicians. He asked for one to bring forth one's essence, and he would do anything to point the way toward the work he wanted done at the time."

"After I was with him awhile," adds Charles McPherson, "I figured that if I could work with this cat, I could work with anyone." As Nat Hentoff observes,

"Mingus' presence serves as a stimulus to his colleagues, and the result is an impassioned, mutual testing of wills and ideas that—when the collective spirit takes fire—spirals into a remarkable organic unity."[128] Ted Curson characterized his stay with Mingus as being like a "university thing. . . . With Mingus, it was more like a school in the real sense of being a school. Mingus was the boss. He gave the orders. He was the musical director and he had ideas on everything." Dannie Richmond, Mingus's drummer of over twenty years, explained that this was because Mingus knew exactly what he wanted the musicians to communicate. He had to work with them individually because they could not just pick it up off the page. He recalled that when some musicians tried to write notes down, "Mingus would say, 'No, no, no! Don't write it down, you play the notes like you're them, that's not what I want.'"[129]

Mingus's 1963 release, *The Black Saint and the Sinner Lady*, showcased the uncompromising musical expression of the intersections between his political ideas and social ideals, between his personal history and his priorities as a composer and mentor of jazz talent. The album, he claimed, is an antidote to the insanity of a contemporary society that would rather blow itself up than create change; it catalogues both an embrace of his musical forefathers and his growth beyond them. A record of his escape from creative and social confinement, it also provides evidence of how to "get out of the observation ward at Bellevue."[130]

The Black Saint and the Sinner Lady documents Mingus's evolving approach to arranging and composing. Rather than notate the music, he used the piano to give the musicians examples of the emotional ideas he wanted them to convey. This process was not without frustration. For example, when Mingus and pianist Jaki Byard had trouble communicating about a particular section, the impasse was resolved by producer Bob Thiele. After Byard's "request to show him or play it himself," Mingus taped certain passages that Thiele then cut into the master. Not all such exchanges were as contested however. Mingus took pleasure in Charles Mariano's "love of living and knowing life and his understanding of the composer's desire to have one clear idea at least musically recorded here for the record." Mariano understood that "tears of sound were what was expected as the intended thought in the background and what also was meant to come out of his alto sax solo." Throughout the liner notes, Mingus comments on the contributions of each of the eleven musicians who provided the album's full, lushly orchestrated sound, achieved in part because Thiele gave him freedom to arrange without the typical "studio rush feel" of his other recordings.[131]

Along with tongue-in-cheek descriptions of the recording process, damning takedowns of jazz critics, praise for the skill of his band members, and celebrations of his own genius, Mingus's liner notes also include a reproach of jazz culture. He condemns a jazz audience who, by relying solely on the recommendations of critics, allows itself to be "brainwashed" rather than take responsibility itself for deciding what constitutes good music. "[T]his means you need an analyst," Mingus observes. In fact, he invited his own analyst, Edmund Pollack, to contribute to the notes, drawing connections with the same narrative issues that concerned him in *Beneath the Underdog*: time, music, and an individual's fragmentation. Though initially reluctant, Pollack eventually embraces the opportunity, reasoning that his training in interpreting "behavior and/or ideas communicated by words and behavior"[132] could be applied just as well to music. Pollack sees the album as a plea, for "all mankind must unite in revolution against any society that restricts freedom and human rights."[133] In Mingus's recording, he discerns the sounds of both an American society inching closer to achieving integration and an individual's continuing emotional evolution. He also hears a religious statement, one in which ecstatic tears of anguish, depression, love, and joy are released. The variety of emotions expressed, he concludes, reveals an essential dynamic of Mingus's personality. Mingus "feels intensely. . . . He cannot accept that he is alone, all by himself, he wants to love and be loved."[134] Pollack writes, "Inarticulate in words, he is gifted in musical expression which he constantly uses to articulate what he perceives, knows, feels."[135]

Bob Thiele produced both *The Black Saint and the Sinner Lady* and *Mingus Plays Piano*, Mingus's only solo piano album. He had signed Mingus after attending the 1962 Town Hall concert and Mingus's performances at the Village Vanguard. Of the Vanguard performances, Thiele remarked that the "music . . . just had to be recorded."[136] What started out as an artistic match made in heaven, however, soon devolved into a brawl in the jazz press. The root of the conflict was their differing ideas about who controlled the recording session. In *JAZZ* magazine (a French publication), Mingus accused Thiele of losing a number of tapes that contained better cuts of the various tracks on *The Black Saint and the Sinner Lady*. He reported spending a number of nights recomposing the missing music; when they had finished recording, the original tapes were then found. An outraged Thiele faulted Mingus in turn, belittling his professionalism and discipline. Thiele's attacks, however, did not manage to refute the truth of Mingus's claims, but to underscore them.

During the contract negotiations with Impulse!, Mingus had made extensive demands, knowing that it was rare for black jazzmen to be adequately compensated for their work. He never hesitated to draw attention to the inequities between musicians and those who profited off their music. Dannie Richmond explains Mingus's position like this: "Man he didn't like jazz critics. . . . He didn't like jazz promoters, he didn't like jazz record producers or jazz executives of all kinds and he didn't like jazz nightclub owners. . . . He felt exploited. If he worked for you, you were exploiting him. The money you paid him was never enough. Maybe it wasn't."[137] When Mingus learned that Thiele was paid every two weeks, he demanded that a similar clause be added to his own contract. "I want to be like an executive—like a white man—I want to be paid every two weeks." As a professional in a world in which musicians depended on infrequent recording gigs, short runs at nightclubs, or long tours, a demand to be paid fairly and consistently could have been viewed as an assertion of dignity, but it struck Thiele as an aggressive display of Mingus's racial biases. "This was *my* first confrontation with certain of Mingus' *Negro and white* views" [italics in original]. Thiele's disdain intensified as their working relationship deteriorated. He characterized Mingus as a race-baiter: "Mingus ranged from friendly tirades about the white oppressor—the & r man in the booth? The engineer?" But described himself as a no-nonsense boss: "I took no BS from Mingus—without any question he sensed that I meant business—I was not interested in racial problems while actually at work in the studio; get to the job, do it well and be done with it."[138]

Whether or not Thiele thought of himself as a racist, he embraced a discourse that valued black jazzmen as vessels for emotion but not as self-determining architects of creative and economically sustaining careers. "I firmly believe that Mingus has much humanity in him—he has basic Christian concepts," Thiele reflected. "Perhaps his trouble is a deep-rooted hatred of white people—*indeed in humanity itself?* . . . Musically, his greatness lies in melodic composition and complete mastery of the bass. I believe that his orchestrating ability is limited—and this, coupled with a strong admiration for Ellington, could be inflicting strong depressant factors on his psyche. Has he completely matured?"[139] Though Thiele disliked having to serve as a "lay psychologist," he had no doubt that Mingus suffered from mental disturbances and was too needy. Mingus, he claimed, could not distinguish between a friendship and a professional relationship. Mingus was someone who "*needed* a friend and some guidance."[140] Despite his expressed concern about Mingus's supposed emotional instability, Thiele couldn't resist the chance to make a record that captured that emotionality for profit and posterity. Thiele's assessment differs wildly from Pollack's, who considered Mingus an advanced social subject, one who has been able to integrate the concentric sites of experience that are his daily life into his identity. The conflict between Mingus and Thiele echoes the disharmony within jazz culture, between the emotional expressivity demanded of jazzmen and the authority to make claims about that emotionality.

After the negative response to the Town Hall concert, the trauma of Eric Dolphy's sudden death,[141] and some irregular gigs, Mingus rebounded, earning critical acclaim with his performance at the 1964 Monterey Jazz Festival in California. One reviewer found that it "may have been the most striking personal triumph in jazz festival history so far." Another reporter noted, "From Mingus sound flowed as naturally as a river tumbling down a mountain until, gathering speed, he was jumping and dancing, exhorting his musicians at the end, the very portrait of a man possessed. The audience gasped when suddenly it ended and roared their approval over and over."[142] In response to a *Down Beat* review of his Monterey concert, Mingus wrote the editors, "No human being could have sat there that Sunday afternoon listening to my live music and, with pencil in hand, say what I was doing. Because if he were there, he, too, was entranced like everyone else was meant to be."[143]

Charles Mingus saw the emotionality of his music as rooted in the traditions of the jazz and classical music he had been steeped in since his childhood in Watts, as well as in the dislocations prompted by his migration east to New York. There he entered a new community whose values seemed, at times, to diverge sharply from the aesthetic, ethical, and political values he'd come to associate with the West Coast sound. Mingus believed in the affective power of music to communicate his thoughts, both to other musicians and to audiences. He urged the musicians he led to respond with their own emotional knowledge. In that process of co-creation,[144] they made something new for audiences. Audiences, in turn, were obligated to respond with their own emotional experiences; because of what they had learned by participating in the musicians' performance, they were responsible for enacting social change.

Across his interviews, liner notes, memoir, and performances, Mingus relies on metaphors of change, tradition, instability, emotion, and insanity to elucidate his goals as a composer and as a black jazzman. He encourages us to think more critically and expansively about the uses to which the jazzman is put as a cultural signifier of truth, emotion, and social ideals. He believed that jazz captures the immediacy of the contemporary moment and is distinctly suited to the project of interpreting and recording the experiences of individuals who may have no other outlet for expression. "Music is another language," he said, "so much more wide in range and vivid and warm and full and expressive of thoughts you are seldom able to convey."[145]

Mingus's desire for music without labels did not preclude him from understanding that what he was creating—and the traditions he drew on—were contributions to a distinctly black cultural project. "Jazz is still an ethnic music, fundamentally. Duke Ellington used to explain that this was a Negro music. He told that to me and Max Roach . . . and we felt good. When the society is straight, when people really are integrated, when they *feel* integrated, maybe you can have innovations coming from someplace else. But as of now, jazz is still our music, and we're still the ones who make the major changes in it." Mingus had a consuming interest in the complex social and personal negotiations required by integration. While he could claim that jazz is essentially an "ethnic music" and that only with genuine integration would that change, it is not so clear that he believed that jazz was "race" music.[146] Though Mingus challenged "race" as an identity, he nevertheless remained committed to a social politics and identity defined by race. He believed black musicians were owed economic and social debts. Jazz was not just black music, nor simply entertainment, nor art for art's sake. It was rooted in a particular experience and reflected ways of being in the world. The twinned bogies of "race" and authenticity obscured the roles played by a deep knowledge about the music's traditions and the disciplined musicianship required to develop emotional articulateness.

Mingus, who never wavered from his conviction that artists should be well compensated for their work, believed he had a duty to raise the public's consciousness of the aesthetic and economic constraints on jazzmen.[147] He was a self-proclaimed "jazz political activist."[148] "I want to talk about musicians' problems. I want to help expose the conditions in which top Negro artists operate—expose the fact that they're paid less than white musicians, and live and die like paupers compared to the white men who copy their music."[149] But Mingus did not just talk about the difficult conditions facing black musicians—he pursued opportunities (such as his independent label Debut and his various publishing companies) to put his music and livelihood in an economically sustainable position. He was determined to leave a legacy.

Mingus bemoaned the fact that critics persistently sought to box jazzmen into ill-fitting categories. When critic Ira Gitler asked him for a self-characterization, Mingus emphasized that his music, as both a composer and a performer, was a primeval, organic, and multivocal expression of himself. "A creative person is not one thing. That's why I'm trying to go back to the beginning to answer the question that's come to me so many times: 'What is jazz? What is my music in relation to jazz and what kind of composer am I or what kind of a bass player am I.'"[150] Being a composer gave him the license to stake out the creative boundaries framing his music and to claim ownership of it both discursively and economically. His approach to composition and performance integrates reflections on music history with forward-thinking assessments of his performance technique and musical goals. It also reveals his strategies for thinking through the complicated questions of what is jazz history, how is jazz a historical record, and how do jazz musicians understand themselves as historical actors.

THREE

"Invisible Lady"

Jazzmen and the Business of Emotional Truth

Mingus was great at getting an idea, like when he said to me "we'll start a
recording company." Like he knew how to go about recording. And he said
to me, "And you find out how to run a record company." . . . And I did it. It
was a wonderful experience because how do you start a record company?
It isn't just making the sessions. It's how do you make a label? How do you
make an album? Who presses it? What does it cost? Who distributes the
records? How do you deal with them? How do you get your money?

Celia Mingus

I'm not interested in making a million dollars but I do want Debut
to be self-supporting so that we can try to put out some good jazz and
also record other jazz artists and jazz groups.

Charles Mingus Jr.

A lot of people don't understand that music is business,
it's hard work and a big responsibility.

Miles Davis

Down Beat announced the birth of Mingus's brainchild, the independent jazz
label Debut, in May 1952.[1] According to an early account of the label's genesis,
Mingus persuaded William J. Brandt, a cigar salesman, to provide the seed

money after a chance encounter. Brandt had planned to join his son at a club where Mingus was performing, hoping to understand what the younger Brandt found so compelling in jazz. Instead of meeting his son, however, Brandt "found pianist Billy Taylor and bassist Charlie Mingus, enjoyed himself immensely and further found, before the evening was over, that he was co-owner of a new record company in partnership with Mingus who had convinced him that money spent at the bar could be better used to further the cause of jazz." Debut remained true to its vision, "best described as pro musician and artistic qualities with loot greatfully [sic] accepted,"[2] throughout its existence. The label's launch promised Mingus financial and artistic independence. Although his experience with Debut was often nerve-wracking and disappointing, it also represents one of the most satisfying roads that Mingus traveled in his career.

Debut emerged from an exploding postwar media landscape, built on the gradual diminution of power of the American Federation of Musicians, the rise of television, and the transformation of radio. Ownership of mass entertainment was increasingly consolidated in the hands of major networks and corporations, while small independent and local stations, record owners, and performance venues struggled to retain their viability as sites for the performance and distribution of various types of music. Across genres, musicians encountered rapidly evolving opportunities. Debut was, for Mingus, one strategy for embracing these opportunities.

By turning attention to the contexts within which Debut operated, we can better understand how jazzmen made a business of selling emotional truth. While a complete history of Debut is beyond the scope of this chapter, aspects of its history usefully illustrate the artistic, structural, and financial challenges and compromises associated with the choice of making a living as a jazzman. I begin by examining why jazzmen, both white and black, decided to become entrepreneurs within the music business. Next I turn to the relationships Mingus cultivated with deejays and fans for insight into his ideas about the demands of working and creating in jazz. I end with Celia Mingus's influential role at the helm of Debut. Through Debut we can trace how ideas about racial difference and emotion shaped narratives about masculinity and the production of a professional jazz culture and jazz audience.

The professional culture that grew up around jazz thrived on the emotional and ideological investments that fans made in the music. Those fans established ways of thinking and writing about jazz, as well as nurturing jazz as a cultural practice. Whether independent label owners, distributors, deejays, or committed hobbyists, they described their experiences within jazz through the language of expertise, which Simon Frith defines as the relationship between knowledge and pleasure, and the cultivation of taste (both their own and that of the consuming public). Jazzmen claimed that part of their talent—their ability to determine who and what to record to capture an audience—was rooted in their emotional connection to the music, as well as in their integrity and their creativity. They became jazzmen because of their obsession with jazz; that obsession produced collective and individual cultural narratives about how their tastes shaped the sound of jazz. These jazzmen considered themselves entitled to claim ownership of jazz because they could feel it and knew how to package that feeling. Their ownership facilitated the music's professionalization and led to the construction of a modern jazz audience that was primarily white, male, and middle class.

The launch of Debut allows us to consider what it meant for black jazzmen like Mingus to claim ownership of the music. A black jazzman seeking control over his music, whether as a bandleader or a record-label executive, confronted the challenges of retaining artistic integrity while pursuing financial independence. Having cultural status as musicians neither inoculated jazzmen from racial prejudice nor provided them with financial security. Real status, black jazzmen understood, depended on claiming ownership of the cultural, social, and economic property their music represented, effectively "increas[ing] the possibility of controlling critical aspects of [their] life rather than being the object of others' domination."[3] For Mingus, with his healthy disregard of white privilege in jazz culture, owning an independent label promised access to more financial remuneration, respect, and control than performance alone did. Mal Waldron recalled Mingus "felt that Debut was his chance to take the business away from the white man. He felt that the musicians were not controlling their own product, and that the man that was controlling it had nothing to do with music and was not really interested in music, but was interested in making money. So he wanted to have control over his music."[4] Mingus's approach to Debut combined a commitment to the history and traditions of jazz, a desire to push the creative boundaries of the music, and a reliance on interpersonal networks to build and sustain the label's commercial viability.[5] He envisaged Debut as one cornerstone of his future creative success as a composer and performer; he also imagined Debut as providing a commercially successful path for himself and the artists he recorded.

The Debut story recognizes how women embraced a variety of roles within jazz to realize their own ambitions. Mingus launched Debut with his wife Celia;

relationships like theirs often enabled women to become jazzmen. Mothers and sisters, for example, were integral performers in many family bands.[6] Other women married into the business, their social status as wives often marking how they participated in the culture. All of these women encountered a complicated web of beliefs about gender, authority, and business—within the music culture and more broadly—reflecting both conservative and progressive ideas about femininity and jazz. A female partner in a small independent label explained, "I mean, what I'm doing is typically a woman's role in the family right? There's your mother who picks up after you and makes sure everything is done. . . . I feel like I take on that primary responsibility of making sure everything is done in the best possible way, you know, the completion of tasks. Men are great initiators, that's their tradition." Maxine Gordon, widow of Dexter Gordon, agrees with these sentiments: "The way we as women are socialized enables us to work, although we don't get any credit. You wouldn't last a day if you did this work to get public recognition."[7]

Celia Mingus shaped Debut as much as Charles Mingus did; she understood Debut as a way to make music that was saying something. Her embrace of jazzmasculinity fostered the interpersonal relationships that sustained Debut as an aesthetic and commercial enterprise; through Debut, Celia assumed a role that recognized her authority as a jazzman. Though women like Celia made the culture functional by nurturing jazzmen and jazz music, they were routinely marginalized. Despite the gendering of emotional labor as women's work,[8] jazzmen embraced the ability to nurture as a fundamental trait of jazzmasculinity, inflecting the term with characteristics such as expertise, discipline, and the mastery of self, others, and the music. These traits were also cast in terms of racial difference. In a culture that celebrated black jazzmen for unmediated emotional expressivity, white jazzmen were admired for rationalizing their emotionality into the management of the recording process. For Mingus to take on the challenge of running a label was to do two things. First, as Mal Waldron noted, it was to resist white control over black cultural traditions and second, it was to embrace the work of institution-building, fathering a historical legacy one record at a time. Without Celia, that plan to make "some good jazz and also record other jazz artists and groups" would have collapsed under its own ideological weight.

"NO PRIVATE INCOME BLUES"

D-day has arrived in the record industry!

Ross Russell

The recording as a means of reproduction is far more vital to an
improvisational music like jazz than it is to, say, classical, band, or show
music. . . . [J]azz is perishably ephemeral, elusive. When a jazz band plays a
number, the particular combination of sounds that emerge will be ones that
have never been heard before and will never be heard again unless,
of course, those sounds are recorded.

Whitney Balliett

Debut followed the rise of other independent labels during the closing years
of World War II. By 1945, in what was then the biggest year for the recording
industry, independents accounted for 50 million of the 350 million records sold.
The easing of wartime shortages made resources for recording more abundant
and affordable, allowing additional independents to enter the field. By the early
1950s, there were an estimated 2,000 independent labels recording across all
genres—rhythm and blues, rock and roll, hillbilly, gospel, blues, and jazz. While
independents were located throughout the country, New York, Chicago, and Los
Angeles were the primary hubs of music activity. The major labels cultivated
extensive distribution and promotion networks, allowing them to reach retail-
ers across the nation and to tap into radio and television outlets. While majors
did operate subsidiary labels in specific markets,[9] their primary advantage over
the independents lay in the diversification of their products. They could rely on
profits from popular artists while they tested niche music. Though independents
sometimes realized great crossover success with artists such as Little Richard and
Fats Domino, their long-term viability was never certain. Perceiving how the
majors were succeeding, one songwriter tried organizing an independent label
association to reap similar benefits for jazz independents. Membership in the
association would ensure that when one area experienced losses, another could
prop up the bottom line.[10] The songwriter understood that the key to succeeding as an independent record label was not simply producing quality music, but
effectively managing revenue and expanding a distribution network.

John Gennari, writing about the career of independent label owner Ross Russell, characterizes jazz in the postwar period as one of racial colonialism. Power
and control over the music rested not with the people who created it, but with

those who seized it. Russell launched Dial with recordings of Charlie Parker, including the infamous session for "Lover Man" during which Russell allegedly stood behind Parker, propping him up until he finished the song. Parker was inebriated, possibly under the influence of heroin, and mentally exhausted. The next day he found himself in jail, where he learned that Russell had released the record without his consent and against his creative judgment. Russell's novel *The Sound* portrays his obsession with Parker, in the character of Red Travers, and the impact of that obsession on his interest in defining and controlling jazz. Gennari reads the novel as evoking the reality of postwar jazz culture: "Red Travers and the other black musicians control the expression of the 'Negro core of jazz' while performing on the bandstand, but every other aspect of the *sound*'s fate as creative property—its codification and commodification as notated and recorded *music*—is controlled by whites."[11]

Described as a "community of addicts . . . almost totally masculine," and "passionate proselytizer[s], and keen follower[s] of the women,"[12] jazz fans who made the decision to run a label were not deterred by a lack of business or technical knowledge, trusting instead on their enthusiasm as an engine for successfully spreading the message to a broader audience. Orrin Keepnews, founder of the Riverside label, lamented, "I ruined a perfectly good hobby by making it my profession. Like other jazz record producers for small labels at the time [1950s], I was a jazz fan who basically decided that I would be a jazz producer and that was it."[13] Their commitment to jazz was ideological. They believed that preserving what they considered "good jazz" on wax, even if they didn't often make a hit record, was as important as their ability to see beyond racial prejudice and value the genius of black jazzmen.[14] The owners of labels like Dial, Atlantic, Commodore, and Blue Note were convinced that their emotional connection to jazz engendered their expertise (both the pleasure they took in the music and their knowledge of different styles of performance), giving them unparalleled insight into what would make a good jazz recording.

Patrick Burke argues that 1930s bachelor culture "consolidate[d] a white identity" among jazzmen who found camaraderie in Swing Street's Onyx Club, where racialized and gendered judgments and expectations about musical labor and authentic expression were formed: "At the Onyx musicians aspired to a state of masculine independence in which they resisted the conventions of the music business and upheld the value of musical and personal self-expression."[15] White jazzmen's taste, intellect, and expertise represented a different sign of racialized masculinity within jazz culture. These jazzmen embraced the production of jazz as a claim for ownership, for racial knowledge, and for a facility for the making of art. A faith in the inherent value of certain genres of jazz, such as Dixieland, motivated their initial interest in recording; gradually that certainty would evolve into an increased concern with dominating commercial markets. These jazzmen did not need to be performers to know how to produce records. They defined their qualifications as label owners by their impeccable taste, a proxy for the authenticity of emotionality that characterized depictions of black jazzmasculinity.

These entrepreneurs often were avid record collectors who had met during the interwar years and developed long-lasting business and personal relationships. At Milt Gabler's Commodore Music Shop on Forty-Second Street, for example, record collectors could browse through stacks of albums and play them in the shop's listening booths before purchase, often spending more time listening to records than buying them. Gabler also hosted Sunday jam sessions at the shop. As he explained the shop's attraction, "The major thing was you met people there that loved music and jazz in particular and you could always find someone you could talk to about your hobby. . . . It became a hangout for the critics, artists, record collectors. We struggled. I wanted to do business. But I never pushed to make a million dollars, or make it the biggest store in New York. I was satisfied with it being the most important jazz store."[16]

Gabler's reminiscences about the beginnings of his career illuminate how much of jazz history, especially that on record, turned on the serendipitous connections forged between likeminded young men. His jazz madness transformed what had been his father's small Eastside radio ship, the Commodore Radio Corporation, into an incubator and repository of jazz talent. He built a "library stock of recordings," drawing in customers from across New York City (and eventually the country) who sought music not easily found in neighborhood shops.[17] Gabler maps the trajectory of gaining expertise and cultivating taste for others in the industry—from pleasure-seeker to hobbyist (slightly more learned than the mere nightclub-goer) to zealous advocate for important jazz. His experience underscores how behaviors, practices, and customs developed to influence how individuals understood and valued jazz as music.

In order to support a life immersed in jazz, however, the desire to produce art needed to be complimented by a desire to make money. Some early jazz entrepreneurs, who initially wanted only to indulge their passions by reissuing hot jazz recordings, soon found themselves taking on new demands and developing new tastes. Alfred W. Lion of Blue Note Records admitted that he had intended his first session in 1939 "only for my pleasure as a fan and collector. But others wanted the record and so I began to sell. That was the beginning of Blue Note. Basically, things haven't changed. I still record what I like." A Berlin native, Lion began living in New York in 1925, briefly returned to Germany in the early 1930s, then fled the Nazis in the mid-thirties, returning to New York. His friend Gabler, who was already producing and stocking Commodore albums at his shop, reluctantly sold Lion's Blue Note albums as well.[18]

Like Milt Gabler, Ross Russell and Bob Weinstock also were storeowners who became label owners. Russell owned Tempo Music Shop in Los Angeles, where he stocked eighty-four independent labels; he founded Dial Records in 1946. Charlie Parker and Arnold Schoenberg were among Dial's most famous artists.[19] Bob Weinstock's record store in New York mainly stocked Dixieland and swing, but his label, Prestige, produced modern musicians like Miles Davis, Lennie Tristano, and Stan Getz. Ahmet Ertegun, son of a Turkish ambassador to the United States, and Herb Abramson founded Atlantic Records in 1949. Though Atlantic made its name recording rhythm and blues artists, it regularly recorded jazz musicians as well, including Mingus.[20]

These staunch fans turned label owners saw a correlation between taste and sales. Producer Bob Thiele, for example, began his life-long obsession with music and jazz when his restaurateur father gifted him a phonograph and some Tommy Dorsey records. As he explained, "since the time I started in the record business as a teenager, I really never made a record anticipating how it would sell. Fortunately, or unfortunately, I think almost every record I've made was done because I personally liked the music. It's as though I was making records for my own collection"[21] Mitch Miller, Columbia's A&R director for popular music, thought a record producer should be willing to say no in order to get a quality recording made. "The trick is self-criticism—good, honest, self-criticism. And I'll keep saying 'no' so long as the guy who buys the records keeps saying 'yes.'"[22] While both Miller and Thiele argue that the audience measures a record label's success, they also hint at a level of disdain for the audience's lack of taste. The true measure of jazz as art, in their minds, is whether they personally approve it; getting consumers to buy their records is merely a validation of that art. They are jazzmen because they control the recording of music, picking the artists who they could sell. Audiences who clamored for anything other than the "real" jazz they produced weren't true connoisseurs of the music.

Such jazz entrepreneurs insisted that they would be content to release albums that would one day be discovered by a wide audience and appreciated for their quality. They felt that jazz had given them succor and, in return, their aesthetic responsibilities were to nurture and develop the music. As Savoy Records' Ozzie Cadena explained, "My dreams are to do as much for jazz as jazz has done for me. Although I'm not spiritually inclined, jazz has given me a sort of spiritual comfort and confidence which, I hope, is also felt as this and future jazz audiences listen to a catalogue of which I am extremely proud."[23] They sought artists who represented certain aesthetic values, principally authentic emotional expressivity, nothing "commercial." Alfred Lion, for example, insisted authenticity was not limited to a particular genre in jazz. "Genuine expression" was the key to the music he recorded,[24] making him "one of the few laymen who not only preserved but also helped shape much of jazz history."[25]

While independent labels reveled in the control they had over creative decisions, these producers also recognized the possibility that their discoveries would be co-opted by major labels. The owner of the small label Jazz: West explained that "The little guys do the experimenting and the inventing; the *bigs* are more at home with the successful formula, usually after the *littles* have made it successful."[26] In response, many white jazzmen questioned whether success often augured capitulation to less stringent aesthetic standards. George Avakian expressed a contrary view; he thought that fifties jazz had matured beyond the danger of adverse influence and as a result, solidified its cultural place and its commercial viability. "It has been said that the public has caught up with the musicians; actually the musicians have caught up with themselves. And the negative side of their past flights into unexpected jazz vistas has given way to positive creation and development on solid ground."[27]

Atlantic began recording jazz musicians in 1955 under the direction of Nesuhi Ertegun, whose experience in music mirrored that of the typical jazzman entrepreneur. He had spent over twenty years engaged in various jazz-related activities—as a writer at the *Record Changer*, a record store owner, a college lecturer, and a supervisor at labels including Good Time and Contemporary—before joining Atlantic as its jazz division head. His first label, Crescent (which was later renamed Jazzman) recorded the Kid Ory Creole Jazz Band; his jazz course at UCLA was the first offered for credit in higher education. Ertegun sold his Jazzman masters to Good Time Jazz in late 1951, then decided to join the label because it offered new recording technologies and new opportunities to reach jazz fans. He found it "very encouraging to see that the kind of music we like sells not only to collectors, but has a strong popular appeal as well."[28] Addressing the question of how to produce quality rather than quantity, Ertegun explained that the difference lay in the label's willingness to nurture the artist. "We don't rush into a recording studio at every opportunity; we try to prepare our sessions with the greatest possible care; every one of our jazz artists has a long-range recording program." Ertegun emphasized that paying for rehearsals and planning recording sessions furthered his goal of creating music for listeners "not only in today's excitable jazz market, [but also with] musical values that are lasting enough to attract listeners ten or fifty years from now."[29] The successful labels, like Atlantic, paid close attention to the business of music recording. While they may have wished to do the altruistic service of recording jazz for posterity, they also cultivated their artists, ensuring they could recoup their investment.

Blue Note, for instance, also used planning sessions and paid for at least two to three days of rehearsals before a session, something that some independents were either too cash poor or commercially shortsighted to do. Recording engineer Rudy Van Gelder's approach to recording shaped much of the jazz sound of the 1950s, particularly that of Blue Note. He saw himself as emotionally invested in the music, sharing "a rapport with the musicians, and [trying] to understand what they were trying to do." He adapted his recording techniques to what he understood jazzmen to be saying musically. "I always felt that jazz musicians should be treated in a way that was a little more as if it were a major effort than the way they had been treated in other places." As recording engineer Joel Dorn explained "To promote jazz, you have to be emotionally involved with the music."[30]

In jazz history, the record is simultaneously a way of identifying a community, a representation of labor (by musicians, record producers, and distributors), and an art object (using technology to capture developments in the music). Those communities, their labor, and their art all retained gendered characteristics of social behavior. White jazzmen who were independent record-label owners created a recording niche out of their experiences in the bachelor culture that marked white male participation in Swing-era jazz. Their approach to recording reflected aesthetic values that prioritized, at least initially, preserving certain genres of jazz on record, promoting the jazz ethos of racial inclusion, and protecting jazz as a culture that celebrated individuality, freedom, and the music as art. White jazzmen saw themselves as nurturing artists, music, and democratic principles. They also saw themselves as endowed with creativity, infallible taste, and the ability to recognize what kind of jazz would sell to the public. They challenged the music industry even as they gradually became a part of its establishment. Their good intentions, however, were sometimes met with resistance from musicians reluctant to relinquish their own control over the music.

MONEY JUNGLE

> I have long contended that the best way to get Jazz to the greatest amount
> of listeners is to educate them in their listening of it. It's the old adage of
> leading a horse to water. You can't make anybody accept Jazz, you can only
> interest them in it by making it interesting to them.
>
> *Charles Mingus Jr.*

For black jazz musicians, starting an independent label seemed one of the most
viable routes for playing their own music. An independent allowed them more
opportunities for choosing which compositions to play and which musicians to
record with.[31] Dizzy Gillespie's short-lived Dee Gee Records was one of the first
independent labels to be both black-owned and run by a jazz musician (following Mezz Mezzrow's King Jazz and Al Hall's Wax). Gillespie recalls deciding, "it
would be desirable to own a record company. . . . I wanted to make . . . records for
myself. . . . With the objective of building a large record company, I invested my
money and talent and tried to become a musical industrialist." Gillespie's decision illustrates the importance jazzmen placed on having creative and financial
control over their music. He soon found out how difficult it could be to run a
label: "We lost the masters, everything, through tax liens. [My partner] took
the blame, and the government just confiscated the masters and sold them to
Savoy or some other company, probably for next to nothing. . . . We made some
very good records, but we lost the company."[32] Dee Gee failed both to create a
well-developed strategy for selling its records and to maintain accurate financial
accounts. While Gillespie was sanguine about the experience, we can appreciate the bitterness he must have felt when he realized that the company had lost
everything to the majors, with little to no remuneration. His creative output and
intellectual property were no longer his own.

With Debut, Mingus embraced the idea that he could compose, perform, and
identify good music—and rely on an audience to trust his taste. But first, the
Minguses had to learn how to cultivate that audience and how to get the music
to them; in other words, they had to learn how to run a label. Learning how to
make records was as much about the mechanics of production as it was about
creative vision. From the beginning, Mingus perceived Debut as a label like any
other jazz independent in the postwar period. He wanted to shape the future
of jazz through releases of contemporary artists like himself. He also wanted to
make a living at selling records. The Minguses relied on the music trades to get

started. As Celia explained, "I just went at it step by step, cutting expenses, writing liner notes, taking photographs. *Billboard* printed a list of the major distributors. Well, that was *gold*. I wrote to each one of them."[33] Celia's experiences echo those of many jazz entrepreneurs who entered the business without mentors.

Drummer Max Roach and his then girlfriend, Margo Ferraci, bought into the Debut partnership, agreeing that, "since people weren't knocking our doors down to make records under our own names, . . . we'd start our own label."[34] Debut was later incorporated, with attorney Harold Lovette as president. Because Roach's "input was financial and as a performer with the company,"[35] Mingus himself assumed nearly complete control over who and what was recorded.[36] As the "Mingus Treasury" could get "mighty low,"[37] both Celia and Charles maintained other jobs to funnel money into the label's operating account while Mingus sought out and produced talent.[38] Though Mingus and Roach were primarily concerned with developing their own artistic careers—negotiating the tension between what Roach described as "trying to play and to learn how to play,"[39] that didn't preclude them from recognizing who was the true musical industrialist.

Roach admitted that simultaneously performing and running a business was more than he bargained for: "You had to lead a band, and compose and perform, and also run up to Boston to deal with distributors; or go down to the docks here in New York and see your records sitting there because you hadn't made the right connections with the unions to ship your stuff to Europe. . . . Just a number of things that befall small businesses. . . . It was too much. . . . Celia perhaps had more problems than any of us. She had to live with it."[40] Celia balanced the overlapping stresses of the label's financial demands and the personal management of Mingus's career, continually reprioritizing her work for the label. Mingus frequently dropped his work at Debut to go on the road with other bands. As she once explained to a client, it was the

> same old story—so darn busy. Mingus went with Art Tatum's Trio last month for an engagement in Miami's Birdland and really left everything on my shoulders. Not only Debut but also helping out in his capacity with the Carnegie Hall Concert which he had to drop out of. It came off very successfully incidentally and another group of musicians are getting together plans for another right after Easter. Mingus probably won't be able to make this next one either as he's now with Teddy Charles' Quartet and they're planning on being on the road for awhile.[41]

Though acknowledging the strain these gigs put on both the functioning of Debut and opportunities for Mingus to perform his music closer to home, Celia appreciated how they enabled her to develop expertise in the business of jazz as both a label owner and manager of talent. "I learned how to do all this simply because there was no one else to do it—our limited budget the first few years allowed for no outside help. . . . I received very complete training in the last four years but I would hardly advise any woman to follow in my footsteps unless she wants her whole life to be aligned with music, as mine is."[42]

Writing in 1954, Harold Lovette predicted that "with all the new material we are recording, [we] expect to be one of the leading jazz labels by the end of the year."[43] Part ideological enterprise, part commercial venture,[44] Debut actively sought a national distribution network. By building a profitable label, Mingus expected to support not only himself, but the other musicians he recorded as well. Celia, Mingus, and Roach envisioned Debut as representing modern music produced and cultivated *by* musicians *for* other musicians and fans. Mingus's own music embraced "radical diversity," with "a proclivity for experimentation, an emphasis on compositional structures, a deep feeling for the blues and the jazz traditions, [and] a stable of strong soloists," often culminating in "an exposition of Mingus."[45] Debut's other recording artists, such as Hazel Scott, Max Roach, and Thad Jones, also typified these traits of experimentation, skill, and self-expression. Given the label's dedication to new, modern sounds, its approach to distribution required a concerted effort at understanding previously unrecognizable networks of power and influence.

Other independents also realized that their longevity would depend on access to profitable distribution networks. In his first two years of operation, Bob Weinstock traveled from city to city on Greyhound buses, contacting local deejays and distributors. This road-warrior approach highlights the role that radio deejays played in creating viable audiences for jazz. Deejays made it possible for labels both to get airtime and to make connections with local record stores and distributors. Although each deejay was part of a local community, that relationship could be used as a stepping-stone to larger markets and more influence on the national scene; he was "the fellow whom the community accepts as an authority on records."[46] Many deejays, like the independent label owners, identified their emotional investment in the music as a characteristic of their creativity and evidence of their status as jazzmen. Just as independent labels were upending established industry practices, deejays and distributors were changing the landscape of popular music.

Radio had been a primary source of music entertainment in the United States since the 1930s. Between 1927 (with the passage of the emergency Federal Radio Act) and 1934 (with passage of the Federal Communications Act) the number of radio stations controlled by networks like NBC and CBS grew from 50 to 300, representing 97 percent of the evening broadcast audience across the nation and generating nearly $75 million in annual advertising revenue. Because the Federal Communications Commission (FCC) restricted the licensing of new stations before and during the war, the networks' dominance became entrenched—a Jim Crow of the airwaves.[47] Between 1947 and 1960, however, the number of AM stations licensed by the FCC grew from 1,062 to 3,456; during the same period, the number of FM stations rose from 146 to 688. While AM reception tended to be slightly noisier than the FM band, AM stations would continue to dominate radio until the early 1970s. In 1950, about 56 percent of AM stations were network-affiliated.

The decentralization of radio encouraged the growth of local independent stations. Those stations relied on "canned" music (recorded music that had previously been restricted "for home use only") instead of live musicians. Recognizing that recorded music would dramatically reduce the opportunities for musicians to earn wages and royalties on their performances, the American Federation of Musicians (AFM) called for recording bans in 1942 and 1948. AFM President James C. Petrillo decried the "power of the record [to contain and reproduce] one's own labors."[48] During the strikes, however, major record labels released the music they had stockpiled before negotiations with the union failed. The new availability of canned music gave deejays the power to control what audiences heard. *Down Beat* reported that there were at least 120 jazz deejays around the country by 1958.[49] Most local deejays did not find their profession to be especially lucrative, however. Some hosted shows on more than one station, while others only used it as a side job. Although most jazz deejays saw themselves as crusaders for the music, their zeal could be tempered by the realities of advertising revenue, as stations often structured their programming based on a deejay's ability to secure sponsorship. Deejays whose jobs depended on attracting sponsorship sometimes had to choose between advocating for jazz as art and pushing jazz as a marketable product, even though some outliers became hugely successful.

Like independent label owners, most jazz deejays embraced their responsibility both to preserve jazz and to serve as a resource for the public. After all, even those audiences who were knowledgeable liked to be reassured about their choices. As Paul Cass observed, "In a sense, jazz is a product that must be presented and promoted to be acceptable to the greatest number."[50] Deejays were there not only to inform audiences about the production details of the recording, but also to guide new listeners to a fuller appreciation and greater consumption of jazz.[51] Sometimes they had to contend with unknowledgeable distributors who didn't make the effort to furnish them with modern music or even to include them on the appropriate supply list. Such distributors would then complain that they couldn't sell the records because there was no audience for them. "Jazz doesn't sell?" Deejay Willis Conover countered: "Get the records to the guy who has built an audience for you! If the records don't sell then—somebody goofed *before* distribution."[52]

Throughout the fifties, *Metronome* chronicled the efforts of industrious jazz deejays to get "modern" music on the air, documenting the breadth of the jazz audience, and developing a framework for understanding how the music was to be heard. The featured deejays were picked for their skill at nurturing an increasingly expert and nominally more liberal jazz audience.[53] Bob Smith of Vancouver, for example, explained that his "show fills an aching void in these parts for the modern type of jazz," and claimed that he tried "to keep [his] own personal taste as broad as possible, knowing that without Lester there would have been no Stan and without Roy there would have been no Dizzy." Hal Uchida of WMID in Atlantic City was an avid fan of Stan Getz, "who brought jazz out of the cellars and really put it on the concert stage." As Uchida explained, his "only aim in radio at present is to make some people dig the sounds and hope they'll convert, because jazz has so much to offer to the trained ear. . . . Jazz also expresses freedom from prejudice—in no other art form are the barriers of racial prejudice pulled down as in jazz."[54]

Willis Conover disliked the term "disc jockey," preferring something more along the lines of "auditor-editor" since he had to "listen, study, think, edit, outline, and speak." A jazz show was not just a slapdash blend of tunes, but a well-conceived and organized program of music. "There's a definite relationship between records, a definite balance, some sort of underlying stated or unstated theme to the program."[55] *Metronome*'s featured deejays condemned those whom they thought lacked knowledge because such deejays ceded control of the show to the audience.[56] A good deejay, they argued, one who put thought into organizing and curating their shows, followed a consistent pattern. As Allen Scott insisted, "Record identifications are a must. Important members of the personnel, where and when the recording was made, and facts of general interest about the artists and their subsequent work accompany the selections."[57] To aid deejays,

Metronome published index-card cutouts featuring capsule information about the different artists they were likely to play. The *Jazz Review* lambasted this approach with ads such as "New Parlor Game for Jazz Fans: Program ideas for jazz disc jockeys. Loads of fun. Amaze your friends with 'Big Band Sidemen who never soloed,' 'Husband and wife teams trading fours,' or 'left-handed drummers.' Comes with dual turntables, complete instructions, and a copy of Cab Calloway's *Jive Dictionary.*"[58]

In the late fifties, as public outrage grew over the revelation that television game shows were being fixed, deejays came under scrutiny for the practice of payola, the promise to play music in exchange for something of value (like cash). The jazz press fixated on payola even though the payments themselves had never been illegal; not reporting such payments, however, was against the law. The public excoriated deejays who accepted payola as a "group of smart operators . . . waxing wealthy on the product of other persons' talent and ability."[59] Whether they chose to use payola to their advantage or not (the specter of pay for play continues to haunt the music industry), independent labels did succeed in helping deejays introduce the public to a multitude of new sounds over the airways.[60]

Jazz deejays were competing for airtime in a commercial landscape in which their "modern" music of choice often did not fit the programming priorities of many stations. Despite a postwar boom in jazz sales, other genres like rhythm and blues, country, and rock and roll crowded the airwaves. As Arnold Hartley, vice president and program director of New York's WOV (once a jazz station), observed in 1957, "People who like jazz have evolved into a specialized esoteric cult of the elite. Jazz no longer has a hold on the mass audience, nor even a large segment of the public, so we no longer feature it. We must appeal to the masses."[61] Although jazz shows were not securely entrenched on radio, some stations attracted a loyal audience. Writing for *Jazz Review* in 1959, Mimi Clar described the strategy of a California station featuring jazz all day. KNOB's program philosophy emphasized diversity, "the 'variety approach'—jazz for housewives, Latin jazz, dinner jazz . . . . 'Jazz for Housewives,' for instance, gives listeners the best in that class of prettier, milder jazz. The 'Housewives' show repeatedly builds to musical peaks and then descends: Sinatra and Ray Bryant might start a portion of the program and would gradually work up to Herbie Mann, Modern Jazz Quartet, and finally Sonny Rollins. Theoretically, the housewives will sit through Rollins because they know they can expect more Sinatra later on."[62]

Entering this complex field of changing markets and tastes, Celia and Charles Mingus laid the groundwork for a label that exemplified their commitment both to the music and to the individuals who made the culture such a dynamic scene. Mingus believed in his ability to identify good music. Like Gabler, Thiele, and other label owners, he would allow his own taste to dictate the content of recording sessions. Unlike those labels, however, the owner's own music would provide a creative building block for sessions. Mingus's relationships with deejays, distributors, critics, and fans were symbiotic. Each benefited financially, while each also expanded their understanding of the constraints that they as jazzmen labored under. Mingus saw these relationships as an opportunity to nurture his audience and to aid other people who were working to build a lasting jazz legacy. He seized the chance to explain his music, to discuss the challenges of creating, and to describe the impulses for presenting the music the way he did.

Mingus learned firsthand of the difficulties confronted by jazz deejays in general and black deejays in particular from Bob Summarisse, a former classmate at Jordan High. Mingus began corresponding with Summarisse after a chance encounter with Bob's brother Rudolph at the Bengasi in Washington, where Mingus was playing with Stan Getz. After reminiscing over old times, Rudolph suggested that Mingus contact Bob, who was both a deejay and a record storeowner. In his reply to Mingus's letter, Bob wrote, "Give my regards to my brother if you should see him again and tell him to be sure to write home. No ones heard from him in months."[63] Excited about Mingus's music, Summarisse offered to distribute Debut records, explaining that he was "the only Negro disc-jockey in the whole Northwest and I try to make my program as educational and entertaining as possible therefore any direct news is highly appreciated." In mid-1953, Summarisse's show was airing seven days per week; by the following year, he had been cut back to one night a week for eighty minutes. In spite of the decrease, he was nevertheless confident that "trully [sic] modern" music would continue to be aired regularly. Although he knew of other deejays in the area who would willingly "spinn [sic] modern platters," his was the "only show that plays everything including the 'funky blues.' . . . [S]ince I've been in the record business, I've changed my format somewhat but I still devote about 50% of the show to modern sides."[64]

Audiences had scant access to such music in regions where there was limited airtime (on both television and radio) and a dearth of performance venues. The few jazz stations in those areas competed with an ever-increasing number of Top 40 stations. Debut experimented with strategies for getting airtime on jazz shows like Summarrisse's. Celia Mingus believed that if deejays were truly committed to the music then they wouldn't mind sharing the financial burden of generating new listeners. More listeners would benefit the station, the deejays, and the label. She offered what she hoped would be appealing terms for access to Debut's music: "[W]e will [send samples] postage C.O.D. so that they will be sure to reach you. By mailing direct, we have often had our records get into the hands of disinterested persons at a radio station who would put them on a shelf somewhere to collect dust!"[65] Debut also provided deejays with information about the recordings that deejays could use to teach their audiences about what the musicians were trying to accomplish.

Jack Garret, an eighteen-year veteran of the tenor sax, saw deejaying as an intellectual project. Family ties carried him from Atlantic City to Mississippi; antijazz sentiment drove him from Vicksburg to Starkville. His insistence on educating his audience about the music led him to leave one station for another, one that allowed "chatter about records."[66] He provided his listeners with an all-around education in jazz, from early to modern, in the hope that jazz would triumph on the air. Garret's commitment to promoting jazz and his interest in Debut led Mingus to share why he had partnered "Precognition" with "Portrait" as Debut's first release. They were complementary sides, using the same instrumentation to different effect. "I have backed 'Precognition' which is strictly for jazz fans with 'Portrait' which I feel will appeal not only to the jazz fans but to the general public." Mingus assured Garret that he was the only deejay whom Mingus attended to personally and, outside of some New York deejays, he was the only one to receive all their releases.[67]

Mingus refused to become a jazz cliché, either as a performer or composer. He was always on the lookout for new ways to communicate with his audiences and to expand their jazz horizons. He was concerned not only with promoting his albums, but also with framing the discourse by which they might be understood and criticized, recognizing this as important for the way he would be situated within the jazz tradition. Through Debut, Mingus often challenged distributors' and deejays' approaches to marketing jazz. As one branch manager divulged, his distribution company had "learned long ago that it is a waste of time to try to sell anything but very commercial records to some accounts in our territory. Even if they get them to try and sell them, we get them back before too long as they just don't have the personnel who know enough about this type of merchandise to push it and therefore, they don't get that type buyer in their stores." As a result, this distributor explained, "Portrait" was "a little too 'way out'" for the average jazz buyer.[68] Despite the efforts of deejays and the jazz press to foster a mainstream acceptance of jazz, educating audiences about its developments through curating shows around genre, instrument, musician, and other themes, "modern music" such as Mingus's still seemed unfamiliar, out there, beyond category. But Mingus was not easily deterred. He and Celia embarked on an extensive public-relations campaign, an attempt to give the critics something to write about. By using liner notes, interviews, and correspondence to frame the music, they also shaped the aesthetic discourse around it.

Mingus imagined that a ballad would be the best way to introduce a "new field of listeners" to the music he was exploring—jazz composition with classical instruments. Mingus once used the term "jazzical" to identify these musical expressions, "because they contain both old and new classical forms as well as old and new jazz forms."[69] He thought these progressive compositions could appeal to "more cultural and intellectual music lovers,"[70] giving them a better model of what composers like him were doing in the jazz idiom. Mingus reasoned that by using "instruments (like the bassoon, oboe, violin, cello) in our music, it would open everything up" and a more mainstream acceptance of jazz would be inevitable.[71] The April 1952 recording of "Portrait" and "Precognition" by the Charles Mingus Quintet featured an interracial and mixed gender ensemble: Lee Konitz, George Koutzen, Phyllis Pinkerton, Mingus, and Al Levitt, with Jackie Paris on vocals. According to Mingus, the moods of each song were different, but equally compelling—and Jackie Paris's intimate style was well suited to "Portrait."[72] Mingus's lyrics for "Portrait" portray a seductively romantic image of nature, showing him "[p]ainting [his] own pictures in tone."[73] (The spare orchestration behind Paris's voice was made lush three years later, when Debut rerecorded "Portrait" with Thad Jones and the Charles Mingus Orchestra.[74])

Celia Mingus sent review copies of the record to Flo Hansen, a copywriter and host of a "women's world" program on KFRE in Fresno, California. In a prefatory note, Celia introduced the music first, and then Mingus.[75] Though uncertain as to Hansen's taste in jazz, she hoped that Hansen was one of the "more cultural and intellectual music lovers" who could appreciate the aesthetic direction that Mingus was taking with both "Portrait," a ballad, and the instrumental "Precognition." Because the Minguses felt that "Jazz in essence is purely an American art," they were "trying to encourage interest in it from a higher level such as those interested in the classics instead of the wild-eyed, screaming, frantic bobby-soxers who are mostly under the delusion that jazz is 'anything that's loud and fast.'"[76] After playing the songs for a number of people, Hansen responded encouragingly. "It is not a 'commercial' type recording as you probably know and the shock was too much for many of them, but I didn't let it deter me. Sometimes I let them read your letter first—sometimes afterwards. . . . [P]erhaps in repetition lies its value." Some listeners weren't able to categorize Paris's distinctive voice. "By the way," Hansen wrote, "they also want to know—is Jackie a man or a woman? I don't know what difference it makes, but that's one of the questions."[77] Although the saxophone was disturbing to some listeners who "couldn't surmount their prejudice against jazz in any form," Hansen went on, both sides could be appreciated as "musician's music" which, after awhile, "gets under one's skin."[78]

To deejay Hal Zogg's bulletin that "Portrait" and "Precognition" were being favorably received, Mingus, commented "in all modesty," that the news proved Zogg's listeners "evince a very high caliber of music appreciation."[79] To another deejay, Mingus recommended the strategy of Jack Garrett on WJQS in Jackson, Mississippi. Garrett lured listeners with the music they wanted to hear; after they learned to trust him, he began slipping in more modern jazz and teaching them how to appreciate the newer, more progressive sounds.[80] Nat Hentoff apprised Mingus that "Reaction of the listeners to your record has been excellent—particularly to *Portrait*. That's the side, after several listenings I prefer. Precognition, though stimulating, is somewhat stiff."[81] Charles Delauney, editor of *Jazz Hot*, validated Mingus's concerns about the "need of creating new sounds, and chang[ing] our ears from the same arrangements which are too often played and played again by the various bands without any attempt of changing it." He invited Mingus to write an article about his musical experiences, assuring him that "every local musician and jazz enthusiast will read" it.[82] French critic Marcel Fleiss, though willing to help Mingus, was not as confident as Delauney about there being a warm reception for the music: "the French public don't like to [*sic*] much modern jazz."[83] Nevertheless, he thought "Portrait" and "Precognition" were good and he looked forward to receiving more Debut records.[84]

While musicians, record companies, deejays, and magazines all claimed ownership of jazz, fans were no less vociferous. As we have seen in his exchanges with Gary Soucie, Mingus maintained relationships with his fans, engaging them with his theories about what makes a jazz composer and offering them advice about pursuing their own creative dreams, though he warned that he would never insist that anyone make a particular career or romantic decision.[85] Nonetheless, Mingus always embraced the chance to talk about his music (and himself) with interested listeners. Debut offered numerous opportunities to do just that. The label advertised that it was always looking for new jazz talents and that it liked "to help jazz fans whenever and wherever they could."[86] Often, jazz hopefuls would ask if it would be possible to send in tapes for consideration, and Debut would comply.[87] Sometimes fans requested advice on music merchandising, or on songwriting and singing for the label. In those instances, Celia Mingus would direct them to more appropriate venues by offering the names and addresses of local distributors or other record companies.[88]

Many jazz fans pursued opportunities for creating a space for the music. In fact, the jazz monthlies encouraged fans to recognize their financial and musical responsibilities, admonishing them to patronize nightclubs and concert halls and to become knowledgeable "beyond the ooh-and-ah school of music apprecia-tion."[89] Mingus's fans regularly updated him about their efforts to promote the jazz cause. When Jerry Walker was preparing to open a nightclub in Ann Arbor, Michigan, in the late 1950s, he understood the need for a pedagogical network for jazz fans in the area. His club would be "dedicated to the promotion of jazz . . . to give [it] the strongest backing and support it has ever received in the midwest. This nightclub will also be sponsoring a Jazz Unlimited Club open to all who are interested in learning about or further understanding the jazz scene." Club membership would require application, and preliminary responses gave Walker "reason to believe that this will be a strongly supported venture."[90] John Brown, of the Fortesque Jazz Club in Chicago, argued that if record companies, booking agents, and jazz musicians "would fully realize that they too have an obligation and would make a real effort to aid Jazz Clubs, Jazz Workshops and Societies all over the country more could be accomplished that would promise more work for the musicians, more records sold and quite naturally, more money for the booking agents."[91]

According to producer Ed Michel, Debut "was the small label's small label."[92] In an era when jazz remained a contested site for ownership, Mingus pressed his claim as both a musician and an independent label owner. Through Debut, he could open his audiences' ears to the new sounds characterizing modern jazz, particularly that music which was integrating classical and jazz traditions. "The company [was] dedicated, as Mingus says, to the proposition that jazz can be played just from being read, and also that Charlie Parker was a new beginning in jazz and not a suspended ending for everyone else to go on copying from."[93] The musicians he recorded tell us about the jazz being played at the margins and at the vanguard. Debut allowed Mingus both to nurture jazz and to nurture the individuals who were central to producing jazz—deejays, distributors, musicians, and fans. Though the ability to nurture is typically construed as an expression of femininity, jazzmen embraced the skill as a valuable aspect of jazzmasculinity. To nurture jazz was to instruct consumers on how to be fans, and to preserve and protect the music from unscrupulous people, those who were uncommitted to the ideals advocated by jazz culture.

"CELIA"

It's how I like feeling about her.

Charles Mingus Jr.

It's unbearable, because all of my aspirations of youth are gone,
to have so much energy so I can write all day long, so I did.
That's how I lost all my wives. I was writing music.

Charles Mingus Jr.

Celia Mingus's chronicle of becoming a jazzman, of aligning her whole life with music, starts with a love story. Her first husband was trumpeter Jon Neilson; they had grown up together in California. As she remembered it, "Jon wanted to be a jazz musician so I was trying to find out what the jazz scene was, and what that kind of music was about." It was during her early investigations into the jazz scene that she first met Mingus, deciding that he was "a musician who looks like he would have something to say."[94] Their marriage cemented her commitment to jazz. She willingly accepted the challenge of Debut because Mingus "had great confidence in [her]."[95] Critic and long-time friend Nat Hentoff describes Celia as a "woman of a forth-rightness and courage equal to her husband's. She also has a reservoir of perceptive wit, including the easy ability to laugh at herself, that leavens Mingus's frequent somber moods. Like Mingus, she also is an immensely understanding, warm human being who does not stifle her emotions."[96]

Celia's jazzmasculinity is rooted in affect—her feelings (love, commitment, intellectual interest) about the music and musicians, her ability to direct those feelings into the management of the label, and her willingness to be emotionally open and take professional risks. Her status as Mingus's wife placed unexpected demands on her, but also allowed her the room to grow as an individual and as a jazzman. Her commitment to Mingus drove the success of the label. She nurtured Mingus, provided discipline for the company, and produced a musical legacy. Celia Mingus navigated the independent music business by drawing on her familiarity with the everyday lives of musicians and by constructing a business strategy that relied on interpersonal networks, knowledge about musicians and music, and the dynamism of her individual personality. Elaine Tyler May notes that, in the years after World War II, only one-fifth of employed women found their work to be personally fulfilling. The postwar reconfiguration of gender in the workplace limited the diversity of job options for women, reinforcing "women's subordinated position in the occupational hierarchy."[97] Though Celia found an opportunity to fulfill her ambitions by working at the label, she nevertheless believed that the gendered structure of jazz culture limited the number and types of employment available to women.[98] Celia's role in Debut expands our conceptions of how women shaped jazz culture. While she may not have eliminated barriers to increased representation of women in the business of making and selling jazz, she does represent a window onto how women shaped jazz in their image. Celia made Debut work in a way that Mingus could not.

Celia understood that the predominantly male world of the record business was rife with gender stereotypes. The roles Mingus, Celia, and Roach performed were not expressly defined initially. Her early tasks in the day-to-day running of the label were largely secretarial: she drafted and signed communications for Brandt, Mingus, and Roach.[99] Her deployment of masculine authority in the early stages of the label's founding, however, allowed her to serve Debut's interests while making a place for herself in a sexist industry. She often used Mingus, whose reputation as "Jazz's Angry Man" was widespread, as both carrot and stick for delinquent clients. As she embraced her authority as a jazzman and asserted her role as primary administrator of Debut's affairs, her name became synonymous with the label and her tactics shifted. She understood the importance of building connections with people who were, like her, invested emotionally in the music. Celia forged bonds with distributors, disc jockeys, and music critics by expressing emotional and personal interest in their lives and in their commitment to the music. Informal, interpersonal connection was crucial for their success. Unlike Duke Ellington's Mercer label, which was initially distributed through Prestige, Debut could not rely on a large corporate infrastructure to track invoices or ensure production values.

Building such ties was essential to providing a foundation for Debut's expansion across the country. In order for the music to be heard, people needed to feel an obligation both to the label and to the people managing the label. Most deejays and distributors requested news updates about musicians, the nightlife, and what was being recorded to expand their own knowledge about the scene. Ohio distributor Rob Gannon found that moving Debut LPs was slow going, but he and Celia's shared musical interests enhanced their ties.[100] In a quick reply to Gannon's request for someone willing to score music for the "modern vocal quartet" he had put together, Celia recommended her "Schillinger teacher at Hartnett's, George Robinson—[who] was writing some crazy things for a vocal quartet not too long ago." Even though she was no longer attending Hartnett's ("I'm giving myself a vacation after a year and a half steady!"), she and Robinson were still in touch and she could provide Gannon with an introduction very easily.[101] She helped Gannon because of her general interest in "reaching that section of the public which is more concerned with the progressive arts."[102] Other opportunities regularly presented themselves for building a network sympathetic to Debut's interests. She and Mingus introduced music critic Ralph Gleason to Bill Coss of *Metronome*. Gleason enjoyed the meeting, not just because he "dug" Coss's work, but also because Coss was "a real good guy and an honest one."[103]

Celia took full advantage of the entrepreneurial and collaborative nature of the independent jazz scene. Other jazzmen encouraged Celia to seek out and maintain her own list of distributors and disc jockeys, particularly because most distributors were "very un-promotional minded."[104] She then asserted control over the distributors, providing them with regional lists of critics and deejays to whom she wanted them to send sample copies, although distributors were given some discretion in deciding on the best candidates for promoting Debut's albums in their area.[105]

To counter the competitive edge that majors had over independents, those involved in the independent scene had to take on a variety of responsibilities. For example, Salt Lake City disc jockey Hal Zogg offered to act as a distributor in Utah because other distributors were "pretty well tied down by their mother companies."[106] Through their relationships with critics such as Ralph Gleason, who regularly reviewed Debut's recordings in his column for the *San Francisco Chronicle*, Celia and Mingus also were able to interest other distributors into taking on their label.[107] Distributors in so-called "jazz deserts" reached out to Debut, offering their services to market in areas such as Colorado, Wyoming, and New Mexico. And when fans pressed distributors to stock Debut recordings, distributors pressed Debut for access. Bob Thoralson of Modern Music House in Billings, Montana, wrote, "My jazz customers have read some good reviews in *Metronome* lately on your LPS. How on earth can I get them?"[108] The independent scene was entrepreneurial, collaborative, and jazz mad.

Despite their enthusiasm, however, not all of the industry's participants were business savvy, and their lack of acumen often affected Debut's bottom line. Still, Celia knew that even if an individual distributor failed at selling a particular album, its participation remained essential to selling future albums. The networks were so small that none could be ignored or cut off permanently. When Celia began corresponding with Audrey Schwarz of College Music Distributing, in Boston, she demonstrated the same informality she employed with other distributors and disc jockeys. Celia admitted to Schwarz that the newly formed label did not yet have a fully developed billing system in place. She intended to rely on College Music's experience while she worked out her own system. "Since we're new in the business, when you do get the records you might let me know how you're usually invoiced."[109] After four months without receiving any money from this distributor, however, Celia saw that this approach would not work. Though hoping to maintain a positive working relationship (Debut had just completed another recording session and needed College Music's network), Celia made clear how important it was to promptly receive all the money due them. "It is a very small amount but since we are a new company operating on a very limited budget and are pressed to meet our own obligations, we would greatly appreciate your check by return mail."[110] Her pleas were sometimes met with similar cries from the distributors, who pointed out how connected they all were and acknowledged that they could only pay their Debut accounts if their own clients paid them first.[111] But Celia wasn't placated. She excoriated College Music for their lack of payment. "I trust that when you started in business you received better treatment from your customers—otherwise I do not see how you could still be in business today."[112] College Music claimed there had been a mix-up with the two checks Debut was expecting—one had been lost, while the other was in the mail. Some six months later, Debut still had not received any money. The label eventually concluded that it did "make one mistake in this entire maze of events and that was sending you the records."[113]

Numerous companies found their way to the "dead" file, for reasons ranging from inexperience, to lack of financial resources, to the seemingly inexplicable. Celia responded with sarcastic incredulity to some of the excuses offered by delinquent accounts for nonpayment. "We sympathize with your position and we have extended our heartfelt sorrow at your 'bad luck.' However, we cannot be sorry and patient forever as we are in business to sell records, not extend condolences!"[114] It was not unusual for distributors to bear the brunt of a record producer's ire. Bob Thiele characterized them as "instinctively and habitually, killer parasites," who were "not basically music people. The old gag was that these distributors were so great they could sell shoes as well as records."[115] But having once been consigned to the dead file did not preclude a company from resurrection—if that distributor could fill a void in a given territory. For example, Debut dropped Commercial Music in St. Louis, Missouri, in early 1957 for nonpayment, but Celia turned to them again in June of that year once their account had been cleared.[116] Records, Inc., in Boston was reinstated because Celia wanted help in promoting Alonzo Levister's new album while he played in the area.[117] The need to gain access to record-buyers often overrode any pragmatic assessments of a distributor's business skills. It was a risk that independents had to take, and Celia didn't shy away from making the hard choices.

Debut expected distributors to zealously promote their records since that was how a distributor would see his own profit; nevertheless, some distributors pursued questionable strategies at best.[118] For example, Robert Chatton of Chatton Distributing Co., in Oakland, sent Mingus a letter breezily announcing his decision to shift the line to another distributor. "By this time perhaps you are aware that we have discontinued your line. . . . We are writing you, however, on behalf of a new distributor who we believe will do a fine job for you. . . . His credit rating seems to be good in these parts."[119] Perhaps stranger still, Music Please & Record Co., of Hubbard, Ohio, requested an invoice for the records it had sold—as if Debut would know what they had been doing in Ohio.[120] One California distributor expected Celia to be sensitive to his circumstances since his was a small company, unable to "lay out a lot of cash for slow moving items." He thought she should be even more sympathetic considering that he had "in fact . . . paid off Disc Jockeys out of [his] own pocket." This was the only suggestion of payola found in the Debut archives, although some deejays and distributors might have occasionally received free records for review.

As a perk for its more diligent distributors, Debut instituted a payment policy intended to mitigate the effects of a price war then underway. In the mid-1950s, the majors were turning away from shellac-based 78s toward the newly engineered vinyl 45s and LPs. Vinyl records were cheaper to produce and distribute than the old shellac ones. And the microgroove significantly lengthened the time available for recording on an album; for example, the music on four 78-rpm discs could fit on a single 10-inch, 33-⅓ LP with four songs on each side. Columbia had introduced a 12-inch LP in 1948; to challenge its increasing popularity, RCA produced the 7-inch 45.[121] Economies of scale enabled the majors to offer distributors lower prices—independents could not compete and many were soon bankrupted. Some independent labels, like Debut, realized that they would have to reissue their recordings on the new LPs in order to remain competitive.

Making sure that records were pressed and mailed without breaking was a constant source of anxiety for Debut. RCA Victor, touting the technological quality of their albums,[122] sometimes leased their studios to independents and even distributed their music on occasion. Though Victor initially seemed like a safe bet to Debut, the finished records belied the advertised quality. Mingus did not "know how Victor [could] put out such material—and still charge more than anyone else."[123] To Celia, "This Victor is a pain in the A flat." To find other options for recording and pressing, Celia had to do a lot of footwork, becoming increasingly literate about the questions that needed to be asked to make an informed decision about which company would get their business.[124]

Celia's experiences reflect how the choice to align one's life completely with music both strained and nurtured individual ambitions that exceeded gendered expectations of a woman's role in jazz culture. For women like Celia, skill in what was typically thought of as women's work (nurturing male ambition and caring for family members) facilitated their initial participation in jazz culture; this provided the ground for them to transform their own and other's expectations of that participation. Bill Evans, the pianist on Mingus's *East Coasting* album (on which the Mingus composition "Celia" is recorded), was managed by Helen Keane from the late 1960s through 1980. Keane, the first woman to be trained as an agent at MCA, remembered how "The men I worked for saw something in me, saw that I had a feeling for performers. So they . . . trained me, all very quiet." She had started working at MCA in the 1950s at age seventeen. After two marriages, children, and a move to competitor CBS, Keane decided that she did not want to be a mother who worked outside the home any longer. "For one thing, I missed the children. So I left CBS and opened my own little management office, right in my apartment." Keane's experiences as a manager and producer trained her to delegate tasks to men who possessed greater technical knowledge without feeling insecure about her demands.[125]

Musicians often relied on their romantic partners to manage their financial affairs, to make it possible for them to do the work of music—to spend their time thinking and playing—rather than scrounging to make ends meet. As Valerie Wilmer observes of musicians in the 1970s, "the male musician without an established name has generally relied on his wife or 'old lady' for economic support."[126] The value of women's support was often couched in terms of racial difference, with white women seen as more accommodating than black women. Lack of accommodation could lead to tragic consequences when an "old lady" confronted the fact that her financial support and sexual loyalty did not ensure a musician's fidelity; a woman's disappointment also could lead to grave consequences for the music itself.[127] Black women who supported their husbands' musical careers labored under the demands of respectability as well. Black jazzmen who had a "happy home" were celebrated, particularly in the black press, for making jazz acceptable to the mainstream and reinforcing conservative gender ideals of female respectability and responsibility.

More established jazz industrialists like Lionel Hampton and Dizzy Gillespie also relied upon the business acumen of their wives. In its praise of Gladys Hampton, for example, an article in *Color* magazine was typical of the time: "Gladys had faith in Lionel Hampton and the drive to encourage his ambitions." The reporter notes that her ability to manage his business affairs had been cultivated in her previous career and from the lessons she had learned from her mother. "A designer of quite a reputation, Gladys modestly says she was 'just a little dressmaker' before she met Lionel. Gladys Riddle was designing creations for such great personalities as Joan Crawford, Marian Davies, Norma Shearer and Lady Mountbatten when she decided to become Mrs. Lionel Hampton."[128] Her position as a respectable black woman factored into Hampton's integration of Benny Goodman's band. As Hampton explained, "[Gladys] had a terrific business, but I had to persuade her to give it up and come travel with us. Benny had said, 'If you come, I want your wife to come.' I guess I was young and pretty wild, and Benny wanted me to have a stabilizer along. He was real sharp."[129] Having Gladys Hampton along when the band traveled the South also could have mitigated potential racial conflicts: what better strategy than to have Hampton traveling with a woman who was both black and his wife?

Hampton was effusive in his praise of Gladys's management of both his band and their life. "We were the perfect team. . . . She was the boss offstage, and I was the boss onstage. A creative person needs someone to run interference. That's what she did."[130] Even some nonmusicians recognized Gladys's management skills. As Malcolm X told Alex Haley, "My boss's wife and Gladys Hampton were the only two women I ever met in Harlem whose business ability I really appreciated."[131]

When asked about working with Hampton, many musicians commented that the Hamptons paid "slave wages," no matter what the venue, and that to ask for a raise was tantamount to offering one's resignation. As Joe Wilder said, "It was sort of a reverse slavery in a way. . . . [Lionel] sort of had an attitude towards the fellows in the band that you can't work any place, because there are so few places for musicians to work and if you don't like the way I treat you, you're out of a job." Cecil McNeely recalled that "Hamp's wife, Gladys, was very protective of Hamp. Nobody stole the show from Hampton."[132] Gladys Hampton exercised an iron fist over the band's affairs. In fact, according to Marshal Royal, "she was the silent leader of the band. She tended to everything."[133]

Dizzy Gillespie similarly praised his wife, Lorraine, for giving him "proper perspective. She gives me the anchor I need."[134] The couple had met when she was working as a dancer in New York nightclubs and he was struggling as a young trumpeter. One critic speculated that it was Gillespie's cooking more than anything else that had won Lorraine over.[135] Drawing on her experience as a professional performer, Lorraine made no bones about telling Dizzy whether he was playing well or not. "She was a dancer, and she says I play off time. I do play off time in the sense of what she's talking about: cham ba dum ba de ba de bund. She remembers the days with Teddy Hill, when I used to make up head arrangements for the band and it used to swing, 'cause she was a chorus girl and they danced their asses off."[136]

Like Gillespie, Raymond Brown also valued his wife's opinions about the music. "I've been digging how my old lady will go to a gig with me and I ask her, 'How'd it sound, baby?' and she'll say 'W-e-e-ll, you just wasn't too strong tonight.' That kind of criticism is so vital. It gets back to that family thing again—you know, no man is an island. He's got to be with somebody else."[137] For Gillespie, it was Lorraine's willingness to put her career before his and "all that grandmother wit" learned during her childhood that provided the foundation for their marriage. Gillespie figured that he successfully avoided the traps that captured so many other musicians because Lorraine was a "staunch defender" who knew all about show business and could separate her love and respect for him as a person from the rumors and hangers-on.[138] As he noted in 1952, Lorraine was "always broad-minded."[139]

Women who were jazzmen—like Hazel Scott, Mary Lou Williams, Lena Horne, Carla Bley, Abbey Lincoln, and Jeanne Lee, among others—also saw their careers shaped by their marriages and relationships with lovers.[140] Scott, who recorded one of her best-selling albums, *Relaxed Piano Moods*, on Debut, found that her marriage to Adam Clayton Powell Jr. propelled her onto the national scene. As the next chapter will demonstrate, Scott's marriage increased the pressure on her to be an exceptional woman—exceptional as a race woman and as a jazzman—even as marriage protected her from the indignities often heaped on women pursuing independent careers. Scrutiny of Scott's performance technique intensified in late 1945 when she left her Café Society to embark on a career as a concert artist shortly after marrying Powell, leading to what became known as "the Hazel Scott incident." Their marriage made her one of the first ladies of black America in the fifties and complicated her positioning within jazz culture. Neither the road to marriage nor its course was easy. Scott and Powell were both dynamic and ambitious. Scott exuded an attractive confidence, marked by a tolerable dose of arrogance, and a healthy measure of race pride. Critic Phil Carter notes that "she was known as much for her insistence on what she believed were her rights as she was for her famous boogie-woogie playing at the piano."[141] Powell, the first black person elected to serve as a New York City councilman, had just launched his career as a U.S. congressman. His base of power was the Abyssinian Baptist Church in Harlem, where he was pastor, a post he had inherited from his father, Adam Clayton Powell Sr., in 1937. The *Chicago Defender* postulated that Powell's decision to marry Scott yielded from his assessment of the prevailing political winds. He was marrying "probably the most famous American woman of West Indian descent" and the union might ease "misunderstandings between Negro American and West Indian Negroes."[142] According to biographer Wil Haygood, Powell masterminded a campaign to get Scott a performance at Constitution Hall in Washington, D.C.[143] That dramatic introduction to President Harry Truman and the nation would profoundly shape the trajectory of Scott's career.

When Debut was founded, Charles and Celia had been married only a year. It was the second marriage for both, but their first interracial marriage. Neither attributed the dissolution of their marriage to the effects of racism. As Celia remembered, "Mingus would say that we stood for something. We are an example to the world that black and white can work."[144] But business concerns did become an obstacle in their relationship, and the demands of Mingus's career threatened to overshadow Celia's independence. As Celia explained, she "found it difficult to function as his wife and his manager. . . . Because he didn't want his wife telling him what to do, and at the same time I couldn't be a manager and not tell him what to do where work was concerned. . . . The only way we could survive at that point, as I saw it, was if I completely sacrificed anything I wanted, and just spent my life doing what Mingus wanted me to do. And I couldn't do it."[145]

Celia left Mingus on April 2, 1958—their seventh wedding anniversary—but she continued to be a part of his life. "Mingus always had a good feeling about me," she recalled. "I guess time proved to him that I was never going to cheat him."[146] After learning of his Guggenheim Fellowship and hearing the details of his book party for *Beneath the Underdog*, she wrote to say, "Sounds like everything is going great for you and we are very happy."[147] The "we" refers to her relationship with Saul Zaentz, owner of Fantasy Records, an independent label and distributor based in California. Celia had found a job there as a secretary thanks to Bill Coss; she and Zaentz eventually married.

With both Roach and Celia gone, Mingus struggled to keep Debut afloat. Although he hoped to develop a partnership with his old friend Buddy Collette, nothing was to come of those efforts.[148] Fantasy Records eventually gained control of the Debut and Jazz Workshop masters; it began reissuing the music in 1962. Though Debut had officially stopped recording in 1957, Mingus never abandoned his desire to own his creative work. He explored other ways of seizing control, including starting another record label and more than one publishing company.[149]

As Debut's history reveals, the story of jazz does not emerge solely from early twentieth-century bachelor culture. Indeed, it is a story of marital and familial relationships in which women were able to cultivate ambitions. Whether thrust into their roles or claiming them on their own, these women developed expertise that contributed to the financial and artistic legacy of jazzmen. During a time when jazz deejays and local stations were attempting to cultivate audiences, jazz-oriented performance venues were becoming increasingly hard to come by.[150] The promotion of jazz during this period depended on an intellectual culture that would introduce artists to the public. While some of this occurred within the jazz press,[151] with *Metronome* leading the effort,[152] much of the music's fan base developed through the critical, personal, and distribution networks so crucial to sustaining an independent label. Aligning her whole life with music, Celia Mingus created a lasting legacy as a jazzman.

FOUR

"Eclipse"

Jazzmasculinity, Race Womanhood, and the Hazel Scott Incident

[Holiday's] tragedy was that she didn't let her natural instincts take
charge and just sing. . . . Instead she began to interpret.

Michael Brooks

The shabbiness, even embarrassment, of Hazel Scott playing "concert boogie
woogie" before thousands of white middle-class music lovers, who all
assumed that this music was Miss Scott's invention, is fully no more hideous
than the spectacle of an urban, college-trained Negro musician pretending,
perhaps in all sincerity, that he has the same field of emotional reference
as his great-grandfather, the Mississippi slave. Each seems to me merely
burlesque, or cruder, a kind of modern minstrelsy.

LeRoi Jones

In 1955, Hazel Scott, Charles Mingus, and Rudy Nichols were filmed in black and
white performing two numbers during that year's March of Dimes Telethon.[1]
Scott's piano is foregrounded on the stage, with Mingus beside her on the left
and Nichols on the drums to Mingus's left. Scott rises from behind the piano
and walks toward the camera. There she reads from the teleprompter positioned
just below the camera's line of sight. Scott wears a strapless cocktail-length dress
with a sweetheart neckline, fitted at the waist. Though imperceptible on film,

the whisper of her skirts, as "always [making] the sound of swishing like sand paper,"[2] is likely audible to those near the stage.

After introducing "Foggy Day," Scott returns to the piano and the camera zooms in, framing her face, shoulders, and décolleté. The camera glances at Mingus and Nichols, but caresses Scott. As Scott sings, she emotes not only through her voice and dynamically rhythmic piano playing, but also through her facial expressions and her body movements. As ethnomusicologist Monica Hairston writes of Scott's work in earlier films, here "Over the course of her performance and in dramatic alignment with key musical moments, she shrugged her shoulders coyly, she lifted one shoulder with playful come-hither teasing, she lifted a hand to accent a phrase, she shimmied, she nodded, closed her eyes or looked off into space, lost in the music, she mugged, raised her eyebrows, winked, and smiled."[3] At the end of the song, Scott retraces her steps to read from the teleprompter. Back at the piano, she sings "Autumn Leaves" in French, her ability to sing in multiple languages a hallmark of her vocal talents and evidence of her "strategic cosmopolitanism."[4] The camera lingers on her face until the final measures of the song, when it spies Mingus's hand slowly drawing his bow across the bass strings.

Earlier that year, Scott had released *Relaxed Piano Moods* (which included a version of "Foggy Day") on Debut. On this album, Scott known for "jazzin' the classics," led a trio that included Mingus and Max Roach, joint owners of the label. For Mingus, who was then exploring the nexus between jazz and classical music, performing with Scott must have been a compelling project. While working frequently as a sideman, Mingus also was teaching the bass, composing, and developing his own band. While his own star was rising, Scott's was burning hotly. Despite having built a career on her technical virtuosity and emotion-laden performances, however, Scott could not satisfy the jazz critics who argued that she was not a true jazzman, unable to perform with emotional transparency and authenticity. She recognized the conundrum. When asked how a "bad write-up" affected her, she remarked that if it was "grossly unfair," she would disregard it completely. "If a critic understands what I was trying to do, then it's beautiful. But if I'm emotionally torn up after a performance and a critic says I skimmed the surface of my material, I want to hit him in the mouth! How deeply involved are you supposed to get?"[5] Scott as angry jazzman tells us as much about the narrow language available for the postwar jazz aesthetic as it does about the scene's gender dynamics. Perhaps in working through her anger toward critics who diminished the emotionality of her music, she unlocked new ways of expressing feeling and explored self-imposed limitations on that feeling. Decades after the release of *Relaxed Piano Moods*, Scott mused on the changes then emerging in her technique, commenting, "My style of playing is much more funky than it used to be, maybe because I'm less self-conscious about it. Max [Roach] and Mingus used to say I was a lady when I played the blues. So maybe I have reached a point where I can relax enough not to be a lady when I play."[6]

Any examination of masculinity in jazz culture is incomplete without analysis of how women participated in the jazz world. In her role at Debut, Celia Mingus's emotional investment, like that of other nonmusicians who sustained jazz, tied her to jazz culture in ways that, as she liked to say, aligned her "whole life" with the music. She modeled jazzmasculinity by putting into practice the values of innovation, collaboration, expertise, and emotionality that defined the culture. Musicians like Hazel Scott performed jazzmasculinity as well, stamping it with her individual voice. When she left the cabaret scene of Café Society for the rarefied atmosphere of the concert stage, jazzing the classics with her "concert boogie-woogie," she demanded we see her as an interpreter of music. Gifted with prodigious skills as a pianist, Scott embraced the cultural signifiers that served other jazzmen as they positioned themselves within jazz culture. She was an artist, not an entertainer; she expressed emotion in performance; she was competitive; she was disciplined; she was a race woman; she was a genius. And yet, even as she exemplified the idealized characteristics of the jazzman, Scott's jazzmasculinity was derided as inauthentic, crude, inappropriate.

Scott's experiences during a pivotal period in jazz, from the mid-forties to the late fifties, reveal how those confrontations sprang from the collisions of a radicalized black community, a white nation insistent on retaining the status quo, and a jazz culture that chewed up black women who asserted their jazzmasculinity. I begin with Scott's emergence as a cabaret performer at Barney Josephson's Café Society to capture how women experienced their jazzmasculinity and its representation as a type of genius. Next I discuss what was known as "the Hazel Scott incident," which embroiled Scott, Adam Clayton Powell Jr., Clare Boothe Luce, and the Daughters of the American Revolution (DAR) in the then-raging debate over whether American racism was analogous to Nazi fascism. I shift into a discussion of Scott's testimony before the House Committee on Un-American Activities, where she attempts to salvage her career from the damage of Congress's anticommunist fervor. As is typical with jazzmen, discourses of rights (civil and social), Americanness, and racial propriety marked how Scott was seen to make music and shaped how her musicking was valued as a cultural practice. Scott's jazzmasculinity was at first a source of support; later, she was punished for embracing those characteristics. Nevertheless, like any other true jazzman, she refused to conform.

Hazel Scott perceived herself (and was perceived by others) as an exceptional artist. Her embrace of that exceptionality also led to her embracing the mantle of race woman. African Americans embraced race men who "establish[ed] race pride," by executing "an aggressive demonstration of their superiority in some field of achievement, either individually or collectively," to the benefit of the race as opposed to themselves solely.[7] Scott's experiences in the fifties—as she built a career, married a race man, and became a public victim of racism—illustrate how jazzmasculinity and race womanhood were often in conflict. A race man who was also a jazzman could articulate his superiority through the mastery of music. Jazz, as Hazel Carby notes, was associated with freedom as an ideal expression of cultural, political, and social values. The race man, like the jazzman, also could use his own experiences in becoming an exemplar of protest and critique. As a figure of protest and critique, however, a female jazzman who embraces her status as race woman exercises a tenuous hold on her audiences. She must be a virtuous, sympathetic figure, at the same time that she articulates anger with the limitations that race and gender have pressed on her.

In the homosocial world of jazz, the moment of recognition of one's relationship to the practice of art, for the jazzman, is experienced as one of sexual desire[8] and the articulation of emotional self-knowledge. But how is jazzmasculinity articulated as a moment of becoming or recognition for women? When freedom characterizes the social, political, and musical zeitgeist of the period, and women musicians are marginalized within the jazz fraternity,[9] what freedoms are they in search of? How is *freedom* emotionally viable as a creative lens for these female jazzmen? How do they remain productive in that creative world? What sexual and gender politics are troubled or reinscribed when a woman is a leader on the jazz scene?[10] Exploring Hazel Scott's career provides entrée into these questions and allows us to see how important her story is to understanding the issues Mingus faced during his early years in New York. Believing himself always to be an underdog, Mingus would no doubt have commiserated with Scott as she exercised her authority as a jazzman and faced consequences that damaged her career, her relationships, and her dignity.

"DEVIL WOMAN"

Another interesting thing—Negro shows before being tampered with
did not specialize in octoroon chorus girls. The girl who could hoist
a Jook song from her belly and lam it against the front door of the theatre
was the lead, even if she were as black as the hinges of hell.
The question was "Can she Jook?"

Zora Neale Hurston

I don't think I'm singing. I feel like I am playing a horn. I try to improvise
like Les Young, like Louie Armstrong, or someone else I admire. What
comes out is what I feel. I hate straight singing. I have to change a tune to my
own way of doing it. That's all I know.

Billie Holiday

[S]he was a woman already and I was still a kid. She always protected me.
She had a very fierce protectiveness where I was concerned.

Hazel Scott

The story of Hazel Scott's genius was widely circulated. Newspaper and maga-
zine accounts depicted her as a prodigy, labeling her "Little Miss Hazel Scott,
Child Wonder Pianist." Born in Trinidad in 1920, she was raised in New York
City during the height of the Harlem Renaissance. She began playing piano by
ear at age four; in 1926 she performed at Town Hall and in 1940 she debuted at
Carnegie Hall. During an audition for Paul Wagner, a professor at the Juilliard
School of Music, the eight-year-old played Rachmaninoff's Prelude in C Sharp
Minor. "She knew she would have to do something to make up for those notes
she could not touch," Arna Bontemps writes.[11] "Wherever the octaves occurred,
Hazel substituted sixths, an odd interval to be sure, and nothing like the effect
the composer intended, but under the circumstances it seemed to Hazel the best
substitute at her command." Wagner acknowledged her gift by placing his hand
on Scott's head and remarking quietly, "I am in the presence of genius." Though
she was too young to be given a scholarship, Wagner took her on as a student,
providing her with free lessons for the next eight years. Scott continued taking
lessons with her mother on other instruments. Her mother, Alma Long Scott,
was a piano teacher and a professional alto and tenor saxophonist, who led her
own orchestra and worked as a sideman for jazzmen like Lil Hardin Armstrong.[12]
Scott's career as a trumpeter was short as, according to one writer, "Hazel feared

that a pronounced embouchure might spoil her looks."[13] As noted in the earlier discussion of Scott's performance of "Foggy Day," her "looks" were an integral part of the persona she presented to audiences.

New York's music scene at the time—from Harlem's big bands, led by the likes of Fletcher Henderson and Chick Webb, to mid-Manhattan nightclubs featuring smaller combos—was jumping. The musicians were predominantly male, with a few bands featuring female vocalists. Female instrumentalists, white or black, were heavily scrutinized, and their femininity was often read as a measure of their lack of musical knowledge, skill, and authenticity.[14] And yet Scott found a home at Café Society Downtown, "jazzing the classics" and mastering "boogie-woogie." Café Society opened in 1938, offering a nightly showcase of cabaret acts—instrumentalists, dancers, singers, and comedians—performing twenty- to thirty-minute sets. Boogie-woogie, a piano style that had emerged in the late nineteenth century, demanded that pianists develop hand independence, with the left hand playing blues-based progressions while the right hand plays syncopated melodies or block chords. Boogie-woogie pianists often performed unaccompanied. During the Swing era, Count Basie, Meade Lux Lewis, and Albert Ammons were its most popular progenitors, while Art Tatum and Teddy Wilson developed boogie-woogie, stride, jazz, and classical traditions into unique and highly influential styles, shaping the ideas of other pianists.[15]

Critic Leonard Feather explains that boogie-woogie in Scott's hands "is, in effect, a synthesis of the artist's impressions of the eight-beat piano style, performed with an instinctive feeling for contrast and climax." Scott maintained aesthetic integrity while simultaneously appealing to a wide audience because what she offered was "not aimed solely at the jazz specialists. . . . [S]he has learned how to combine an innate musicianship and orthodox technique with an unusually commercial quality which is aural as well as visual."[16] Nora Holt, music critic for the *New York Amsterdam News*, found that Scott's "ability to create a new style of improvisations and fantasia in the popular field which embraces the use of all the artifices employed in legitimate music," enabled her to bring a "scholarly approach to the swing division. For this innovation so intelligently handled, she is one step ahead of most instrumentalists."[17] Note that Feather and Holt praise Scott's technical skill, her awareness of the demands of commercial appeal, and her nuanced understanding of the relationship of jazz to other music. Scott's appreciation of these characteristics of jazzmasculinity, including the recognition of jazz as both a business and a form of work, positioned her to chart a career as a successful soloist.

Scott relied on a "proliferating discourse" of racialized and feminized genius to counter the coterie of reviewers who found her style "too gimmicky." A critic for *Time* wrote, "Where others murder the classics, Hazel Scott merely commits arson. . . . She seems coolly determined to play legitimately, and, for a brief while, triumphs. But gradually, it becomes apparent that evil forces are struggling within her for expression."[18] Other critics slammed her approach to and "understanding" of classical music. Though they praised her talent, they advised her to keep to jazz. These critics' aversion to praising Scott for performing classical music seemed to rest on their dismissal of jazz as a complex art, viewing it as little more than a "wild" and "undisciplined" form. Regardless of the facts of her training and skill, these types of reviews put Scott in her place as unqualified and unsuited to performing "real" music in a concert hall. In that sense, they are as scathing in their interpretation of her talent as LeRoi Jones had been when he claimed that the emotionality of her music was inauthentic and laughable (see epigraph to this chapter). Such responses identify the twinned threats many mainstream music critics felt during and after the war—about the quality and strength of women's abilities as instrumentalists on the one hand, and about the increasing dominance of jazz as a popular music, including the specific influence of "black" styles such as bebop, on the other.[19]

Critical focus on Scott's talents eventually shifted from her musical gifts and intellect to her body. This was perhaps a natural progression for a child prodigy. As Scott matured from precocious talent to femme fatale, the increased attention on her femininity and sexuality illustrates both the limited language for women's musical genius and an increasing conservatism around gender during the postwar period. For many, Scott's femininity made her a relatable and accessible star. She was "sweet and hot," and her refusal to wear a girdle seemed evidence that she recognized the "heaven sent" gift of her figure. One writer deemed her a worthy example for "Hundreds of thousands of women of all ages" who "would be more attractive if they leave off their girdles and let themselves fall into normal position." Scott reportedly spent no more than $25 each for the strapless evening gowns she called her "overalls," a term more associated with work than feminine vanity. These gowns showcased the muscularity of her performance and emphasized the power in her arms. This physicality only contributed to her sensuality. "All the lights would go out, Hazel would make her way to the piano, and then suddenly a spotlight would catch her. For a moment the audience would gasp, because it looked as if she were seated there nude—the height of the piano, the bare-shouldered dress, nothing but the golden-brown shoulders and arms, the super-talented fingers."[20] Reviewer Seymour Peck emphasized how her body was as deeply implicated in the performance as her technique. "Her dress represented an interesting compromise with concert-hall tradition. Known for her superbly décolleté costumes, Miss Scott wore last night a black number with a glittery sequin top that covered one arm and shoulder quite without covering. Needless to say, Miss Scott knew which shoulder to keep toward her audience."[21]

Even though Scott's coming of age as a musician was framed within a limiting discourse of femininity, this did not preclude her embrace and expression of masculine authority as a performer and leader. Nor did she disavow her jazzmasculinity when confronted with conservative narratives of gender and racial propriety. Scott's combination of "feminine genius," musical skill, and performance of sexuality plunged her into the limelight, where she navigated the Scylla and Charybdis of fame and ambition. During her residency at Café Society she encountered Lena Horne, unrivaled in her role as glamorous race woman. Ruth Feldstein's depiction of Horne as carving out a space for herself as "a respectable sex symbol," "a distinctly modern black female performer, one who was sexual and respectable, who was desirable yet also unattainable," aptly describes Scott as well.[22] The relationship between Horne and Scott makes clear the minefields racially conscious women faced making their way as artists in New York during the 1940s.[23]

A clip from the 1943 Red Skelton and Eleanor Powell film *I Dood It*, directed by Vincente Minnelli, puts us in the frame for appreciating how Hazel Scott and Lena Horne performed at Café Society. The comedy concerns the antics of an "air-headed pants presser" in love with a Broadway star who yearns after another man for most of the film. One of the subplots involves the producers of a play-within-the-film seeking backers for a new revue featuring Scott and Horne, appearing as themselves. The clip opens by tracking Scott as she enters the theater with her entourage. She begins "trying out" the piano by playing "Takin' a Chance." Her entourage, serving as a well-dressed chorus, drapes themselves across the piano to watch her fingers fly across the keys. A few minutes later Horne rushes in alone, apologizing and attributing her lateness to an inability to find a cab. Seconds later with the lights dim and the spotlight on her she launches into "Jericho." Some minutes later, she stands near Scott at the piano and they close the song in unison. The juxtaposition of Scott's physical and flirty approach at the piano and Horne's theatrical presentation of the song showcases the different styles they brought to the Café Society universe, where politics and art fed one another.[24]

Though Scott and Horne were featured separately at the two Café Society nightclubs—one downtown, the other uptown—the animosity and competition between them was a public secret. According to Horne, "Hazel and I . . . we'd go to hear Billie together, and that's one time we would settle down and not fight. Because here was this voice speaking for the people."[25] The "original 'woman singer'" at Café Society, Billie Holiday had paved the way for both Scott and Horne. Her status as race woman was solidified with her 1939 performance of "Strange Fruit," a song that articulated the heartache, despair, and anger that black communities experienced because of lynching. Her music made that racialized experience accessible so that a broader audience could feel outrage. Holiday exuded authority, femininity, and emotion. Her voice was an instrument finely tuned to the racial, gender, and musical registers of her times. Scott and Horne emulated Holiday in ways that affirmed their identities both as jazzmen and as race women. But their individual efforts to inhabit those identities created tensions between them, providing insight into the pressures they each faced as a performer.

The moments of calm produced after hearing Holiday did not temper the tempestuous feelings between them for long. One evening, the two women allegedly came to blows and "hair pulling" outside of a nightclub for reasons that remain unclear.[26] Though Monica Hairston rightfully characterizes the tabloid story as "a sensationalized query disguised as journalism,"[27] acknowledging the fact of their animosity allows us to explore how they experienced working at Café Society. Barney Josephson, the club's founder, believed the fight was over him—as boss, patron, and potential lover. He had fallen in love with Horne and thought Scott was jealous. "[Lena] became a very passionate thing for me. . . . I though she was beautiful. I didn't think she was really a good singer, and I told her so. But I also told her that she certainly had enough of everything else to make her a big star with her wonderful looks and a manner of performing from her days in the Cotton Club chorus line, walking around the floor to music. . . . She was the first black woman I ever felt that way about. It was that strong that I proposed to her. I asked her to marry me."[28] Despite concluding that Horne was not a great singer, Josephson decided to hire her, not least for her ability to attract white men. Horne elicited desire and he acted on it, as far as she would let him. Josephson claimed never to have felt the same way about Scott, instead taking a paternalistic interest in managing her career. In Josephson's telling, the competition between the two women arises in the typical fashion—as a fight over access to the protection and support of a man. Their competition is a sexual contest rather than a test of musical skill. For Josephson, Horne was just a female singer, albeit not a very good one, while Scott was a passable pianist.

In her own autobiography, Horne politicized the aesthetics of her performance, acknowledging that her development as a singer had as much to do with the quality of the musicians she worked with as it did with her changing political and racial consciousness and her parental responsibilities. Integration made for a better and happier performer, one who could emote freely through song and engage the audience as participants in the performance. She attributed that change partially to Josephson, grateful for his willingness to challenge the status quo; his integrated clubs reflected his recognition of "the true meaning of democracy. He understood that he could not enjoy democracy fully so long as anyone else was denied its blessings." She credited the change in her style to learning "to stop lumping everybody into a group and to recognize that people were individuals, irrespective of color, I loosened up when I sang. I was no longer singing to a roomful of enemies. . . . I was beginning to sing to them as much because I was learning to like them and wanted them to enjoy my performances as because I had to eat."[29] (Not only did she have to eat, but so did her two children.)

At Josephson's behest, Horne began incorporating more "blues" into her repertoire. But he remained concerned about her ability to project racial authenticity, sending her to Holiday for instruction. While continuing her efforts to master her voice and hone her ability to perform, Horne constructed an identity that embraced her jazzmasculinity and her race womanhood; Josephson, however, did not recognize her as a self-determining artist. He believed that if Horne acted "more black," she'd become a better performer, whereas Horne felt that she was already performing a blackness that interpreted and expressed her experiences in both integrated and segregated spaces. To her, the authenticity of her performance of blackness lay in the fact that it was grounded in experiences that she owned and wrestled into a consciousness about the world and her place in it.

Holiday zeroed in on Horne's motivation to hoist the blues of Holiday's signature "Fine and Mellow" from her belly and lam it against the front door of Café Society. According to Horne, "[Holiday] said, 'You've got two babies?' I said, 'Yes.' 'And you take care of them?' I said, 'Yes.' 'Well,' she said, 'sing it. I don't care. Sing anything you want to open your mouth and try to do 'cause you've got to take care of your children. You have to live your life. I'll always be here when you want a friend.'"[30] Holiday offers Horne support, guidance, and friendship. In this anecdote, Holiday figures much as Red Callender and Buddy Collette do in Mingus's *Beneath the Underdog*—as a sympathetic, guiding light for a younger, more naïve musician. Horne had expected Holiday to see her as a competitor and to demand concessions that would appease Holiday's ego as a senior jazzman. But Holiday didn't view her as competition; instead, she encouraged Horne to use her work if she could make a living at it. Holiday did not fear other female performers taking her audience. Her jazzmasculinity was grounded in her appreciation of jazz as work that bloomed when multiple voices had opportunity. She modeled a type of generosity that cultivated individual voices and challenged ideas about ownership, competition, and exceptionality. There are multiple ways of owning a song, and competition should raise the level of skill of all jazzmen, rather than eliminating some from the field or causing sexual jealousy.

In telling of her own coming of age as a jazzman and race woman, Hazel Scott freely admits that she "worshipped" Holiday, even down to modeling her singing style after her.[31] Scott first heard Holiday when she was fourteen, when Holiday was performing with Ralph Cooper's band at the Apollo. "I couldn't believe the way she sounded. I had never heard anything like it in my life." Scott's mother, Alma, and Holiday were close friends. As Scott recalls, Holiday "would be sitting in the kitchen talking to mama, and they would chase me away. She was closer to my age than she was to my mother's, but she was a woman already and I was still a kid."[32]

In *Lady Sings the Blues*, Holiday takes credit for both launching Scott's career and striking a blow at inequality at Café Society.

> One night a little girl came in with her mother and wanted to audition. Barney had turned her down when I heard about it. We had quite a little row in my dressing room over it. I told him to give the girl a chance, what did he have to lose? Barney refused, said she wasn't pretty—she was too dark.
>
> "Too dark?" I asked him. "Hell, this is supposed to be a cosmopolitan joint. What do you care what she looks like as long as she's got talent?"
>
> "Besides," I told him, "I need a vacation and I'm going to take one."
>
> So Barney gave an audition to this dark little girl in her pink mammy-made dress. She played the piano real good. I got my vacation, and Miss Hazel Scott got the job.[33]

Holiday's account underscores the persistent fact of color prejudice at Café Society. By supporting Scott, she forces Josephson to acknowledge the privilege accorded black women who fit an ideal of beauty akin to that of white women. She also illuminates the limitations that black women labored under because of those prejudices. Holiday, again "speaking for the people," draws on her own capital as a jazzman and race woman to make the case for Scott. She constructs Scott as an innocent, "a little girl in with her mother," wearing a "pink mammy-made dress," but one with talent, one who has been denied an opportunity because of color.

The juxtaposition of Josephson's attraction to Horne and his initial dismissal of Scott is a telling reminder of how differently the two women experienced their femininity and how the conditions of their work became embodied in their identities. Josephson tells Horne he wants to mark her: "I want people to know who you are. Let me present you as a Negro performer."[34] He requires her to introduce the blues into her repertoire, "because the people sitting out front, the white people, won't be sure what you are. When you sing the blues they'll think, well, I guess she is [black]." Color prejudice undoubtedly privileged Horne and disadvantaged Scott. Lighter skin provided Horne with opportunity; her politics radicalized her art and gave her a way of being black in an integrated setting. For Scott, a certified genius, color nearly derailed the launch of her career. Scott rarely talked as publicly as Horne did about her ideas on politics or race. And yet Scott's career was perhaps more affected by assumptions of racial privilege, gender difference, and the measure of a jazzman's skill. She had to prove over and over that she could Jook.

"SHOWBIZ, GOD, AND THE RACE"

> You've got to find yourself, where you're at.
> *Betty Carter*

> I told him, "Our orbits are about to collide."
> *Hazel Scott*

Hazel Scott and Adam Clayton Powell Jr.'s August 1945 wedding was front-page news, their reception a political event. After giving her away at a small ceremony in Connecticut, Barney Josephson hosted the reception at Café Society Uptown. On the trip to the church, Josephson rode with Powell. Though initially in favor of their relationship, he had begun to question Powell's motives. In his memoir, Josephson claimed that Powell spent the ride cataloguing Scott's wealth, which Josephson, as her manager during her seven years at Café Society, had helped her to accumulate. Josephson also believed that Powell had induced her to take advantage of his paternal feelings by inviting thousands of guests to the reception, despite knowing that the club could seat no more than 314.[35] He suggests that, in courting Scott, Powell was motivated primarily by a desire for money and a heightened public profile. Speculations about motive aside, that reception cemented the couple as Harlem royalty. An estimated 1500 to 3000 guests, arriving in shifts, attempted to greet the bride and groom that night. Two dozen police officers provided security. "The club became so jammed at one point that an announcement was made over a public address system asking those who had sampled the refreshments to leave so others could move up to the festive board." Though numerous celebrities, including W. C. Handy, Langston Hughes, Frank Schiffman, Mildred Bailey, and Bill Robinson, made appearances, more importantly, the "PEOPLE were truly there," lining the streets, hanging out of the windows in the nearby library. The Powells honeymooned on Long Island, taking over a cottage that "had never been rented to Negroes."[36]

According to rumor, Powell and Scott had been lovers while he was still married to actress Isabel Washington, and many remained sympathetic to the ex-Mrs. Powell.[37] Though Washington had tried to reconcile her past as an entertainer with her new life as the wife of the pastor of an important black institution, she had failed to meet Powell's expectations. Powell attributed the end of their marriage not to the catalogue of doubts his parents had assembled about Washington's suitability—she was older than him, a divorcée, a mother, and a former entertainer—but rather "because one day I caught up with her and then passed. She loved me completely and utterly, yet I grew and she stood still."[38]

Scott and Powell had waited a year after his Reno divorce was finalized to move forward. The wait made them "appreciate [their] later happiness so much more," despite the fact that divorce rumors had to be quashed just months after their wedding. Fans were advised not to "get alarmed about what you hear. Adam and Hazel are doing all right for themselves, thank you and, unlike many of their critics, they are to put it bluntly: 'Saving themselves and the race at the same time.'"[39] Throughout their marriage, Scott navigated the line between the proprieties of being a wife and the exigencies of life as a musician. She cast the requirements of her roles in formal, scripted language that rendered her submissive to the church and her husband, who was willing to accommodate her music within limits. As she observed, "I have always believed that a church belongs to its members and leadership comes from the minister, not his wife. I have always held the view that a minister's wife should assist her husband but quietly, discreetly and always as the subordinate member of the partnership."[40] The Powells had agreed that "The church would make no demands on my time that I was unable to fill or would interfere with my music." But the framing of that decision in these terms of subservience and joint decision making suggests that the fissures in their relationship were already beginning to appear. Despite Scott's efforts to embrace the religious world that Powell occupied, his congregation criticized the pairing, finding Scott, whom Powell had baptized after the marriage,[41] to be so unsuitable a wife that it demanded Powell's resignation. He refused.

Scott relied on conventional gender norms to tell the story of their courtship, admitting they "didn't do the usual things people do in such situations." The melodrama of their early romance gave way, strategically, to a sentimental story of true love. She describes a courtship based on conversation, mutual respect, and common interests. As to the question of marriage, "It was just suddenly there, it happened so quickly. Of course, Adam wasn't free to marry me right away and because of that a proposal of marriage might have been considered not only premature but also indelicate. After he secured a separation from his first wife, the atmosphere was clearer and we could both consider marriage." Their conventional marriage story, told to popular, mainstream black publications, was a concerted effort to skirt the fallout from Powell's divorce from Washington. It also put Powell in a dominant position over Scott's ambitions, though she vowed to "continue to work at [her] career and take care of [her] home as well." So committed was she to sustaining her career, Scott decided to leave the relative security of the nightclub for the greater respectability of the concert stage. The decision to seek out greater credibility and respectability as an artist paid off right away. Scott was booked for "35 weeks straight at a guaranteed minimum of $1,500 per appearance, or 60 per cent of the takings, whichever is greater."[42]

Powell initially felt no qualms about the arrangement. As he explained, "With this brilliant girl, moving ahead in her career, I felt that I had a marriage that would last. And when in October [they married in August] we learned that she was pregnant, then I knew this would be the kind of family in which, while each of us made a separate contribution, we could at the same time live together as a unit. I was totally wrong." Was Scott too independent for Powell? Too arrogant? Too desirous of maintaining the career she had worked her entire life to achieve? Powell attributed their eventual divorce to what he characterized as Scott's moral failings, her drinking, and her poor self-esteem. "Hazel tried her best to help me in the church. But I think she resented the people, because subconsciously she realized that they were the ones standing between us. I tried my best to help her in her career, but here again I probably subconsciously was jealous of her work and the affection she gave it."[43] Like the spouse of many a jazzman, Powell had to compete with the music for his wife's attention. Unlike other jazzmen, however,

Scott had to couch her priorities in such a way as to make her ambitions palatable both to her husband and to the public.

The Powells were celebrated in *Ebony* as the "chief exponents" of the "modern school of ministerial matrimony." In 1956, Scott explained to *Ebony* readers, "How [She] Found God in Show Business." The three photos in the story's opening layout represent her different personas: nightclub entertainer, concert artist, and preacher's wife. The largest of the photos denotes her nightclub guise: black strapless, split-skirt dress and fishnet stockings. In the second photo, she is "demurely gowned" in white and cloaked in the front by the piano, the image of a concert artist. The last photo captures a loving family scene: Scott, Powell, and their son Skipper reading from the Bible. Scott explained her multiple personas by quoting Psalm 150: "Praise Him with trumpets, with dance." As she observes, "I used to be afraid of failure, of dying. I used to be afraid of expressing myself, afraid of getting old. I had all of the old fears and worries. And then I found the answer. The greatest Man who ever lived said it: 'Fear not, I am with thee always.'" In exposing these various sides of herself, Scott experiences a sense of freedom that had eluded her in the earlier part of her career. Expressing her lack of fear in religious terms is a socially permissible way of articulating her experience of freedom, a freedom from self-doubt, from death, from the loss of beauty. For Scott, music provides a voice that speaks for something beyond her self.[44]

The marriage seemed one of equals, each championing the career of the other. Scott supported Powell's political rallies; Powell attended Scott's performances. And yet, in the mid-fifties, they began living publicly separate lives. Scott moved to Paris, purchased a new house, and sold the Mount Vernon home the Powells had shared. During this time Scott often insisted on the stability of their relationship, once joking "We dig each other the most" when asked about rumors of her dating other men. The Powells' marriage officially ended in 1960, perhaps due to Powell's philandering and criticism of Scott's drinking and music-making, or perhaps from the impact of her being blacklisted.[45]

The tumultuous course of their marriage suggests the difficulties Scott faced in reconciling her experiences as a middle-class black woman aspiring to fulfill an idealized domestic role within a conservative institution, and her experiences as a jazzman who navigated a complex culture in which the expression of personality traits such as arrogance, discipline, and a particular type of racial pride could be valued (were it not for her sex). Scott's negotiation of those competing roles sheds light on how jazz culture provided musicians with opportunities to express, in music, the complexity of lives lived both within and without the boundaries of the jazz world. Familial relationships provided foundational experiences for many jazzmen, whether as fathers and husbands or as mothers and wives. Like Charles Mingus and Lena Horne, Hazel Scott tried to integrate all of the aspects of her life into an embodied identity as a jazzman. Her experiences suggest that women like her may not have found any more freedom in jazz culture than they found outside it. The tension between the expectations of race womanhood and jazzmasculinity subjected musicians like Scott to a discursive maelstrom that had real social costs. The pressures to conform to conventional expectations of gendered performance were strong within the black community, even in a politically advantageous love match. Imagine the stakes, then, when a jazzman, making moves across racial lines, must depend on eliciting strong emotional connections with strangers to advance her career and acknowledge her humanity.

THE HAZEL SCOTT INCIDENT

There are 15,000,000 Hazel Scotts in this country—
not with her talent, but with her color.
William O'Dwyer

In September 1945, the national chapter of the Daughters of the American Revolution (DAR) refused Scott permission to perform at Constitution Hall in Washington, D.C. The story broke soon after Japan's surrender and just weeks before the DAR was to celebrate its fiftieth anniversary.[46] The DAR had adopted a "white artists only" policy in 1932. Controversy over the policy first erupted in 1939, when the DAR barred contralto Marian Anderson from performing. Then first lady Eleanor Roosevelt championed Anderson's right to sing at Constitution Hall by resigning her DAR membership. Soon other powerful politicians came to Anderson's defense, among them Secretary of the Interior Harold Ickes, who arranged for Anderson to perform on the steps of the Lincoln Memorial. Her performance before a crowd of 75,000—along with countless others who heard the radio broadcast—was a public moral reproach to segregationists. Some time after the performance, Anderson reflected, "I could see that my significance as an individual was small in this affair. I had become, whether I liked it or not, a symbol, representing my people." As a symbol, Anderson's experience framed her as a heroic black woman, her art the epitome of cultural expression.[47] Anderson was a race woman whose exceptional talent provided a framework for challenging social ideas about race, art, and segregation. Her respectability, as an artist and as a black woman, grounded support for her in the face of racist exclusion.

The Hazel Scott incident called on a different set of tropes about artistic value and respectability. Her music, jazz as opposed to opera, raised questions about whether she was a true artist or merely an entertainer who latched on to "gimmicks" to make a living. As the wife of one of the most powerful black men in the United States, Scott represented conflicting narratives about womanhood and race. Her status as a jazzman challenged assumptions about musical genre, authenticity, and genius. But her choice of jazz rather than classical music compromised her status as a race woman. Out of that seeming conflict, Scott managed to create an identity that embraced both jazzmasculinity and race womanhood, and that led others to embrace that identity as well. The Hazel Scott incident thus illustrates the intersection of formal politics and popular culture that marked the postwar black social landscape, demonstrating that "aesthetic judgments should not be confined to the artistic realm and cannot be detached from political considerations."[48] The multiple, organized efforts to allow Scott to perform at Constitution Hall were as much about affirming her talents as they were about striking a blow against segregationist practices. They were political grenades launched through an aesthetic weapon.

After the DAR rejected Scott's initial request to perform, Adam Clayton Powell went immediately on the offensive. Recognizing the political leverage to be gained, he confronted President Harry Truman, questioning the legality of the DAR's continued practice of segregation in light of its status as a tax-exempt organization, incorporated by Congress. Truman, in a letter released to the *New York Times*, expressed dismay over the DAR's actions and affirmed his stance that no race held exclusive domain over artistic talent. To believe otherwise was to act like a fascist for, as Truman pointed out, "one of the first steps taken by the Nazis when they came to power was to forbid the public appearance of artists and musicians whose religion and origin were unsatisfactory to the master race." Despite Powell's pleas, however, Truman insisted that he could not interfere; because the DAR was a private institution. Bess Truman's subsequent attendance at a DAR tea given in her honor (despite her own note to the Powells deploring "any action which denies artistic talent an opportunity to express itself because of prejudice against race or origin"),[49] led Powell to declare: "From now on there is only one First Lady, Eleanor Roosevelt; Mrs. Truman is the last. . . . You cannot do business with un-Americanism and still say you are not taking sides with it. When Hitler became known as a Fascist, we broke relations, including attending his teas."[50]

In one of her few public discussions of the incident, Hazel Scott wished Bess Truman "had refused to go because in the midst of this unfortunate discrimination her presence there gives sanction to their action against me. . . . If I weren't allowed to use the hall because my music was unsuitable, it would be a different matter. But to refuse to let me play there because of race is both stupidly reactionary and vicious."[51] Scott's criticism of Bess Truman suggests the ways white women could elect to ignore prejudice against black women, even against those who seemed to represent tenets of respectability. Scott also raises an important question about how prejudice colors how we hear music across racial lines.[52] She imagined herself as a concert artist whose art was respectable, suitable for a national stage such as Constitution Hall. She was invested in the idea that art should transcend racial and gender politics. But for this particular audience of white people, her music is indelibly marked as black and disreputable. The "stupidly reactionary" denial by the DAR was a knee-jerk insistence on racist practices, a deliberately cruel attack aimed at inflicting maximum injury. Such actions capture the mental and physical landmines navigated by black jazzmen during Jim Crow.

What did Powell hope to achieve by being critical of Bess Truman? It certainly did not endear him to President Truman, who never invited Powell to the White House again (and did not reflect on the matter in his own memoirs).[53] He dismissed Powell as a "high-brow preacher from New York [who had been] annoying [him and Bess]. He's a Congressman, a smart aleck and a rabble rouser. He got nowhere."[54] Truman received numerous letters from Americans both supporting and decrying his stance on the DAR. Because he condemned the policy but did not take any measures to challenge it, some saw him as tolerating the untenable fact of the nation's capital as a segregated city, as well as shirking the responsibility of "legislating if necessary, against the discrimination of people on the ground of race, color, or creed." Others saw him as infringing on a private institution's right to discriminate, or upsetting the Southern way of managing "race relations."[55] Despite the widespread attention to the issue, however, Truman did not publicly mention the incident again.

Black editorialists like Dan Gardner of the *New York Amsterdam News* believed that Powell had compromised the pending political appointments Truman had offered "the Race" and overreached his political status by using the incident to speak for all Negroes instead of just his wife. Gardner argued that as a "quasi-social equality" issue, the "question of boogie-woogie in Constitution Hall" did not merit as much effort as the more salient "economic" issues that returning black soldiers were facing due to the housing shortage and lack of employment. But the *Pittsburgh Courier* supported Powell's demands. Noting the DAR's claim to be a private institution, adhering to "local customs" of segregation, the editors countered that "Constitution Hall should be opened freely to all who wish to engage it or it should be closed to the public," especially as the main issue revolved around "whether an organization which receives economic benefits from all the taxpayers should continue to do so if it discriminates against any of them in the rental of its premises." Despite the merits of the case, however, the editors believed Powell had ceded moral ground with his statements against Bess Truman. It was not the place of black Americans to criticize people on the grounds of their associates, as that was a ploy central to segregationists' logic. "We only insist that racial prejudice and color discrimination not be supported at Government expense."[56] Taking another tack, editors for the *Afro-American* noted that the numbers of black soldiers fighting in the Revolutionary War, combined with the low birth rate of Revolution-era families, could lead one to question who really composed the DAR membership rolls. "Is it possible that the Daughters of the Confederacy are taking it over, lock, stock, and barrel?"[57]

Powell looked to congressional colleagues to take action against the DAR and in defense of his wife. New York's senators Robert F. Wagner and James W. Mead declared that "[t]he attempt to extend race prejudice into the field of art and music . . . does violence to the memory of the patriots who risked their all to establish our Constitution and the example of all who fought in this war." Representatives Helen Gahagan Douglas of California and Emanuel Celler of New York introduced bills to revoke the DAR's tax-exempt status along with the 1895 congressional act incorporating the DAR.[58] Some in Congress, including unregenerate racists like Representative John E. Rankin of Mississippi, supported the DAR. His claim that protests against the organization were "Communistic" in origin provoked outbursts in the House gallery.[59] Redirecting the blame, Senator Theodore G. Bilbo of Mississippi, chairman of the committee that could review efforts to revoke the DAR's tax-exempt status, argued that the United States would be better off attacked by atomic bombs than forced to give up segregation, which was "as American as any of the other well-known institutions and ideals which have come to us through the one hundred and fifty years of our national existence."[60]

Powell organized a "People's DAR" (Drive Against Reaction) as a branch of his People's Committee, "turning over the un-American discrimination of my wife, Mrs. Hazel Scott Powell, to you leaders. If the individual were any other than my wife, I would lead this fight. However, I assure you that I will support you every step of the way."[61] The People's DAR's first efforts included planning a concert for Scott at Carnegie Hall and organizing a mass meeting of over 5,000 people in New York, inviting the city's mayoral candidates. At the meeting, candidate Newbold Morris, a member of the Sons of the Revolution, challenged the DAR to "say so in the open if they are out to destroy democracy."[62] Though mayoral candidate William O'Dwyer did not appear, his spokesman insisted that O'Dwyer's "program for real freedom does not include the Bilbos or the D.A.R. at their present standards."[63] But those who supported Powell and his People's DAR also demanded support in return. They wanted Powell to press the issue of integration in Washington, D.C. The National Negro Council urged him to "make the nation's capital a decent place to live for every American citizen and human being, despite Senator Bilbo and others wedded to Jim Crow, like their Nazi brethren, so properly condemned by President Truman."[64]

At the core of these debates was the question of what it meant for America to be a democracy in the aftermath of World War II. African Americans had pressed the Double V campaign during the war; now that the war had been won, they, as well as some white Americans, questioned how the United States could lead the fight for democracy abroad while discriminating at home. The Hazel Scott incident raised a moral problem the nation as a whole had to remedy. Mary McLeod Bethune, then chairwoman of the National Council of Negro Women (NCNW), likened the actions of the DAR to those of the Germans and Japanese. "The Axis propaganda to the smaller nations tried to discredit the United States on the grounds that its democracy was not sincere. The D.A.R., by its official action, now picks up where the Japanese and the Germans left off." The NCNW called for the principles of the recently created U.N. charter to be applied to the United States.[65] As James Nabritt of Howard University noted, "We should continue to press for use of Constitution Hall and embarrass America at home and abroad until just democracy exists in this country."[66] To get the DAR's attention, a letter-writing campaign was proposed and the addresses of the women comprising its board posted in the Afro-American.[67] The Hazel Scott incident galvanized social outrage against the institutionalization of racism in the nation's capital.

Congresswoman Clare Boothe Luce launched a prolonged attack on the DAR's policy, turning her membership in the organization into a political cause célèbre. A member of the Putnam Hill Chapter in Greenwich, Connecticut, Luce believed she could "democratize from within." Wife of Henry Luce, one of the most powerful men in publishing and communications, Clare Boothe Luce had already created a name and career for herself before entering Congress. She worked at *Vanity Fair* as a writer and managing editor in the early thirties, and her play *The Women* had opened on Broadway in 1936. As a representative of the Fourth District of Connecticut from 1942 to 1947, Luce served on the House Military Affairs Committee, broadcast weekly speeches, and introduced legislation on issues ranging from equal pay to the atomic bomb. Although she would later have close ties to Presidents Eisenhower and Nixon, Luce's relationship with Truman was quite vexed, stemming, the rumors held, from Luce having insulted his mother on the House floor.[68]

Luce's two-pronged approach was designed to appeal both to the consciences of DAR members and to a broader cross-section of Americans. Working through various media outlets and through internal chains of communication at the DAR, Luce challenged white Americans' acceptance of segregation. She announced that if the Putnam Hill Chapter refused to censure the Washington chapter, she would resign membership from the chapter and seek admittance to a new chapter willing to protest this "un-American" practice. When her chapter rejected censure, 48 to 2, Luce resigned as promised. Newspapers across the nation reported the story. After the vote, Putnam Hill member and former national vice-president Grace Hall Brosseau commented that Luce's resignation "does not matter. Mrs. Luce has never been to a meeting during her five years of membership." (Brosseau did not acknowledge, however, that more than three times the regular number of members had attended that particular meeting.)[69]

Luce reported that the Putnam Hill Chapter "declined to support my request that the chapter protest the undemocratic action of the Washington chapter in denying the use of Constitution Hall to an American artist who happened to be a Negress."[70] Despite this setback, Luce believed she could prove that the organization's founding principles continued to be important and could serve as a national model; she and other members could "reinstate the D.A.R. in the public mind as a symbol of continuing democracy."[71] The privileges granted the DAR by the public demanded an "inescapable responsibility to keep faith with the democratic traditions of the U.S."[72] With the advice of public relations guru Edward Bernays, Luce then launched a national campaign to eradicate the "white artists only" clause from the by-laws of Constitution Hall.

After a series of spring visits drumming up support for the DAR's fiftieth anniversary, Mrs. Julius Y. Talmadge, the national president, had touted the history of the organization in her May 1945 report and praised Constitution Hall's increasing accessibility to the public.[73] She lamented the fact that members could not hold their annual convention there, however, as the Department of Transportation had requested that all organizations restrict their travel, including canceling their annual conventions, to conserve national resources and facilitate the movement of active-duty servicemen to and from their posts. Although the fighting had ended, Talmadge emphasized that this did not signal the end of patriotic duties. She encouraged individual chapters to increase their endeavors and celebrated the new strength of the organization (arising from the inclusion of descendants of Revolutionary War privates).[74] Though Talmadge may have believed the new membership pool was fortifying its democratic bona fides, black women criticized the continuing racial barrier to membership. As Thomasina W. Johnson, a lobbyist for Alpha Kappa Alpha Sorority, noted, "The first blood that was shed so that there might be a DAR was shed by Crispus Attucks, a colored man." By refusing the inclusion of Negro descendants from the Revolutionary era, "One can only say that such fascism clothed in such patriotic trappings is only a warning of things to come."[75] As did other civil rights organizations of the period, the women of Alpha Kappa Alpha Sorority highlighted the link between white American racism and the scourge of fascism. Later that summer, in its own attack on fascism, the DAR resolved to support the formation of a permanent committee on un-American activities in the House of Representatives. The resolution sought to "express continued belief in the purpose of this committee, and urge that the committee continue to render service in perpetuating vigilance as a price of liberty."[76]

By December 1945, Luce had become a member of the Eunice Dennie Burr Chapter in Fairfield, Connecticut.[77] PM magazine, though often critical of Luce's political positions, saluted her insistence that "The basic democratic issues of freedom and equality for all, regardless of race, creed or color, is as worth fighting for today as it was in 1776."[78] Indeed, other DAR chapters and individual members also were willing to raise their voices in protest.[79] Less than a week after her transfer, Luce sent letters to various DAR members indicating her plans to create a committee "which will work to bring our Society once again into line with its best American traditions" and urging members to support rescinding the ban on black performers at Constitution Hall.[80]

Luce delivered radio speeches on at least two occasions condemning the whites-only policy. Her speeches characterized the Hazel Scott incident as evidence of Americans' own "un-American" actions in embracing the theories of racial superiority that were the foundation of Hitler's persecution of the Jewish people.[81] Luce anchored her pleas in the lessons of the DAR's founding, which itself was a protest against the discrimination practiced by the Sons of the American

Revolution, who had excluded women from participating in that organization "simply on the basis of their sex, and nothing else, nothing else at all." She argued that the DAR risked its moral authority when it denied two women the right to perform in the "People's house" simply because of their color.

Members of the DAR knew Constitution Hall as "Our Home, Sweet Home." The events held there ranged from closed meetings to musical performances open to the public. Though Congress had appropriated funds for the hall's construction and maintenance, most members considered it as belonging to a private institution; the organization justified its whites-only policy because "local practice" in the District of Columbia permitted segregated schools, restaurants, and even neighborhoods (through restrictive covenants).[82] Luce countered the local-practice argument by investigating the issue with the district's corporate counsel, who explained that while there was no explicit law of segregation, there was no explicit practice of integration.

The *New York Times* editorialized that "The D.A.R. can't be an exclusive social club and also a public institution. . . . It can't consistently hang its case for segregation, as the executive committee tries to do, on 'prevailing custom.'"[83] According to Luce, the DAR's reliance on custom and practice regarding race relations led to "inertia and a slavish obedience to precedence and mores" in a way members wouldn't have accepted when it came to gender discrimination. "For many who would not bow down to men are often grovalling [sic] slaves to manners. But mostly prejudice put it there. Un-American prejudice." Like some black journalists who commented on the issue, Luce attributed the DAR's inertia to the inclusion of "daughters of Lee, as well as of Washington" among its membership, and observed that "The Washington Board is controlled by reactionary prejudiced women from below the Mason Dixon Line. They do not reflect the attitude of the majority of the fine patriotic women of the D.A.R. throughout the country." Luce insisted the organization's focus should turn to the inheritance of "spirit" rather than "blood," arguing that the "white body" of the DAR was itself blackened by the continued prohibition of black artists from Constitution Hall. In a commemoration of President Washington's birthday, Luce railed, "Washington is the mightiest name on earth because he believed in civil liberties for all our citizens—and that means, today, for Marian Anderson and Hazel Scott too. And that means he would not think highly of any DAR who in the year 1946 will continue to countenance the exclusion from Constitution Hall in our nation's capitol, great and gifted artists for no other reason, none, none, none—than that their faces are of a darker hue."[84]

Luce received mail both from her own constituents and from individuals across the nation about her advocacy. The language used by these correspondents reveals a broad anxiety about the stability of the definitions of "Americanness," democracy, and American character. Some letter writers homed in on the moral doubts raised by the incident, though the specific questions varied according to an individual's positions on segregation and racial equality. Depending on the writer's perspective, Luce could be seen as wearing the minstrel's mask, as the dupe of a vast communist conspiracy, or as a true American. At a time when postal rates meant that one's thoughts literally cost just a penny, Luce received a postcard inquiring "So you're going on blackface this time are you Clare??"[85] On her decision to transfer her membership to another chapter, one wrote, "If you want to do a real courageous thing then I suggest that if the House of which you are a member does not back you up in your stand on this matter, you resign from that body. That would be a really courageous action. To resign from the Putnam D.A.R. means nothing, and I hope they accept your resignation without delay."[86] Luce's reputation as a socialite left her open to personal attacks, while her position as a politician led many to accuse her of seeking the "sexy" issue of the day—The Negro Question—to keep in the public eye.[87]

Despite the public criticism heaped on the DAR during the previous six months, the organization decided to maintain its stance on the "white artists only" clause at their annual congress in May 1946. A rebel committee formed by Luce, the Committee Against Discrimination in the Use of Constitution Hall, was dismissed as an unauthorized group and prohibited from using the terms "D.A.R. and Constitution Hall" without permission from the national body. During the first evening's formal convening of the congress, President Talmadge told the membership that "Politics and publicity have lurked behind every curtain in every attack on our management of Constitution Hall." Talmadge claimed that though she did not herself believe in racial discrimination, she alone could not act to change the clause. She did promise, however, that the board would review the decision, even though "The woman [Scott] is not a great artist, no matter what color she is."[88] The board voted to review the matter at a later date, and its decision to keep the "white artists only" clause was met with "a great applause."[89]

As the Hazel Scott incident morphed from the denial of a proposed booking into a national debate about integration, democratic principles, and antifascism, Scott herself was oft-talked about but little heard from. Her race was interchangeable with her music, making both unsuitable for Constitution Hall. Though Scott represented some ideals of respectability and femininity, the fact of her blackness precluded recognition of her genius. When Marian Anderson had been denied Constitution Hall as a venue, she was provided an even larger stage on which to perform. Scott was not accorded similar treatment, though she did accept an offer to perform at the all-white National Press Club's annual dinner, a decision she would later regret.

Upon learning of her upcoming performance, black journalists condemned the National Press Club for its adherence to segregated practices and asserted that Scott would be a hypocrite for performing there after the DAR incident. "If this is the extent of democracy being practiced by the National Press club, then we would find some difficulty in reconciling Miss Scott's appearance at the dinner with the dramatic protestation of justice often voiced by her husband."[90] Less than two weeks after agreeing to perform, Scott declined the invitation. Her terse response to the public criticism appropriated the black journalists' condemnation of the club, affirming that she stood in solidarity with the "colored journalists [who] have been excluded from the press galleries of the House and Senate."[91] Scott's thinly veiled criticism of those journalists for publicly taking her to task rather than communicating with her privately was likely provoked by the constraints she faced as Powell's wife.

"PATRIOTIC VIRGINS AND UN-AMERICAN ACTIVITIES"

The Hazel Scott incident illustrates how women could become galvanizing figures for cross-racial identification, a role usually limited to black men. Out of her humiliating rejection by the DAR, Scott engendered sympathy, outrage, and activism from both jazz fans and others who rejected the premise that the fact of her blackness made her ineligible to play in one of the people's houses, Constitution Hall. The response demonstrated a national desire for civil liberties—for the rights to associate freely, to experience the democracy that had been fought for during the war, and to insist that color prejudice should not hinder the expression and development of talent. Between the political vortex stirred up by the DAR and her appearance before the House Un-American Activities Committee (HUAC), analysis of which closes this chapter, Scott comes to recognize herself fully as an artist. It's in her HUAC testimony that Scott identifies her role as a jazzman with the ideals of American democracy. Recognizing the symbolic register that the jazzman represents, she uses it to defend herself as a public performer, refusing to see a conflict between her jazzmasculinity and her race womanhood.

In 1950, Scott was honored by the city in which she had been prevented from performing in 1945. "The District Commissioner and a committee came down to greet me [at the armory], and they gave me the Key to the City. So now I've got the Key to the City—and what can I do with it in Jim Crow Washington!" The honor recognized her stance on "the rights of Negro entertainers to dignity," and her vanguard work in film, where "She was the first Negro to sign a movie contract stipulating she was to appear as herself, and not in some 'degrading role.'"[92] Despite the esteem with which the black and jazz press held her throughout the forties, Scott's star began falling soon after receiving the keys to Washington, D.C. After being listed in *Red Channels: A Report on Communist Influence in Radio and Television* in June 1950, Scott lost her nationally broadcast variety show, the first ever to be hosted by a black artist. Scott reportedly had over a dozen potential sponsors for that show, but the listing prevented her from solidifying any of those relationships.[93] The show was canceled only one week after her appearance before the House Un-American Activities Committee. It would take six years before another black entertainer, Nat King Cole, would again host such a program.[94] Scott lamented the social panic of the time: "Steps must be taken to halt the hysteria which is threatening the careers of some of our best entertainers." Despite being falsely accused, she refused to be identified with either "the political right or the political left . . . whatever flaws exist in American democracy can be corrected without the aid of Communism."[95]

Scott was only one of several black entertainers, artists, and intellectuals to appear before the HUAC. The committee's primary target was Paul Robeson, who was called to account for his embrace of civil rights, anticolonialism, and unions. Jackie Robinson and Josh White were among those who appeared before the committee to repudiate Robeson and the politics he embraced. Josh White appeared voluntarily to clear up "misconceptions," and, as Richard Iton describes it, "to perform patriotic fidelity."[96] As part of his testimony, he performed the antilynching elegiac "Strange Fruit," which he had taken to performing at Café Society after Billie Holiday left the club. White believed in protesting against injustice, but did not think that joining Communist organizations was the proper route to creating change. He was especially critical of Robeson, rejecting the notion of Robeson as the ideal race man, and even the idea of a race man at all. White pled ignorance about having performed before subversive organizations—if he had done so, it was only at the behest of his management rather than due to any true sympathy on his part.[97]

By 1948, Barney Josephson's Café Society clubs had been permanently closed as a result of the Red Scare and HUAC's contempt conviction of his brother Leon.

A previous association with Josephson was another reason why black artists such as Scott, White, Robeson, and Horne found themselves testifying before the committee. With the nightclub on their résumés, these artists were tied to the Popular Front and assumed to have Communist sympathies.

During this same time, most civil rights organizations also were distancing themselves from any hint of Communism or affiliation with the Soviet Union. Even so, any black protest, whether from the NAACP, the National Urban League, or the National Lawyers Guild, was labeled subversive and un-American.[98] As Coleman Young explains, "It was all but impossible for a black person to avoid the Communist label as long as he or she advocated Civil Rights with any degree of vigor."[99] Saving the race under these conditions often, but not always, required rejecting former allies. Lena Horne, for example, refused to name names; instead, she aligned herself with Robeson, deflected attention from her interracial marriage, and affirmed her unshakable racial identification. Her erstwhile rival, Hazel Scott, tried to split the difference between Horne and White.

Under Adam Clayton Powell's direction, Scott voluntarily appeared before HUAC in 1950. Newspapers reported on her testimony without much commentary,[100] though the *New York Amsterdam News* defended Scott's position (she had pre-released her statement), maintaining that art should not be bound by race or politics. Her testimony, more than any of her other published statements during this period, reveals the anger she felt about the impact of politics on her career. Scott must have long known that she was under government observation. Over the previous ten years, she and Powell had been involved in several FBI investigations. The first came in 1941, a relatively minor incident in which Scott had been the target of a potential blackmailer who claimed to be an FBI agent. Although the FBI investigated the case for several months—requiring the cooperation of Barney Josephson, Café Society, and Scott—it was ultimately unable to identify the blackmailer.[101] In 1942 the FBI began investigating Powell, whose militancy and cooperation with Communist organizations during the Depression had drawn the attention of the New York office, substantiating their request for surveillance.[102] Documented alongside his political maneuverings were his marriage woes.

While Lena Horne celebrated Barney Josephson's patriotic spirit, claiming that he knew the "true meaning of democracy," Hazel Scott wanted nothing but distance from her former boss. Although she credited him with nurturing her career, Scott claimed ignorance of his politics, despite his well-known political leanings. In 1944, a reporter for Powell's community newspaper, *People's Voice*, had wondered at the extent to which Josephson's artists shared his views, and "whether or not a definite policy is used to educate politically artists who work these spots." Josephson believed, the reporter noted, that by "treating artists as people, giving them good working conditions and their contact with liberal thinking people who frequent the clubs," artists would come to their own conclusions. Indeed, Josephson insisted that only with understanding of the issues affecting people of color and the working class could an artist fully express herself. "He attributes much of this change in his artists, from artists merely with talent to artists with talent plus a social view point, to Paul Robeson whom he admires." Josephson embraced integration as a social good. He was especially proud to have "been able to help lead the way to a better understanding between the races."[103] By the time Scott appeared before HUAC, however, she had apparently rejected this view of him.

In her testimony, Scott proposed "positive methods by which to deal with Communists in the entertainment profession," stressing the importance of labor unions, her membership in them, and the role they played in safeguarding democracy.[104] She contended that the committee's hearings were worse than a criminal proceeding for she was presumed guilty with no opportunity to prove her innocence. She proposed that HUAC should act as if the "entertainment unions . . . oust any Communist member, but only through orderly procedures presenting opportunity for rebuttal and defense." According to Scott, musicians' and artists' unions should boycott radio networks, sponsors, and performance venues that fired entertainers on the basis of a listing in *Red Channels* or some other mark of "disloyalty." Scott tried to convey a sense of the real economic impact that the committee's investigations were having on people's livelihoods, a crucial concern of jazzmen who often lacked control over how and when they were paid.

Scott expressed contradictory beliefs when defending her own livelihood. She was fiercely anticommunist and adamant that art could be divorced from politics. Though she insisted that she be recognized as a musician foremost, she also felt that it was as a musician that she could be most effective in the battle to influence American minds, committed as she was to "furthering American freedoms." This part of her testimony reveals her efforts to bridge what she perceived as the gap between being a jazzman and a race woman. Speaking before the committee, she implicitly attributed her increasing sophistication about politics to her marriage to Powell. She acknowledged that she began scaling back her memberships in the 1940s—even changing her management—as she became increasingly well versed in the politics of other entertainers, including Paul Robeson, whom she had once idolized.[105] Although her statement opens by noting that she appears before HUAC as "a musician," not "as the spokesman for any group—economic, political racial, religious, profession, or artistic," the language of her testimony, despite questioning the validity of the hearings, is replete with terms like "perversion," "patriotic virgins," and "reputation," echoing the language of HUAC's efforts to "purge the perverts."[106] Scott asserted that "Loyalty is a moral question and communism—a disloyal affiliation—is therefore a perversion." As for the negative effects of the committee hearings, Scott claimed that entertainers were "the real voice of America" and HUAC's investigations tainted their main currency. "Every human being values his reputation. But two groups above all others must guard their reputations with particular vigilance, since their very existence depends upon the respect and favor of the general public: the public official and the public performer. Both must be particularly jealous of their good names. You gentlemen are elected by the people, just as my colleagues of the musical and theatrical world are elected by their public."[107] Scott railed against the damage done to her reputation, feeling the impact on her marriage, her career, and her sense of self.

In 1972, Scott sat down for an interview with Arthur Taylor, the drummer and compiler of the classic collection of musician-to-musician interviews, *Notes and Tones*. Over twenty years had passed since her HUAC testimony and yet, many of the concerns she articulated then still figured in her thoughts about the role of the musician in a racially stratified society. She remained the angry jazzman she had been during the forties and fifties, when she was trying to establish a career that both complemented her talents and respected her dignity as a black woman. Part of what led fans and critics to see Mingus as Jazz's Angry Man was his insistent focus on addressing the economic issues facing musicians as they worked to earn "beans and greens" for their families. When Mingus recorded Scott for Debut, it's likely they discussed the persistent dilemma of earning a living as musicians and creating music that spoke to them as artists. The album Scott made for Debut is perhaps her most well regarded recording. In her conversation with Taylor, Scott noted that she had recently decided to start her own production company for the very same reasons Mingus had: she wanted the power to record music the way she wanted to play it, to finally address the neglect she had experienced from other recording companies over the course of her career. "The music business is just like every other business," Scott said. "You're exploited or you're the exploiter."[108]

Scott's desire for both independence and control over the music she performs echoes the desires of most jazzmen. Scott understood that such control not only would increase her ability to make a living, but also would engender more freedom in her ability to express herself. She describes her self-produced album, *Hazel Scott Live at the St. Regis*, as a revelatory moment. "For the first time I'm satisfied with how I sound on record. When I heard it, I said, 'That's my voice, and that's the way I sound on the piano.'" It's a moment of self-recognition and pleasure, an appreciation of the sound of freedom. Scott describes feeling more contentment in music than she had when younger; that feeling is a result of growing in her skill as a musician as well as allowing herself to be present in the moment of performance. "I have to play for myself first. When I was a kid, it was a lot of flash and please the audience, but not now. I have learned that if I can please myself, the audience will go along, because they're getting a better performance."[109]

Scott was a musician who embraced the seeming conflict between jazzmasculinity and race womanhood. Before her move to Paris, Scott "was down South desegregating audiences in town after town and getting out one jump ahead of the sheriff."[110] Her race consciousness, the roots of which she attributes to her father's Garveyism, compelled her to actively push for dismantling segregation; this commitment did not diminish during her time in Europe, despite the difficulties she encountered maintaining her career. Her ideas about integration evolved over time. During the incident with the DAR, integration meant the assertion of social equality and the ability of a black woman to represent the ideals of American democracy; later, she gained an awareness that integration would not in and of itself create change on an individual basis. Rather, she had begun to conceive of integration as the necessary demand for human rights: "Every human being is entitled to have a decent job, a decent place to live in, medical care, education and the comfort of knowing he's giving his best to his children."[111] It's what white people had and it's what black people deserved.

FIVE

"The Chill of Death"

The Sway of Charles Mingus's Black Jazzmasculinity

For years I've been trying to say all this. The problem is I can't get
started. I mean I keep trying to whisper sweet-somethings
in this crazy pony's ear while she's trotting and galloping and bucking
me heavenward. But there's no way to either begin or end what
I need to say about Charles Mingus.

Al Young

For years, Charlie Mingus was called all sorts of names,
was accused of being "hateful" and of always "pitching one."
But all he wanted was to be heard!

Nina Simone

The music producer Hal Willner organized the 1992 tribute album *Weird Nightmare: Meditations on Mingus* around Mingus compositions played on instruments invented and built by composer Harry Partch (1901–1974), who "once described himself as a 'musician seduced into carpentry.'" Willner employed a "dream" house band—Keith Richards, Vernon Reid, Chuck D, and Don Byron, among them—to interpret the music. He explains his choice of Partch instruments as a decision made out of respect for Mingus's willingness to experiment creatively. "Although the album has its own sound and 'vibe,' I believe it also serves as an homage to Mingus' composing talents and spirit. Not many composers' works could handle the approach this album took, but Mingus' music creates a whole other world here. I'm sure he would approve."[1]

As Norman Granz did for Billie Holiday after her autobiography was published, Willner juxtaposes portions of the manuscript of *Beneath the Underdog* with different Mingus compositions, among them "Jump Monk," "Self Portrait in 3 Colors," "Pithecanthropus Erectus," and the intended Holiday vehicle, "Eclipse." Willner's "Eclipse" also includes Mingus's poem "The Chill of Death." Written in 1939, "The Chill of Death" was not recorded until 1972, on the album *Let My Children Hear Music*. That span of years underscores a fear that had long brought Mingus to the brink of despair—that he was not given opportunities merely because he was a black man. Mingus knew he "would probably get it recorded someday. But when you have to wait 30 years to get one piece played—what do you think happens to a composer who is sincere and loves to write and has to wait 30 years to have someone play his music? That was when I was energetic and wrote all the time. Music was my life. Had I been born in a different country or had I been born white, I am sure I would have expressed my ideas long ago."[2]

Mingus often decried what he saw as the fatal flaw of the music industry—the perpetuation of Jim Crow practices in a self-professed democratic and freedom-loving culture. Like other musicians of his era, Mingus embraced music as political expression. Often, he used his music to make explicit his critique of racism and racists, both inside and outside the industry. And just as often, the industry proved his claims held merit, particularly when it came to letting Mingus speak freely. "Fables of Faubus," initially an instrumental work recorded for Columbia on his album *Mingus Ah Um*, is one of the most frequently covered of his compositions. But Columbia refused to allow him to record the lyrics for which the song is now well known. Mingus, through call and response with his long-time drummer Dannie Richmond, had improvised the lyrics during performances, homing in on the absurdity of Arkansas governor Orval Faubus, who mobilized the Arkansas National Guard to keep the Little Rock Nine out of Little Rock Central High School. Though the 1954 Supreme Court decision *Brown v. Board of Education* had struck down the "separate but equal" cover of racist practices in education, the country was slow to accept the presence of black children learning alongside white children. Critic Nat Hentoff, then head of the independent label Candid, gave Mingus the freedom to record the lyrics with the song in 1960, under the title, "Original Faubus Fables."

For Mingus, the journey toward the recording of "Original Faubus Fables" was characteristic of the resistance he met in creating jazz that could be heard for its musical inventiveness, its critical perspective, and its expression of personality. In 1971, during the same year in which his memoir *Beneath the Underdog* was published, Mingus was nominated for a Grammy for the liner notes to the album *Let My Children Hear Music*. In "What Is A Jazz Composer?" (as the notes were titled), Mingus walked the line, as he'd always done, between championing modern, experimental approaches to composition and disparaging some of those very same efforts. He embraced modernism in jazz as being inclusive of, as Ingrid Monson observes, "a constellation of ideas about form and content, abstraction, individuality, iconoclasm, rebellion, the autonomy of art, authenticity, progress, and genius."[3] Mingus wanted his children, both actual and metaphorical, to have access to live music that was emotionally sustaining, "to have music," and "to hear live music," not noise. In the notes, he offers his ideas on what that music could be, along with describing some of the roadblocks to creating it.

Playing with feeling has its place; in fact, it is precisely what appeals to many in the jazz audience.[4] However, "valid" expression lies in the musical depiction of the emotion the musician has felt, the beauty he's witnessed, and the experiences of the life he has lived. Therein, Mingus writes, is the difference between a creative musician and someone who is "stealing or copying a form of music that is not his own." More than mere "feeling," Mingus desires melodic thought, a musical idea that, though spontaneously composed, is fixed enough in the musician's mind that it can be performed again and again. The soloist takes what was perhaps banal, familiar, or unremarkable, and creates a "new complete idea with a new set of chord changes," a "new melodic conception." A thought like that should warrant repeating. According to Mingus, "empathy" for the musicians' musical outlook corresponds to appreciation of their technique as jazz composers.

Mingus valued "spiritual music," music with feeling and emotion that "came from the heart, even though it's composed." In his opinion, "That's what often happens in jazz: I have found very little value left after the average guy takes his first eight bars—not to mention two or three choruses, because then it just becomes repetition, riffs and patterns, instead of spontaneous creativity. I could never get Bird to play over two choruses. Now kids play fifty thousand if you let them. Who is that good?" Musicians have been letting the concept of novelty distract them from what the audience wants. "At one time" in jazz, "[y]ou played your ad lib solo, you created it, and if it was worthwhile, then you played it in front of the public again." He recalls being a kid listening to Coleman Hawkins and Illinois Jacquet, both of whom "memorized their solos and played them back for the audience, because the audience had heard them on records." An improvised solo should clearly relate to the tune being performed; it should "belong" to the composition, as well as have movement or be "developed" from one musical place to another.[5]

In this respect, Mingus is expressing ideas that his idol, Duke Ellington, also articulated. It was Ellington's "firm belief that there has never been anybody who has blown even two bars worth listening to who didn't have some idea about what he was going to play, before he started." Ellington insisted that jazz is "a matter of thoughtful creation, not mere unaided instinct." Indeed, "Improvisation really consists of picking out a device here and connecting it with a device there, changing the rhythm here and pausing there; there has to be some thought preceding each phrase that is played, otherwise it is meaningless," and "nothing more than musical exercises."[6]

Among Mingus's favorite jazz composers were Art Tatum, Bud Powell, and Dizzy Gillespie, but none stood higher than Charlie Parker, the "greatest genius of all" for having "changed the whole era around." These musicians were his contemporaries; they shared a commitment to composing in ways that innovated new rhythmic and melodic concepts. Mingus never doubted that he was himself a composer but felt that he was never properly recognized as such. "Back to the record: the music on this record is involved with my trying to say what the hell I am here for. And similar ideas . . . But mainly I am saying: Do you really know Mingus, you critics?" Mingus did not believe he had been born free; as a result, he felt that he had much he needed to say. Over the nearly four decades of his career, his efforts to communicate his ideas were a constant struggle.

With *Let My Children Hear Music* and its liner notes, Mingus argues for the continuing importance of jazz in two ways. One draws on his experience as a student of Lloyd Reese. Reese taught Mingus how to listen and how to compose based on what he had heard—essential training for musicians who wanted to produce complete musical thoughts during their solos. Raised on classical music and the choir, Mingus learned from Reese how to extract the individual lines played by the different instrumentalists on classical recordings. Whereas Mingus had initially heard "a whole lotta shit going on . . . too much to figure out," he gradually learned to "decipher" what was being played and thereby understand its musical structure. This understanding of structure fundamentally shaped his approach to composition and its possibilities for expressing multilayered musical concepts.

Mingus's second argument credits jazz with creating generations of virtuosos, often unacknowledged as such because of the American bias toward perceiving classical musicians as more skilled. Mingus observes that jazz musicians have expanded the ranges of their instruments in ways that confound classical musicians. "And take Jimmy Knepper. One of his solos was taken off a record of mine and written out for classical trombone in my ballet. The trombone player could barely play it. He said it was one of the most technical exercises he had ever attempted to play. And he was just playing the notes—not the embellishments or the sound that Jimmy was getting." The ghettoization of jazz musicians limited their explorations to only a few instruments—trumpet, saxophone, trombone—instead of the broader expanse of instruments found in the symphony. Mingus believed that if "his children" heard music and embraced it fully, we would see a widening of the scope of what are considered jazz instruments, from the bassoon to the English horn, French horn, cello, and so on. He acknowledged that European musicians had already recognized this fact and begun turning toward jazz in more significant numbers.[7]

While *Let My Children Hear Music* shows Mingus's concern with claiming his legacy, his performance of "The Chill of Death" reveals the continuing seductiveness of the death wish, which had fixated him for years. We can hear this preoccupation in his memoir, where he castigated Fats Navarro for falling prey to it; we also hear it in his regularly voiced fear that he would die before fully presenting his musical ideas. In this composition, Mingus depicts Death as a beautiful woman, evidence that he knew his own weaknesses well. The song's protagonist greets Death. Like a lover, she throws her arm around him, but he resists the embrace, thinking it is not yet his time. She warns that he will not cheat her this time. But cheat her he did. In the decades after his death, Mingus's influence on other writers, musicians, and artists has steadily increased, his music a touchstone for their own creative experiments and a model for their willingness to plumb the reticences of their "black" interiors. In ending this book, I explore three moments that capture the impact Mingus made on those who knew and loved him, moments that focus, as I have done throughout, on the sway of Charles Mingus and black jazzmasculinity.

"GOD MUST BE A BOOGIE MAN"

[H]e thought I was a nervy broad.

Joni Mitchell

Time never ticked so loudly for me as it did this last year.
I wanted Charlie to witness the project's completion. . . .
I know it would have given him a chuckle.

Joni Mitchell

Mingus's autobiography, *Beneath the Underdog: His World as Composed by Charles Mingus*, demands that its audience embrace a racialized masculinity that is fractured, obstreperous, profoundly creative, and alternately in love, making love, and loving. Throughout his life, Mingus challenged deeply held cultural narratives about the ways in which black men speak and in which they are heard. His collaboration with Joni Mitchell on the album *Mingus* (1979) reflected his desire to push the boundaries of autobiographical performance. As Mitchell observes, "It was as if I had been standing by a river—and Charlie came by and pushed me in—'sink or swim'—him laughing at me dog-paddling around the currents of black classical music." They worked together on all the songs except the one she completed after his death, "God Must Be A Boogie Man." Mitchell inhabits Mingus's voice precisely when his body and his ability to perform begin to fail him, attempting to represent the fractured subjectivity Mingus staged in *Beneath the Underdog*. She retells the book's opening by listening intently to the rhythm of the narrative and improvising a melody of her own interpretation. "I tried to take those pages and use the meter and everything to the melodies of his that I was using, but the words wouldn't adhere. So then I let them have their own syncopation and wrote my own melody."[8] She sings,

Which would it be
Mingus one or two or three
Which one do you think he'd want the world to see
Well world opinion's not a lot of help
When a man's only trying to find out
How to feel about himself
In the plan oh
The cock-eyed plan
God must be a boogie man![9]

Mitchell had responded to Mingus's siren call—she took his material and created something new, something that would both please him and satisfy her artistic truth. "I was after something personal—something mutual—something indescribable." Mitchell adopts marginalization as a source of creativity in the *Mingus* "audio paintings."[10] Their collaboration illustrates the challenges, both personal and critical, that a fearless embrace of racialized subjectivity in performance produces.

It was masquerading as a black man on the cover of her tenth album, *Don Juan's Reckless Daughter* (1977), that led Mitchell to *Mingus*. (She says that album made Mingus call her.) Mitchell was then in her jazz period (1974–1980), and viewed black masculinity and jazz as avenues for creative freedom and exploration, even though some critics felt that her turn toward jazz made her music, like free jazz itself, inaccessible. Although her stylistic shift from a pop and folk style to jazz and rock seemed like a radical move, her jazz leanings were rooted, as they were for many jazzmen, in a youthful moment at a record store. As a teenager, she had bought the Lambert, Hendricks, and Ross album, *The Hottest New Sound in Jazz* (1960). Mitchell committed the album to memory, playing it continually, teaching herself how to sing each song the group performed. "I considered that album to be my Beatles," she claimed.[11] Kevin Fellezs describes this origin story as the launch of her "musical migrations," the "generic border crossing" she performed by creating an "illegitimate and liminal space—a broken middle between pop and jazz," which plied "the waters between high art aesthetics and a popular music career."[12] Like Mingus, Mitchell was creating no thing we had heard before, widening the scope of our understanding of what emotionally resonant music can be. She describes her jazz turn as an almost involuntary recruitment, as if she were "being sucked into jazz projects and working more and more with jazz musicians." Mitchell found herself being challenged musically, and as a result experiencing greater freedom to express her ideas. "I find I'm more understood there, and the heavier the player that I work with, the [easier] it is to communicate."[13]

On the cover of *Don Juan's Reckless Daughter*, Mitchell dresses in costume. Coincidentally, Mingus frequently dressed according to the persona he was then performing—conking his hair when a teenager, sporting a bowler hat and three-piece suit in his English chap phase, or donning farmer's overalls during the period around the 1962 Town Hall concert. Mitchell's jazz-rock fusion album showcases her growth as a singer and instrumentalist, as well as her ability to create collaboratively with other musicians, like celebrated electric bassist Jaco

Pastorious. Though widely praised, the album was also characterized as "weird," as "schizoid Joni balances her several personalities (folk, rock, jazz, classical) in a mish-mash of music and words."[14] Wesley Strick, referencing the career of the legendary blackface entertainer, described the cover as "Joni Goes Jolson." He finds Mitchell assuming three "disguises": "Real Indians—the North American kind—tend to recur ('They cut off their braids and lost some link with nature.') throughout the lyric, as do Black Men, mostly pimps with dizzy, adoring White Broads."[15] Indeed, her disguise as the black male pimp or "black dandy"[16] is foregrounded on the cover.

Dave Surratt describes her multiple musical personas as "Joni the jazz-head ('Cotton Avenue'), the expansive strings-arranger ('Paprika Plains') and the Latin sound experimentalist ('The Tenth World')."[17] A number of reviewers found that Mitchell's lyrics were too romantic, that she had gone to the well of lost love and her fascination for black people[18] once too often for lyrical inspiration, risking turning off listeners who were familiar with her other albums. Janet Maslin called Mitchell pretentious, a song lyricist who "belabors" the form, and an "uninterest-ing chronicler of experience other than her own."[19] According to Steven Holden, writing in the *Village Voice*, "Sexual prostitution becomes Mitchell's ultimate metaphor for exploitation and imperialism." That metaphor, Holden argues, grounds the "most perfect song" on the album, "Off Night Backstreet," in which Mitchell imagines her lover as her pimp, "wheedling him in the sultry tones of a cunning prostitute."[20] Mark Kernis finds the same song "downright chilling despite being a brilliantly focused composition—spare but emotionally dense."[21]

The critical response to the album echoes some reviewers of *Beneath the Underdog*, who believed that Mingus's multiple personas and sexual confessions were a literal sign of excess, of uncontrollable sexuality, masking an inability to express a genuine interior landscape. Anxious to protect their rights as songwrit-ers, composers, and performers, Mingus and Mitchell both draw upon images of the pimp and prostitution to critique the music business, experiencing their work for record companies as being like that of a "sharecropper."[22] Just as Mingus understood that critics did not always know what they were talking about, Mitch-ell believed that critics of *Don Juan's Reckless Daughter* weren't savvy enough to see where she was going musically or to comprehend that the music was a commentary on the exigencies of the period. Just as Mingus had railed against the injustices of segregation and Jim Crow, Mitchell railed against contemporary practices of prejudice and discrimination. In a 1985 interview, she explained that her work was a reaction to the times, that "[b]asically it has to do with turning your back on America and heading into the Third World . . . at the time Muslims were messing around in Washington, there were radical tensions. I was disillusioned." She suggests that her musical personas were created out of a desire to understand and capture the experience of those most affected by the era.[23]

As a musician and writer, Mingus dramatized his racial and gender experiences, using a wide-ranging field of emotion and multiple personas to confess the truth of his story. *Beneath the Underdog* allows us to understand how Mingus came to see his experience as a black man as having an indelible imprint on his music. He believed that, through music, he shared an emotional language with his audiences, and that those listeners who were honest and open could really hear him. Despite Mitchell's reputation for being too confessional, she also remained a cipher.[24] Like Mingus, Mitchell imagined various personas to compose music that revealed her experiences and connected her to an ever-present audience. However, Mitchell's desire to situate herself within a different musical tradition, to use personal experience to challenge conventional narratives about racial and gender subjectivity, is regarded, as it was for jazzman Hazel Scott, as evidence of her inauthenticity rather than an expression of sublime artistry. Earlier in her career, Mitchell's deeply personal songwriting revealed a realist attitude toward composition. Keith Fellezs argues that Mitchell's later "inauthentic performativity" was the root of her genius, that "the artifice of authenticity—in other words, inauthenticity—was not necessarily a false experience. . . . Inauthentic performativity, then is a methodological tool Mitchell utilized to create a public persona through which she may readily construct artworks that resonate 'truthfully' with audiences."[25]

According to Leonard Feather, Mitchell need not have worried about undertaking the collaboration. With her album *Mingus*, Mitchell does for Mingus the man what Mingus the composer did for Lester Young with "Goodbye Porkpie Hat"—create a tribute of "great emotional power."[26] The album's elegiac theme continues in the controversial interludes between songs: snippets of Mingus caught in conversation, about the luck he has had in his life and his plans to be buried in India. (These plans had been made long before he became ill.) Sue Mingus had provided Mitchell with the tapes during the ten days she spent with Mingus in Cuernavaca. The collaboration had started earlier, in New York, where she and Mingus would listen to music and discuss plans—she demurred to his original suggestion of an album based on T. S. Eliot's *Four Quartets*.[27] Mingus composed four of the six songs, while Mitchell wrote the lyrics and sang. At the recording sessions, the musicians included members of the jazz-fusion band,

Weather Report—Jaco Pastorious, Wayne Shorter, Peter Erskine, and Don Alias—along with Herbie Hancock and Emil Richards. Mitchell also acknowledged the musicians who'd helped her experiment with musical ideas before the recording, including Mingus's long-time drummer Dannie Richmond, Phil Woods, Gerry Mulligan, and Eddie Gomez, among others.

Mitchell's approach to performance—experimental, experiential, conceptual—made her a compelling collaborator for Mingus at a time when, despite his encroaching physical disability, he nonetheless wanted to keep creating and telling his truth through music. *Mingus* is both a beginning and a requiem, a swan song and a breakthrough, the culmination of one, if not two careers, to hear Mitchell tell it: "When I did the Mingus project, I was advised what it would cost me[.] I took that seriously but I couldn't believe that I would lose my airplay." Expressing a mixture of regret and conviction, Mitchell notes that the album "kicked me right out of the game. It was a great experience, one of my fondest. . . . I would do it today even knowing what it costs, but it certainly cost me. It took me some years to get back in it."[28] Through *Mingus*, Joni Mitchell attempted to bridge the gap between her evolution as a musician and Charles Mingus's phenomenological aesthetics of black masculinity. It was an "intimate process," with Mitchell spending time "sitting around in Charles' shoes. It seems like it might have been a hard thing for [her] to see his point of view, but it wasn't." The success of the enterprise resides in the risks Mitchell was willing to take as a singer, lyricist, and composer to meet Mingus, the composer always searching and questioning.[29]

Adrian Piper's performance of black masculinity as the Mythic Being (1972–1976) plumbs the line of racial ambiguity and gendered experience that Mingus did so vividly throughout his career. "I am a conceptual anomaly who elicits xenophobic responses from most people," Piper explains. "So it is in my own interest to confound crude stereotypes and bring the viewer to a greater awareness and acceptance of anomaly, singularity, and individual complexity."[30] Just as Mingus understood and represented himself as a racial outsider, aware of his own epidermalization, Piper crafts art out of her own experience of otherness. With *The Mythic Being*, she intended to stimulate new thoughts in her audience about their relationship to race at the very moment that they encounter difference. In the notes she wrote as she was developing this art project, she envisioned the "M.B.—an attempt to glean raw art information *only* from the circumstances of my own life and not from current styles in the art world—to use my continuing & ever-expanding past as a source of information." Piper documented her performance of black masculinity on video, revealing her physical transformation from a young, slight, fair black woman, into a threateningly inscrutable man of color. She sported an Afro and a mustache, often masking her eyes with dark sunglasses. She walked Manhattan streets as the Mythic Being (also known as the Angry Man), reciting different passages from her journals as mantras. According to Piper, using intimate autobiographical passages from her diary as mantras allowed them to become "meaningless sounds, depersonalized expressions ascribable to anyone and everyone: They are common property."[31] In viewing *The Mythic Being*, we see how embodying black masculinity could inform her phenomenological aesthetics and contribute to her understanding of how the visual informs subjectivity. Her body becomes the instrument on which questions of race and gender are scored, improvised, and applauded.

Piper explains her ability to work successfully, and simultaneously, as an artist, a philosopher, and a yogi with a battle metaphor. "I have survived in each of these respective fields through camouflage." Her camouflage is performance; her three personas constitute a creative, fractured, yet singular, identity. Her willingness to give each persona full expression is a challenge both to the parochialism of audiences and to the expectation that she make conventional choices in her public and private lives. Her use of "survival" as a descriptor for her work emphasizes her belief in the *necessity* of art-making to her life. "Not to be able to realize or express the self I am in action is to die a slow and painful death."

We can interpret Piper as exploiting the distinction between the autobiographical and the personal in becoming the art object. Her work serves as a critique of racial identity and the assertion of agency, publicly and privately.[32] Piper is motivated, John Bowles argues, by a belief that there is no innocent viewer; rather, the viewer is always in a position of privilege and thus implicated in the performance or the artwork. Piper's work disturbs that privilege, encouraging us to accept the burden of racialized subjectivity in a belief that acceptance liberates consciousness. That burden isn't the sole province of black people—Piper sees her work as a demand that white people also take responsibility for seeing themselves as racialized subjects. Through her art, she provides them an entrée. According to Sidonie Smith, Piper embraces her role as the "art object, as she deploys a rhetoric of self-revelation to become the text with which the viewer interacts. . . . The artist's self, Piper suggests, exists to be *worked*," "disrupt[ing] and transform[ing] viewers' ways of seeing in order to create the social conditions for full subjectivity."[33] Though not a musician, Piper's insistence on working the self through her art practice calls to mind the way jazzmen like Mingus saw their music as racially specific and yet also universal to the human condition. To see the other in oneself, the fact of difference, was to feel communion across that difference.

Through Mingus, Mitchell, and Piper, we are privy to the negotiations that black men, white women, and black women field as they attempt to express racialized gender identities within the context of jazz, performance art, and the everyday. Black masculinity is the sign that motivates their phenomenological aesthetics, their embodiment of difference as radical articulation of self and others through art practice. We might not be too far wrong in describing each as failing spectacularly to create performances that resonate with audiences beyond those already predisposed to embrace representations that challenge preconceived ideas about how one engages with art, who the subject of an art-work is, and how we appreciate the real in those performances. But they succeed phenomenally in making us aware that art demands a readiness to be exposed, on the part of the artist and the audience, to have our difference scrutinized, reviled, and valued beyond the exploitation of the market, in reminding us that art demands a willingness to be free.

PASSIONS OF A MAN

If the ultimate sources for poetry and jazz are the life of the emotions, the extreme difficulty of describing that life, and the great spiritual cost of *not* trying to describe it, then poetry and jazz are rooted at the very center of what it's like to be human.

William Matthews

Mingus viewed music as an elixir, an antidote to the poison, a religious calling. In a phone conversation with Mingus, the only word you could be sure of was the last one, "love." I got a lot from him.

Janet Coleman

In 1989, a decade after Mingus's death, writers Janet Coleman and Al Young published a shared account of their friendship with him, *Mingus/Mingus: Two Memoirs*. Charles Mingus had proved a catalyzing force in both their lives. According to Coleman, she and Young were "both, at that time, beatniks and English majors at the University of Michigan. . . . The coincidence of us . . . knowing him never seemed remarkable to Mingus, nor did the fact that we seemed to turn up everywhere." Swept up into his orbit, these "Mingusologists," as Coleman describes themselves, soon learned of the opus he was working on, the manuscript that would become *Beneath the Underdog*. Mingus shared his manuscript, alternately titled "Half Yaller Nigger" or "Half Yaller Schitt-Colored Nigger," with Coleman. Desirous of approval, he asked for her impressions: "Does it sound clear? Does the writer sound convincing? Has he been dead and alive?"[34]

Mingus dangled the enticement of collaborating with him on preparing the manuscript for publication before them both, though Young never saw it. Mingus always promised that he would give Young a draft to review "tomorrow." But "Tomorrow never came. It never happened; we never got to first base with this Me-Author-You-Editor idea of his. The following day and all the subsequent days and nights I tried to get to see that manuscript of his, Mingus—sometimes firmly, other times gracefully—blocked the way or froze on me."[35]

Despite that disappointment from his jazz hero, Al Young wrote numerous "musical memoirs," such as *Drowning in the Sea of Love*, reveling in the extent that Mingus's music acted not just as a soundtrack for his coming of age, but also as a particularly expressive language for articulating an emerging sense of being as a black man.[36] Young writes, "Like a blithe and beautifying fungus, Mingus mushroomed inside me, killing off forever the notion that music or anything else had to go or be or stay a certain way." Mingus's appeal lay in his openness to making music that documented his spiritual questing, his longing for human connection, his desire to best his contemporaries, and his grief over lost loves and friends. In living a life full to bursting of emotionality, Mingus presented to listeners a model of embracing emotions. To Young, Mingus is "purr and thunder."[37]

In a vignette titled after Mingus's "Nostalgia in Time Square," Young tells of the brief relationship he had with a woman when he first arrived in New York, a story of sexual innocence confronting the hard edge of the city. They take a walk together in Times Square "back before genitals and orifices were being packaged." Her sudden silence after their walk, when it seemed that she had something "urgent and deep" to say, continues to haunt him.

> It is this remembered silence of ours that has hovered for decades in a secret part of me that would come out sounding—were it ever orchestrated—like Mingus's subway-grounded, wounded, slash-and-burn landscape of love. Sometimes, standing at the edges of "Nostalgia in Times Square" and listening to it without regard for history or time, this piece sounds to me the way God might've

described how it might feel to go spirit-slumming and wind up side-tracked and unheard from on some festive back street.[38]

Young's affecting, poetic portraits reveal how his feelings for Mingus reflected and influenced not only his search for identity as a writer, but also the stuttering, turbulent, rapturous experience of coming of age in the fifties and sixties. Mingus's music allows him to untether sexuality from silence, giving him permission to represent desire in his own writing. Yearning for love and spiritual intimacy, Mingus's passions give voice to melancholy, to an ever-present desire to be known, in a blues-based shout that cries out for feeling.

In *Mingus/Mingus*, Young describes the ecstasy he experienced when first hearing Mingus on *Pithecanthropus Erectus*. The music caused him and his friends to "look up from the shoes we were shining and take time out to do some serious talking about those shrieks and moans Mingus and his sidemen were hurtling at us along with all that new-sounding energy." One by one, he and his friends moved from Detroit to New York where musicians were "*doing* that shit. . . . They just come right on out with it."[39] Both a deejay and a musician, Young was a frequent haunter of record shops; he made a study of Mingus's music from "Mingus Fingers" through the Debut releases, then on to the albums then coming out on Atlantic, Candid, and others. Sides like "Portrait" and "Precognition" gave him "the same feeling I still get whenever any kind of genuine joy goes percolating through my nervous system. This new music . . . a little like bebop, a little like classical, a little like pop—was, all in all, like no music I had ever experienced before. It made me feel like living forever."[40] As Mingus had always asserted, his music was evidence of his soul's immortality. Young discovered that he, like Mingus, was "basically a happy, truth-starved person, and fundamentally pretty straight," with music playing "a shining role in [his] spiritual development."

The poet William Matthews, describing himself as "a weird white be-bop groupie," echoes Young's sentiments about the influence of Mingus and other musicians of the era—including Sonny Rollins, Ben Webster, and Lester Young—in giving himself permission to conduct a "personal archeological exploration" in his poetry. Through their music, he learned to "forge an introduction to [his] emotional life and not to be terrified of it."[41] Matthews, like Young and Mingus, discovered that music and its representation—whether in memoir, poetry, or another form—provided not only a framework for understanding one's emotional life, but also a grammar for expressing and depicting the value of emotions. These men's willingness to understand that their gender did not preclude a healthy ability to master and appreciate emotions suggests why so many people saw in jazzmen models for a good life. The language of emotions in jazz provided a vernacular for belonging, practicing the ethical treatment of the self and others, imagining a new vision of society, and developing an ever-evolving skill in portraying experience through creative practice.

Mingus believed he made art with a purpose—whether to challenge views about what constituted fair wages for artistic labor, to resist limiting the possibilities envisioned for jazz as a compositional form and for jazzmen as musicians, or to counter the destructive discourses and dynamics around race and color both within and outside of black communities. Mingus artfully juxtaposed revolutions in black protest and on jazz records, reflecting his view that aesthetics were bound to judgments about ethical behavior and social equality. He considered his music as art weaponized for the liberation of black people. During his *Down Beat* blindfold test in 1960, he asked Leonard Feather to turn off an album because he'd "rather talk about something important—all the stuff that's happening down south."[42] Eric Dolphy had hipped him to the fact that "there was something similar to the concentration camps once in Germany now down South . . . and the only difference . . . is that they don't have gas chambers and hot stoves to cook us in yet," said Mingus. In solidarity, he "wrote a piece called *Meditations*, as to how to get some wire cutters—before someone else gets some guns to us."[43] "Meditations" premiered at a 1964 benefit concert for the National Association for the Advancement of Colored People (NAACP); the composition was a call to arms, a shield against the slow death racism promised black people. Not simply a defensive strike, the music represented Mingus's belief that jazz could create change through the sharing of political, emotional, and musical ideas and experiences. Jazz was a way of being and relating to others. By taking on the issues confronting jazzmen and the people they spoke for, Mingus embraced the idea that music is a dialogue, that it is prescriptive, that it can be the grounds for radical thinking.

Mingus's declaration of a fractured self in *Beneath the Underdog* was a demand that he be seen as a multilayered personality with conflicting ambitions and desires. To express his love of the music and the people within it, he expressed his disappointment, his rage, and his humor. Mingus challenged himself, as he challenged others, to tell the truth even if it damaged his own relationships, because he valued the idea that only through honest expression could he accurately and creatively make music that was saying something. His insistence on truth-telling regularly got him into trouble—whether it was having to pay for physically assaulting a valued collaborator, losing professional opportunities, or failing at relationships. Nevertheless, we can admire his tenacity and clarity of vision. He sought in his music a presentation of his better nature, his higher self, and he prescribed the same for his audiences. Thunderously, Mingus purred, "Let my children hear music."

EPITAPH

He died, still looking for life, in Cuernavaca, Mexico in 1979.

Nat Hentoff

Don McGlynn's 1998 documentary, *Charles Mingus: Triumph of the Underdog*, riffs off the title of Mingus's 1971 memoir. As the film opens, Mingus's voice plays over images of him walking around New York City. He describes his essential dilemma—that he is a "famed jazz musician, but not famed enough to make a living in this society called America." Preparation for the performance of Mingus's masterwork, *Epitaph*, at Lincoln Center in 1989, loosely frames the film.[44] The late composer Gunther Schuller conducted the work. Schuller described Mingus as the first Third Stream composer, the one who combined classical and jazz traditions in his compositions, cooking up a "bouillabaisse that doesn't show its seams." Trumpeter Wynton Marsalis, who performs in the concert, finds Mingus "is not victimized by a style," that he is "trying to relate [his music] to something human." Mingus, says Schuller, depicted "exactly who he was in his music." He ranks him "high up there" in terms of American composers in general, and alongside Duke Ellington, Mingus's musical hero, in particular. ("I was born loving Duke. . . . I would still choose Duke.")[45] At last, Mingus was defined as a composer.

Ellington had celebrated his seventieth birthday at a two-day festival held in his honor at the University of California, Berkeley, in 1969. Sue Mingus believes that Ellington's performance of Mingus's "The Clown" turned Mingus back on to music after the fallow period of the mid to late sixties. Many of his close friends believed him to be clinically depressed at the time. The depression led to several breakdowns, including one that kept him at Mount Sinai for a few months in 1967 and was certainly connected to the events that led to his eviction from his Great Jones loft in 1966, documented in Thomas Reichman's cinéma-vérité film, *Mingus 1968*. Mingus had intended to turn the loft into a music school. Writer Janet Coleman remembered that the "answering pick-up was 'Music, Art and

Health, who's calling?' He was planning a school that would incorporate all the arts in a healthy atmosphere." Mingus once told her that he had employed "a minister, a Zen teacher, Charles Rice, who teaches karate, and Katherine Dunham for dance and witchcraft."[46]

In *Mingus 1968*, Reichman juxtaposes clips of Mingus in performance with images of him in conversation as he waits for the evictors. We witness the sanitation department trucking off all his belongings—his music scores, his basses, and the various other personal effects he had collected over a lifetime, including the typewriters he had been using to draft his autobiography. There are scenes of Mingus with his youngest children, Carolyn and Eric, in the loft and in Central Park. He admonishes his daughter to love only one man. Mingus explains his philosophy about love: "Give me three days and three nights, Pithecanthropus Erectus. Some woman to take time out and make a little love. My religion is that everyone should kiss and make love."[47] Estranged at the time from both his wife, Judy, and his lover, Sue Ungaro, Mingus found himself emotionally unmoored. Carolyn would later say that her father "wanted to be emotional. . . . As much as he was guarded, he wanted to be vulnerable. . . . , to feel that pain. It was a conscious thing. He wanted to set himself up for that suffering, and he picked the women who could do it best."[48]

Recalling that time, Judy Starkey Mingus McGrath says that Mingus was in a constant struggle both to make music and to make a living at making music. He had not released a studio recording since the 1964 album *Mingus Plays Piano*. The breakdown that led to his being admitted to Mount Sinai stemmed from that constant stress. "It would just tear your heart out if you could picture this man who was a great presence in one of those striped hospital robes and medicated. It's like there's this person inside who can't get out. . . . Back then it was standard; they'd think he was a violent black guy, and want to keep him immobilized [on thorazine]. But he was like a zombie."[49] Mingus would remain on thorazine for several years, requiring drastic efforts to wean him from the drug.

Gradually, Mingus began composing and performing locally again. He entered a new phase of his career in which he could bask in the recognition he'd long desired and begin making a substantial living as a musician. *Charles Mingus in Paris*, released in 1970, started an avalanche of new, acclaimed albums—among them *Let My Children Hear Music* (1971), *Mingus Moves* (1973), and *Changes One* (1974). Sue Mingus became a jazzman herself, managing Mingus's career and protecting his music. President Jimmy Carter hosted him at the White House.

Mingus's newly invigorated career proved essential to his ability to cope with the illness that had been plaguing him off and on for a few years. In the mid-seventies, he was diagnosed with amyotrophic lateral sclerosis (ALS), the progressive neurodegenerative disease associated with baseball player Lou Gehrig. Mingus eventually lost the use and control of his extremities, requiring a wheelchair. He and Sue relocated to Cuernavaca, Mexico, in search of a cure, having given up on traditional courses of treatment. Despite his physical decline, Sue remembers that "he never cursed the gods." Of her visit to Cuernavaca, Celia Mingus Zaentz recalls, "He ruled the house. You didn't just go there and sit around. He orchestrated everyone."

Buddy Collette came to Cuernavaca when Mingus called, knowing it was time: "He said, 'I've got to see you. Come.' That's about all I heard. And I said, 'I'll be there.'"[50] For a few years, Collette had noticed Mingus slowing down, sometimes unable to respond physically to his neurological commands. Now, he had to face the fact that Mingus was nearing the end. They spent their last days together sitting in companionable silence. Collette recalls that even though the disease had advanced to the point where it was difficult for Mingus to speak, his eyes still communicated his pleasure and sadness. Despair permeated the air, according to Collette, as Mingus was given various dubious remedies in an effort to halt the disease's progression. Collette believed the strain was making everyone go slightly mad; he encouraged Sue to bring Mingus back to Los Angeles where he, Grace Mingus, and others were eager to support her in caring for him. He believed Mingus wanted to come home too.[51]

Home was always Los Angeles, of course, though he'd spent more than half his life in New York. Home was the friends like Buddy Collette, who had known him since boyhood and knew how to calm him when he was in one of the rages that masked his insecurity and creative anxiety. Home was the bass, the piano, and his sheet music. Though Mingus died before making it back to Los Angeles, he nevertheless seemed to orchestrate a final performance, reminding many of his "mystical" powers. Just days after Mingus died at the age of fifty-six, exactly fifty-six whales were reportedly stranded on the sands of a Mexican beach —a fitting send-off for a man who had long imagined the circumstances of his death. His "end was planned. Planned, but well."[52]

NOTES

Preface

Epigraph from liner notes by Nat Hentoff for *A Modern Jazz Symposium of Music and Poetry with Charles Mingus*, Bethlehem 20–40092.

1. Nichole T. Rustin, "'Blow Man, Blow!': Representing Gender, White Primitives, and Jazz Melodrama through *A Young Man with a Horn*," in *Big Ears: Listening for Gender in Jazz Studies*, ed. Nichole T. Rustin and Sherrie Tucker (Durham: Duke University Press, 2008), 361–92.

2. Nichole T. Rustin, "'Mary Lou Williams Plays Like a Man!' Gender, Genius, and Difference in Black Music Discourse," *South Atlantic Quarterly* 104.3 (Summer 2005): 445–62; 460.

Introduction

Chapter epigraphs from liner notes to Charles Mingus Jr., *Let My Children Hear Music*, and from Nat Hentoff, *The Jazz Life* (New York: Dial Press, 1961), 142, emphasis in the original.

Epigraphs to section "There Is No Guilt in Love" from Charles Mingus, *Beneath the Underdog* [1971] (New York: Vintage, 1991), 191; and Albert Murray, letter to Ralph Ellison, March 11, 1957, in *Trading Twelves: The Selected Letters of Ralph Ellison and Albert Murray*, ed. Albert Murray and John F. Callahan (New York: The Modern Library, 2000), 155.

1. From the liner notes to *Mingus Plays Piano*, Impulse! IMPD-217.

2. "Some people think that a composer is supposed to please them," Mingus said, "but in a way a composer is a chronicler, like a critic. He is supposed to report on what he has seen and lived" (from the publicity for Quintessence Jazz Series, n.d.). Likewise, while Max Roach affirmed the belief that one can create art simply for art's sake, it is also true that "the artist is like a secretary . . . : He keeps records of his time, so to speak." Quoted in Arthur Taylor, *Notes and Tones: Musician to Musician Interviews* (New York: Perigree Books, 1977), 112.

3. Mingus, "Open Letter to Miles Davis," *Down Beat*, November 30, 1955.

4. Charles Mingus to Barry Ulanov, May 9, 1952, Charles Mingus Collection (CMC), Library of Congress.

5. Ronald Radano, *Lying Up a Nation: Race and Black Music* (Chicago: University of Chicago Press, 2004), 12, 15.

6. Martin Jay, *Songs of Experience: Modern American and European Variations on a Universal Theme* (Berkeley: University of California Press, 2005), 1, 6–7.

7. Ibid., 407.

8. Guthrie P. Ramsey, Jr., *The Amazing Bud Powell: Black Genius, Jazz History and the Challenge of Bebop* (Berkeley: University of California Press, 2013); Penny Von Eschen, *Satchmo Blows Up the World! Jazz Ambassadors Play the Cold War* (Cambridge: Harvard University Press, 2006); Ingrid Monson, *Freedom Sounds: Civil Rights Call Out to Jazz and Africa* (Oxford University Press, 2010); Paul Allen Anderson, "'My Foolish Heart': Bill Evans and the Public Life of Feelings," *Jazz Perspectives* 7.3 (2013): 205–249.

9. According to Martha Nussbaum, "If we think of emotions as essential elements of human intelligence, rather than just as supports or props for intelligence, this gives us especially strong reasons to promote the conditions of emotional well-being in a political culture: for this view entails that without emotional development, a part of our reasoning capacity as political creatures will be missing." Nussbaum, *Upheavals of Thought: On the Intelligence of Emotions* (Cambridge University Press, 2001), 3. Jazz musicians expressed similar sentiments, believing that in their expressions of emotion through music, they were articulating insights vital to the functioning of an integrated society.

10. Nussbaum, *Upheavals of Thought*, 52.

11. Ibid., 11.

12. Ibid., 76. Nussbaum writes that these judgments shape how the culture evolves and how individuals interact within it, forming "the geography of one's emotional life . . . . The background emotion acknowledges dependence on or need for some ungovernable element in the world; the situational emotion responds to the way in which the world meets or does not meet one's needs." Ibid., 74–75.

13. See, for example, Leonard Meyer, *Emotion and Meaning in Music* (Chicago: University of Chicago Press, 1961), and Jerrold Livingson, "Emotion in Response to Art," in *Emotion and the Arts*, ed. Mette Hjort and Sue Laver (New York: Oxford, 1997), 28, 29.

14. Nussbaum, *Upheavals of Thought*, 60.

15. Hazel Carby's work on Miles Davis raises some of the questions I'm interested in here. She examines how Davis imagined through jazz and his bandmates' "intimacy and interdependence," enabling "an unconventional, gendered vulnerability." I'm extending the scope of that emotionality to jazz culture as a whole and arguing that the emotionality was conventional, a defining characteristic of how jazzmen valued their relationships with one another. Carby, *Race Men* (Cambridge: Harvard University Press), 144, 155–156.

See also Patrick Burke, "Oasis of Swing: The Onyx Club, Jazz, and White Masculinity in the Early 1930s," *American Music* 24.3 (Autumn 2006), 320–346; Eric Porter, "'Born out of Jazz . . . Yet Embracing All Music': Race, Gender, and Technology in George Russell's Lydian Chromatic Concept," in *Big Ears: Listening for Gender in Jazz Studies*, ed. Nichole T. Rustin and Sherrie Tucker (Durham, NC: Duke University Press, 2008), 210–234; Rustin, "'Blow Man, Blow!'" in *Big Ears*, 361–392; and Trine Annfelt, "Jazz as Masculine Space," Kilden Information Centre for Gender Research in Norway, http://kjonnsforskning.no /en/2003/07/jazz-masculine-space, last accessed October 16, 2013. (I want to thank Martin Niederauer for bringing Annfelt's article to my attention.)

16. See Sherrie Tucker, *Swing Shift: "All-Girl" Bands of the 1940s* (Durham, NC: Duke University Press, 2000); Angela Davis, *Blues Legacies and Black Feminisms: Gertrude "Ma" Rainey, Bessie Smith, and Billie Holiday* (New York: Vintage, 1999); Hazel Carby, "'It Jus Be's Dat Way Sometime': The Sexual Politics of Women's Blues," *Radical America* 20.4 (1986): 9–24; Farah Jasmine Griffin, *If You Can't Be Free, Be a Mystery: In Search of Billie Holiday* (New York: One World/Ballantine, 2002); and Rustin and Tucker, *Big Ears*.

17. See Guthrie P. Ramsey, *Race Music: Black Cultures from Bebop to Hip Hop* (Berkeley: University of California Press, 2003); Ronald Radano, *New Musical Figurations: Anthony Braxton's Cultural Critique* (Chicago: University of Chicago Press, 1994); and John Gennari, *Blowin' Hot and Cool: Jazz and Its Critics* (Chicago: University of Chicago Press, 2006).

18. See Eric Porter, *What Is This Thing Called Jazz? African American Musicians as Artists, Critics, and Activists* (Berkeley: University of California Press, 2002); and Steven Isoardi, *Songs of the Unsung: The Musical and Social Journey of Horace Tapscott* (Durham, NC: Duke University Press, 2001).

19. Because the idea of jazzmen's genius was so tied to the assumption and privileging of masculinity as the site of emotional truth, authority, and authenticity, such women were regularly excluded from the jazz fraternity. See Tucker, *Swing Shift*; Porter, *What Is This Thing Called Jazz?*; Griffin, *If You Can't Be Free, Be a Mystery*; and Davis, *Blues Legacies and Black Feminisms*.

20. According to Sara Ahmed, when emotions "stick" to certain bodies, those individuals become objects and their status as Other depends on value claims about their bodies. She writes, "Such objects become sticky, or saturated with affect, as sites of personal and social tension. . . . Of course, emotions are not only about movement, they are also about attachments or about what connects us to this or that. . . . What moves us, what makes us feel, is also that which holds us in place, or gives us a dwelling place." Ahmed, *Queer Phenomenology: Orientations, Objects, Others* (Durham, NC: Duke University Press, 2006), 10–11.

21. Ibid., 11, 13. Similarly, Paul Allen Anderson explores how the label of "poignancy" stuck to Bill Evans throughout the 1960s. Poignancy was an "evaluative adjective" that was used to masculinize the perceived sentimentality of his music; the term gave gender

cover to critics who praised his work. "Poignancy in jazz was implicitly gendered as non-feminine when described as believably dramatic (rather than sentimentally exaggerated or melodramatic) and quietly tender (rather than cloying or bombastic)." Anderson, "My Foolish Heart," 209, 227. Divorced from the desire to express subjective experience, however, the poignant performance faces the danger of becoming nothing more than a performance.

22. Evelyn Brooks Higginbotham, "African American Women's History and the Meta-language of Race," *Signs* (Winter 1992): 251–74.

23. Tony Whyton, "Crosscurrents: The Cultural Dynamics of Jazz," in *Jazz Debates/ Jazzdebatten*, ed. Wolfram Knauer, Darmstadt Studies in Jazz Research, vol. 13 (Jazzinstitut Darmstadt, 2014): 165–74.

24. Elsa Barkley Brown, "'What Has Happened Here': The Politics of Difference in Women's History and Feminist Politics," *Feminist Studies* 18.2 (Summer 1992): 298.

25. Ruth Solie, ed., *Musicology and Difference* (Berkeley: University of California, 1995), 6, 9, 10.

26. Brown, "What Has Happened Here," 297.

27. Joan Wallach Scott, "History in Crisis: The Others' Side of the Story," *American Historical Review* 94.3 (June 1989): 690; Joan W. Scott, "The Evidence of Experience," *Critical Inquiry* 17 (Summer 1991): 777, 779–780.

28. D. Soyini Madison, "The Dialogic Performative in Critical Ethnography," *Text and Performance Quarterly* 26.4 (2006): 320–24; E. Patrick Johnson, "Queer Theory," in *The Cambridge Companion to Performance Studies*, ed. Tracy C. Davis (Cambridge: Cambridge University Press, 2008), 161–81.

29. Charles Mingus Jr., liner notes, *Jazzical Moods*, Fantasy OJCCD-1857–2.

30. Imamu Amiri Baraka, "Numbers, Letters," in *The Black Poets*, ed. Dudley Randall (Toronto, New York: Bantam Books, 1971), 219.

31. James Moody, "I'm in the Mood for Love," *King Pleasure*, Slay'D 5000.

32. Amiri Baraka, *Blues People: Negro Music in White America* (New York: Quill William Morrow, 1999 [1963]), 152.

33. Eric Porter, "'It's about That Time': The Response to Miles Davis' Electronic Turn," in *Miles Davis and American Culture*, ed. Gerald Early (St. Louis: Missouri Historical Society, 2001), 130–47.

34. Burnett James, quoted in Benny Green, *The Reluctant Art: Five Studies in the Growth of Jazz* (New York: Horizon, 1963), 47.

35. Wynton Marsalis with Selwyn Sefu Hinds, *To a Young Jazz Musician: Letters from the Road* (New York: Random House, 2005), 41–42.

36. Ibid., 118. See also Tracy McMullen, "Identity for Sale: Glenn Miller, Wynton Marsalis, and Cultural Replay in Music," in Rustin and Tucker, *Big Ears*, 129–154.

37. See particularly bell hooks, *Ain't I a Woman? Black Women and Feminism* (Boston:

South End Press, 1981), *Feminist Theory: From Margin to Center* (Boston: South End Press, 1984), and *Yearning: Race, Gender, and Cultural Politics* (Boston: South End Press, 1990).

38. Mingus studies are expanding, including new biographies, analyses of his autobiography, and studies of his work as a composer. I am indebted to work by Brian Priestley, Gene Santoro, Jennifer Griffin, Salim Washington, Eric Porter, Scott Saul, and Fred Moten, among others, for contributing insight into Mingus as a man and musician.

39. For example, consider Ken Burns's ten-episode *Jazz* documentary, in which Burns argues that the story of twentieth-century jazz is that of Duke Ellington and Louis Armstrong. Although he argues that Mingus was Ellington's heir as a composer in one episode, Burns extends little effort in developing an understanding of Mingus's career and work.

40. Nichole T. Rustin, "'Mary Lou Williams Plays Like a Man!' Gender, Genius, and Difference in Black Music Discourse," *South Atlantic Quarterly* 104.3 (Summer 2005): 445–462.

41. Amiri Baraka, *The Autobiography of LeRoi Jones* (Chicago: Lawrence Hill Books, 1997), 65.

42. Christopher Harlos, "Jazz Autobiography: Theory, Practice, Politics," in *Representing Jazz*, ed. Krin Gabbard (Durham, NC: Duke University Press, 1995), 134.

43. Ibid., 141.

44. Elizabeth Alexander, "Can You Be Black and Look at This: Reading the Rodney King Video(s)," in *The Black Interior: Essays* (Graywolf Press, 2004), 175.

45. The section heading comes from Mingus, *Beneath the Underdog*, 140. Hereafter, citations for this source will be given parenthetically (by page number) in the text.

46. When asked by Nat Hentoff what the composition "Celia" meant, Mingus replied, "It's how I like feeling about her." Mingus quoted in Nat Hentoff's liner notes to *East Coasting*.

47. See Davis, *Blues Legacies and Black Feminism*, especially chapters 5 and 6, which focus specifically on the sexual politics of Holiday's "love songs" and the social critique embedded within "Strange Fruit"; and Griffin, *If You Can't Be Free, Be a Mystery*, which examines the various myths of Billie Holiday and attempts to define black women's genius as jazz artists. The documentary *Strange Fruit* (California Newsreel, 2002) explores a number of these concerns as well. Eric Porter's discussion of Abbey Lincoln's growth as a singer examines how Billie Holiday's aesthetic choices shaped Lincoln's vision of what was possible as a singer and composer as well as how Holiday's choices are given meaning as black feminist praxis. See also Lara Pellegrinelli, "Separated at 'Birth': Singing and the History of Jazz," in Rustin and Tucker, *Big Ears*, 31–47.

48. Judith Halberstam, "The Good, the Bad, and the Ugly: Men, Women, and Masculinity," in *Masculinity Studies & Feminist Theory*, ed. Judith Kegan Gardiner (New York: Columbia University Press, 2002), 345, 362.

49. Rustin, "'Mary Lou Williams Plays Like a Man!'" 457.

50. Ibid., 459.

51. Halberstam, "The Good, the Bad, and the Ugly," 345.

52. Ibid., 353.

53. Sherrie Tucker draws attention to how to listen to what female jazzmen tell about themselves, noting that, "A woman who repeatedly insists, 'We were real musicians,' is baffling to the feminist historian until she or he understands that the narrator is pushing against power structures of discourse, commodification, and practice that greatly affected how she was seen, how she saw herself, and what she had to prove in order to live her life and do her job." Tucker, *Swing Shift: "All-Girl" Bands of the 1940s* (Durham, NC: Duke University Press, 2000), 26–27.

54. Rustin, "'Mary Lou Williams Plays Like a Man!'"

55. Susan McClary, *Feminine Endings: Music, Gender, and Sexuality* (Minneapolis: University of Minnesota Press, 1991), 28.

56. Ibid., 21.

57. Ibid., 24. McClary builds on philosopher Mark Johnson's work on metaphor which, he explains, shows "the indispensability of embodied human understanding for meaning and rationality." Johnson, *The Body in Mind: The Bodily Basis of Meaning, Imagination, and Reason* (Chicago: University of Chicago Press, 1987): xiii–xvi. Similarly, Harris M. Berger focuses, through "stance," on "structures of lived experience and the culturally specific ways in which people make meaning by fitting expressive forms into the context of those structures." Berger "recognize(s) that experience is fundamentally social, not radically individual, and emphasize(s) that all of social life is shot through with affect." He also posits a useful distinction between two types of experience, explaining that experience can refer either "to the concretely lived world of objects grasped and actions taken—to the contents of consciousness," or "a much looser notion of one's experience of holding a generalized position in society." Berger, *Stance: Emotion, Style, and Meaning for the Study of Expressive Culture* (Middletown, CT: Wesleyan University Press, 2011), 5, 139 n7, 148 n5.

58. Ruth Feldstein highlights the rarity of black women as subjects in discourses about jazz and art in her study, "'I Don't Trust You Anymore': Nina Simone, Culture, and Black Activism in the 1960s," *Journal of American History* 91.4 (March 2005): 1349–79. See also Sherrie Tucker, "West Coast Women, a Jazz Genealogy," *Ethnomusicology* 8.1 (Winter 1996–97): 5–27.

59. Carby, *Race Men*, 139.

60. Porter, *What Is This Thing Called Jazz?*, 31.

61. Feldstein, "I Don't Trust You Anymore," 1356.

62. McClary, *Feminine Endings*, 13.

63. Tucker, *Swing Shift*, 27–29.

64. See Gillian Siddall, "'I Wanted to Live in That Music': Blues, Bessie Smith and

Improvised Identities in Ann-Marie MacDonald's *Fall on Your Knees*," *Critical Studies in Improvisation/Etudes critiques en improvisation* 1.2 (2005), http://www.criticalimprov .com/article/viewArticle/16/45, last accessed September 9, 2012.

ONE "Self-Portrait in Three Colors"

Chapter epigraphs from Grace (Mingus) Washington, letter to Charles Mingus, September 12, 1961, Charles Mingus Collection (CMC), Library of Congress; and Mingus, *Beneath the Underdog*, 3. Hereafter, page references to *Beneath the Underdog* will appear parenthetically in text.

Epigraphs to section "'Background for Thought'" from George Simon's review of Mingus's composition, "Background for Thought," performed in May 1954 at the Museum of Modern Art in New York City, in *Metronome*, May 1954; and Al Young's review of *Beneath the Underdog* in *Rolling Stone*, June 10, 1971, 52. (Young, a friend of Mingus, fittingly identifies more than three Mingus selves in his review.) For more on the slippage between "negro" and Jew in psychoanalysis, see Claudia Tate, "Freud and His 'Negro': Psychoanalysis as Ally and Enemy of African Americans," *Journal for the Psychoanalysis of Culture & Society* 1.1 (Spring 1996): 53–62.

Epigraphs to section "'All the Things You Could Be by Now If Sigmund Freud's Wife Was Your Mother'" from Richard Wright, "Psychiatry Comes to Harlem," *Free World*, September 1946, 45–51; and Charles Mingus, letter to Barry Ulanov, May 9, 1952, CMC.

Epigraphs to section "*Mingus Mingus Mingus Mingus Mingus*" from the dedication and caveat pages opening *Beneath the Underdog*; and Ann duCille, *Skin Trade* (Cambridge: Harvard University Press, 1996), 63. The title of the section comes from the 1963 album *Mingus Mingus Mingus Mingus Mingus*, Impulse!, A-54.

1. Dufty is often referred to as Holiday's ghostwriter. For a discussion of why "collaborator" is more appropriate than "amanuensis," see Maya C. Gibson, "Alternate Takes: Billie Holiday at the Intersection of Black Cultural Studies and Historical Musicology," PhD dissertation, University of Wisconsin-Madison, 2008. Mingus credits Nel King with being the only white person capable of editing his manuscript. She did not, as an amanuensis would have done, write any portions of it.

2. Billie Holiday and William Dufty, *Lady Sings the Blues* (New York: Doubleday, 1956), 5.

3. Quoted in Jesse Hamlin, "Billie Holiday's bio, 'Lady Sings the Blues,' may be full of lies but it gets at jazz's great core," September 18, 2006, http://www.sfgate.com/entertain ment/article/Billie-Holiday-s-bio-Lady-Sings-the-Blues-may-2469428.php, last accessed May 30, 2016.

4. Griffin, *If You Can't Be Free, Be a Mystery*, 48.

5. As Christopher Harlos writes, "any critical assessment of what a given jazz autobi-ographer is up to means considering the various components of a writing subject who also happens to be a jazz musician." Harlos, "Jazz Autobiography," 137.

6. For example, consider the following comments by Quincy Jones who, having spoken of his deep adoration for Miles Davis, assesses the truth in an autobiography that Davis wrote with Quincy Troupe. In short, he thought Troupe let Davis "go to far. It is a rough thing, but it is Miles. One hundred and forty motherfuckers on every page. But a lot of that shit he made up. He made up that shit about Quincy [Jones] and Marlon Brando giving Frances an engagement ring. I said, 'Miles, you know that's bullshit.' 'Man, that fucking sounds good.' Miles was a serious dramatist, you know." Quoted in "I Just Adored That Man," Quincy Jones interview by Gerald Early, in *Miles Davis and American Culture*, ed. Gerald Early (St. Louis: Missouri Historical Society Press, 2001), 43.

7. Ajay Heble, *Landing on the Wrong Note: Jazz, Dissonance, and Critical Practice* (New York: Routledge, 2000), 91, 96.

8. Rudolph Byrd, "The Tradition of John: A Mode of Black Masculinity," in *Traps: African American Men on Gender and Sexuality*, ed. Rudolph P. Byrd and Beverly Guy-Sheftall (Indianapolis: Indiana University Press, 2001), 1–24.

9. W. E. B. DuBois, *Dusk of Dawn: An Essay toward an Autobiography of a Race Concept* [1940] (New Brunswick: Transaction Publishers, 1984), xxix.

10. Alexander, *The Black Interior*, ix, x–xi.

11. Frantz Fanon, *Black Skins, White Masks* (New York: Grove Press, 1994), 231.

12. In her analysis of women's autobiographical practice, Sidonie Smith examines the "performative nature of the entire autobiographical enterprise," including how the repre-sentation of excess reveals what Teresa De Lauretis has called "resistance to identification." Smith posits that through reading these performative excesses, we can understand how the autobiographical subject identifies or disidentifies with, solidifies or upends gender norms. Sidonie Smith "Performativity, Autobiographical Practice, Resistance," in *Women, Autobiography, Theory: A Reader*, ed. Sidonie Smith and Julia Watson (Madison: University of Wisconsin Press, 1998), 111, 113.

13. See E. Ann Kaplan's essay, "Is the Gaze Male?" in *Powers of Desire: The Politics of Sexuality*, ed. Ann Snitnow, Christine Stansell, and Sharon Thompson (New York: Monthly Review Press, 1983), 309–27; and Deborah McDowell, "Pecs and Reps: Muscling in on Race and the Subject of Masculinities," in *Race and the Subject of Masculinities*, ed. Harry Stecopoulus and Michael Uebel (Durham, NC: Duke University Press, 1997), 361–86.

14. Robyn Wiegman, *American Anatomies: Theorizing Race and Gender* (Durham, NC: Duke University Press, 1995), 7.

15. Sidonie Smith, *Interfaces: Women, Autobiography, Image, Performance* (Ann Arbor: University of Michigan Press, 2002), 227.

16. George C. Wolfe, *Jelly's Last Jam* (New York: Theatre Communications Group, 1993), 22.

17. Vivian Mingus, interviewed by Shelby Jones in *The Mingus Sisters Speak*, disc 1, Lacecap Records, 2001.

18. Jack Kelso, quoted in *Central Avenue Sounds*, ed. Clora Byrant, et. al (Berkeley: University of California Press, 1997), 145, 222.

19. Hentoff, liner notes to *Mingus/Oh Yeah*, re-released on *Passions of a Man*, Rhino R2 72871, 100.

20. Navarro died in 1950 at the age of twenty-four due to complications from tuberculosis and heroin use. Ross Russell, "The Legacy of Fats Navarro," *Down Beat*, February 19, 1970, 14–16, 33; Barry Ulanov, "Fats Navarro," *Down Beat*, November 1947, 19, 38–39; Dizzy Gillespie quoted in Ira Gitler, *Jazz Masters of the 40s* (New York: Da Capo Press, 1966), 101; Carmen McRae quoted in Jack Chambers, *Milestones: The Music and Times of Miles Davis* (New York: Da Capo, 1988), 142.

21. Grace Mingus, interviewed by Shelby Jones, *The Mingus Sisters Speak*.

22. Ibid.

23. Grace Mingus and Vivian Mingus, interviewed by Shelby Jones, *The Mingus Sisters Speak*.

24. See *Beneath the Underdog*, 72.

25. Quoted in *Central Avenue Sounds*, 95. Woodman goes on to say, "Well, he always liked to fight, and always had a reputation. When he got old, he followed his reputation. Any musician will tell you that."

26. Britt Woodman, in *Central Avenue Sounds*, 121.

27. Michael Uebel, "Men in Color: Introducing Race and the Subject of Masculinities," in *Race and the Subject of Masculinities*, ed. Harry Stecopolous and Michael Uebel (Durham, NC: Duke University Press, 1997), 5.

28. Charles S. Johnson, "A Phenomenology of the Black Body," in *Traps: African American Men on Gender and Sexuality*, ed. Rudolph P. Byrd and Beverly Guy-Sheftall (Indianapolis: Indiana University Press, 2001), 225, 226, 229 (italics in the original).

29. Ibid., 229.

30. Ibid., 230–31 (the terms are mine, the descriptions Johnson's).

31. Ibid., 232.

32. Alexander, "Can You Be Black and Look at This?" in *The Black Interior*, 204.

33. Hollie I. West, "Bass Viol Book," *Washington Post*, May 15, 1971.

34. Andrea Queely recognizes "the pimp" as the "persistent myth of Black hypermasculinity." "Hip Hop and the Aesthetics of Criminalization," *Souls* 5.1 (2003): 1–15; 13. See also Robin D. G. Kelley, "Miles Davis: The Chameleon of Cool; A Jazz Genius in the Guise of a Hustler," *New York Times*, May 13, 2001.

35. Review of *Beneath the Underdog* in *Publisher's Weekly*, n.d., Mingus Clippings File, Institute of Jazz Studies, Rutgers University, hereafter IJS.

36. Mingus says he composed "All the Things You Could Be by Now If Sigmund Freud's Wife Was Your Mother" while in Bellevue. Rather than reveal insight about Mingus's experience of Freud as a tool for disciplining his personality, he says that the name actually "means nothing." In fact, "The title probably came from the way the audience was reacting one night." The time frame for the composition of the song is at least two decades previous to its first recorded performance on the album *Charles Mingus Presents Charles Mingus*, recorded in 1960. The Bellevue incident, according to *Beneath the Underdog*'s chronology, probably occurred in 1959.

37. Mingus, "A Living Benefit for Mingus," 1968. Critic Bill Whitworth observed, "While jazz fans, music magazines and musicians puzzle over such outbursts from a man many of them consider to be a genius, Mingus has a simple explanation for it all. He says he is going crazy." Bill Whitworth, "The Rich Full Life of Charlie Mingus," *New York Herald Tribune*, November 1, 1964, 13.

38. Bud Powell, who suffered from mental illness and spent extensive periods in mental institutions, tended to self-medicate with drugs and alcohol. When a court determined he was not fit to manage his own career and finances, he was put under the guardianship of Oscar Goodstein. Guthrie Ramsey, *The Amazing Bud Powell: Black Genius, Jazz History, and the Challenge of Bebop* (Berkeley: University of California Press, 2013).

39. Kevin McNeilly argues, "The 'lobotomy' which Mingus fears is a symbolic castration, an act of taming which threatens to homogenize his multiplicitous self, to convert his split subjectivity into a pallid, speechless whole; Mingus resists the dehumanizing 'Dr. Bonk' by discursive doubling, trashing plain language and so refusing to allow his talk be made coherent, understandable, assimilable." "Charles Mingus Splits, or, All the Things You Could Be by Now If Sigmund Freud's Wife Was Your Mother," *Canadian Review of American Studies* 27.2 (1997): 61.

40. Olly Wilson, "The Black American Composer and the Orchestra in the Twentieth Century," *The Black Perspective in Music* (1985): 26–34; 32. See also Ben Sidran, *Black Talk* [1971] (New York: Da Capo Press, 1983), 159.

41. Bill Whitworth, "The Rich Full Life of Charlie Mingus," *New York Herald Tribune*, November 1, 1964, 13, 15.

42. Sarah Ahmed defines "orientated" in her *Queer Phenomenology: Orientations, Objects, Others* (Durham, NC: Duke University Press, 2006).

43. Thomas Carmichael, "*Beneath the Underdog*: Charles Mingus, Representation, and Jazz Autobiography," *Canadian Review of American Studies* 25.3 (Fall 1995): 30, 32, 34.

44. Christopher Harlos, "Jazz Autobiography: Theory, Practice, Politics," in *Representing Jazz*, ed. Krin Gabbard, 131–66 (Durham, NC: Duke University Press, 1995), 141, 143, 145. I try to illustrate moments of Mingus's playfulness and humor in telling his story, as

Hortense Spillers does in her reading of Frantz Fanon. See "All the Things . . . ," in *Black, White, and in Color: Essays on American Literature and Culture* (Chicago: University of Chicago Press, 2003), 392.

45. McNeilly, "Charles Mingus Splits," 45, 46, 58, 59.

46. Sherrie Tucker, "When Did Jazz Go Straight?: A Queer Question for Jazz Studies," *Critical Studies in Improvisation* 4.2 (2008).

47. Hentoff, "A Volcano Named Mingus," *HiFi Stereo Review*, December 1964, 53.

48. Ibid., 55.

49. Hortense Spillers, *"The Crisis of the Negro Intellectual:* A Post-Date," in *Black, White, and in Color*, 457.

50. "In other words, the social subject of 'race' is not only gaining access to her own garbled, private language, as psychoanalysis would have it, but to language as an aspect of the public trust." Spillers, *Black, White, and in Color*, 396.

51. Spillers, *Black, White, and in Color*, 426.

52. Claudia Tate, *Psychoanalysis and Black Novels: Desire and the Protocols of Race* (New York: Oxford University Press, 1998), 10, 54.

53. Marlon Ross, "White Fantasies of Desire: James Baldwin and the Racial Identities of Sexuality," in *James Baldwin Now*, ed. Dwight A. McBride (New York: New York University Press, 1999), 25.

54. Ibid., 27, 36.

55. Ibid., 23, 39.

56. Audre Lorde, *Zami: A New Spelling of My Name a Biomythography* (Freedom, CA: The Crossing Press, 1982), 179–80, 226. See also Donna Penn, "Sexualized Woman: the Lesbian, the Prostitute, and the Containment of Female Sexuality in Postwar America," in Joanne Meyerowitz, ed., *Not June Cleaver: Women and Gender in Postwar America, 1945–1960* (Philadelphia: University of Pennsylvania Press, 1994), 358–381.

57. Delany, *The Motion of Light in Water: Sex and Science Fiction Writing in the East Village, 1960–1965* (New York: A Richard Kasak Book, 1993), 315, 317.

58. Rudolph Byrd, "The Tradition of John: A Mode of Black Masculinity," in *Traps: African American Men on Gender and Sexuality*, ed. Rudolph P. Byrd and Beverly Guy-Sheftall (Indianapolis: Indiana University Press, 2001), 1–24; Eric Porter, *What Is This Thing Called Jazz? African American Musicians as Artists, Critics, and Activists* (Berkeley: University of California Press, 2002), 139, 143; Scott Saul, *Freedom Is, Freedom Ain't: Jazz and the Making of the Sixties* (Cambridge: Harvard University Press, 2003), 173–74, 178.

59. See also McNeilly, "Charles Mingus Splits," 45–70, 62.

60. Daphne Brooks, *Bodies in Dissent: Spectacular Performances of Race and Freedom, 1850–1910* (Durham, NC: Duke University Press, 2006), 4–5.

61. Charles Fox, "Unzipped," *New Statesman*, September 17, 1971, 375.

62. Jonathan Yardley, "Agonies of a 'Mongrel,'" *New Republic*, July 3, 1971, 29.

63. Burt Korall, "Mingus on Mingus," *Saturday Review*, July 31, 1971.

64. Phillip Larkin, "Jazz-Man's Sound and Fury," *Daily Telegraph*, August 26, 1971.

65. Peter Davies, "Tarnished Personal Image," *Western Mail*, August 28, 1971.

66. Jerry DeMuth, "Sex between the Riffs," *Chicago Sun Times*, n.d.

67. Crispin Sartwell, *Act Like You Know: African-American Autobiography and White Identity* (Chicago: University of Chicago Press, 1998), 6. See also Eric Lott, *Love and Theft: Blackface Minstrelsy and the American Working Class* (New York: Oxford University Press, 1993), 6.

68. Yardley, "Agonies of a 'Mongrel,'" 29.

69. Neil Tesser, untitled clipping, n.d., CMC.

70. Clive James, "Jim Crow in the Jazz World." *Observer*, August 15, 1971.

71. See also McDowell, "Pecs and Reps," 367.

72. Kobena Mercer, *Welcome to the Jungle: Identity and Diversity in Postmodern Politics* (New York: Routledge, 1994), 259; see also, Gerald Early, "On Miles Davis, Vince Lombardi, and the Crisis in Masculinity in Mid-Century America," *Daedulus* 131.1 (Winter 2002), 154–59.

73. Ingrid Monson, "The Problem with White Hipness: Race, Gender, and Cultural Conceptions in Jazz Historical Discourse," *Journal of the American Musicological Society* 48.3 (Fall 1995): 396–422. See also Monique Guillory, "Black Bodies Swingin': Race, Gender, and Jazz," in *Soul: Black Power, Politics, and Pleasure*, ed. Monique Guillory and Richard C. Green (New York: New York University Press, 1998), 191–215.

74. Radano, *New Musical Figurations*, 12; Scott DeVeaux, "Constructing the Jazz Tradition," in *The Jazz Cadence of American Culture*, ed. Robert G. O'Meally (New York: Columbia University Press, 1998), 525.

75. Jed Rasula, "The Media of Memory: The Seductive Menace of Records in Jazz History," in *Jazz among the Discourses*, ed. Krin Gabbard (Durham, NC: Duke University Press, 1995), 136, 150. See also John Gennari's "Jazz Criticism: Its Development and Ideologies," *Black American Literature Forum* 25 (Fall 1991): 449–523.

76. William H. Kenney, III, "Negotiating the Color Line: Louis Armstrong's Autobiographies," in *Jazz in Mind: Essays on the History and Meaning of Jazz*, ed. Reginald T. Buckner and Steven Weiland (Detroit: Wayne State University Press, 1991), 56.

77. David Solomon, November 11, 1964 memo to A. C. Specktorsky, Jack Kessie, and A. J. Burdrys, Charles Mingus Collection, Library of Congress.

78. Larry Adler, "Six Letter Life," *New Society*, September 2, 1971.

79. Marcellus Blount and George P. Cunningham, eds., *Representing Black Men* (New York: Routledge, 1996).

80. Charles Mingus, *Mingus Plays Piano*, Impulse! IMPD-217.

81. Liner notes to *Mingus Plays Piano*.

82. Ibid.

83. Wahneema Lubiano, "But Compared to What? Reading Realism, Representation, and Essentialism in *School Daze, Do the Right Thing* and the Spike Lee Discourse," in *Black American Literature Forum* 25.2 (1991), 253–282.

84. Guthrie Ramsey, Jr., "Them There Eyes: On Connections and the Visual," in Kellie Jones, *Eye-Minded: Living and Writing Contemporary Art* (Durham, NC: Duke University Press, 2011), 351.

TWO "West Coast Ghost"

Chapter epigraphs from *Beneath the Underdog*, 4; an ad for the album, *Mingus at Monterey* (1964); Nat Hentoff's liner notes to *East Coasting*, Bethlehem BS 6019; and Whitney Balliett, "Jazz Records," *New Yorker*, June 18, 1960, 131.

Epigraph to section "'Mingus Fingers'" from Yusef Komunyakaa, "Copacetic Mingus," in *Pleasure Dome: New and Collected Poems* (Middletown: Wesleyan University Press, 2001), 111. Mingus wrote "Mingus Fingers" while he was with the Lionel Hampton band and recorded it on November 11, 1947 for Decca. He also recorded the song for Dolphin's of Hollywood as Baron Mingus and His Rhythm in November 1948; *Charles "Baron" Mingus West Coast 1945–49*, Uptown UPCD 27.48.

Epigraphs to section "*East Coasting*" from *Beneath the Underdog*, 191; and Eddie "Lockjaw" Davis, in Valerie Wilmer, *Jazz People* (New York: Da Capo, 1970), 39. The section title is from Mingus's album, *East Coasting*, Bethlehem BS 6019.

1. Richard Hadlock, "Charles Mingus' Barely Tamed Show-Stopper," c. 1965, Mingus Clippings File, IJS; Gene Lees, "Caught in the Act," *Down Beat*, n.d., Mingus Clippings File, IJS.

2. One marvels at the disconnect between representations of Mingus's body, as a site of excess and outsized rage, and its reality. Consider Joel Dorn's accounting of his first interview with the "larger than life" Mingus. "If you would have asked me that day how tall he was, I would have said at least 6′ 4″, maybe taller. Over the years I've made it a point to ask people, especially those who saw him in person, "How tall was Mingus?" Invariably they always say, 6′ something. He wasn't. His exact height was 5′ 9¾″. But his presence, his genius, his passion, his madness, his imperial Mingusness—they were six-four." "How tall was Mingus?" from liner notes to *Charles Mingus Passions of a Man, the Complete Atlantic Recordings, 1956–1961*, Rhino R2 72871, 8. Poet William Matthews refers to Mingus's body as "that Parthenon of fat" in his poem "Mingus in Diaspora," which opens with this stanza: "You could say, I suppose, that he ate his way out, / like the prisoner who starts a tunnel with a spoon, / or you could say he was one in whom nothing was lost, / who took it all in, or that he was big as a bus." *Search Party: Collected Poems of William Matthews* (New York: Houghton Mifflin Harcourt, 2004), 243.

3. Whitworth, "The Rich Full Life of Charlie Mingus," 13. Mingus is not the only angry

jazzman but for some reason, his anger precludes him from being easily packaged. See stories about Cab Calloway and Gillespie in Scott DeVeaux, *The Birth of Bebop: A Social and Musical History* (Berkeley: University of California Press, 1997), 182, 178–179.

4. Nat Hentoff, "Mingus Dynasties," *Village Voice*, March 22, 1979, 34.

5. Nat Hentoff, "Mingus in Job Dilemma, Vows 'No Compromise,'" *Down Beat*, May 6, 1953.

6. Grace Mingus, *The Mingus Sisters Speak.*

7. See Brian Priestley, *Mingus: A Critical Biography* [1983] (New York: Da Capo, 1984), 4–8.

8. Quoted in Bryant et al., *Central Avenue Sounds*, 168.

9. Ibid., 137.

10. Ibid., 96.

11. Vivian Mingus, *The Mingus Sisters Speak.*

12. Quoted in Bryant et al., *Central Avenue Sounds*, 105.

13. Ibid., 123–24.

14. Ibid., 140.

15. Buddy Collette with Steven Isoardi, *Jazz Generations: A Life in American Music and Society* (London and New York: Continuum, 2000), 21.

16. Quoted in Bryant et al., *Central Avenue Sounds*, 137.

17. Collette, *Jazz Generations*, 21.

18. Pepper Adams, "Reminisces: Charles Mingus," http://www.pepperadams.com /PepperOnMingus/Page04.html, last accessed September 5, 2015.

19. Collette, *Jazz Generations*, 21.

20. See also transcripts of Collette's oral history with Steven Isoardi, September 13, 20, and 28, 1989, Central Avenue Sounds, University of California [hereafter cited as UCCAS], 150–51 (tape 3, side 1, September 13, 1989).

21. Red Callender and Elaine Cohen, *Unfinished Dream: The Musical World of Red Callender* (New York: Quartet Books, 1986); and interview with Patricia Willard, May 25, 1982, Jazz Oral History Project (JOHP), Smithsonian Institute, Institute of Jazz Studies, Rutgers University.

22. Quoted in Bryant et al., *Central Avenue Sounds*, 142–43; Ted Gioia, *West Coast Jazz: Modern Jazz in California, 1945–1960* (Berkeley: University of California Press, 1992), 40.

23. Quoted in liner notes to *Mingus Plays the Piano*, Impulse!, p. 11. The piano remained a critical and versatile secondary instrument for Mingus—he would sound out compositions to band members or take over at the bench when the piano player wasn't playing what he wanted to hear.

24. David Bryant quoted in Bryant et al., *Central Avenue Sounds*, 175.

25. Mingus interview with Sy Johnson, February 19–22, 1978, transcript of cassette 1–2, Jazz Oral History Project, Smithsonian Institute, 5. Listen for example to Ellington's

famous Fargo, North Dakota, November 7, 1940, date on the Jazz Classics series. For other bassists who soloed before Blanton, see David Chevan, "The Double Bass as a Solo Instrument in Early Jazz," *Black Perspective in Music* 17 (1989): 73–92. Mingus had, according to biographer Brian Priestley, a "guitar-picking style" with his right hand, which Percy Heath said allowed Mingus to use "different [right-hand] fingers to play successive notes in a phrase." Priestley, *Mingus*, 54.

26. Douglas Flamming, *Bound for Freedom: Black Los Angeles in Jim Crow America* (Berkeley: University of California Press, 2006), 92.

27. See Jacqueline Cogdell DjeDje and Eddie S. Meadows, eds., *California Soul: Music of African Americans in the West* (Berkeley: University of California Press, 1998), including Michael B. Bakan, "Way Out West on Central: Jazz in the African-American Community of Los Angeles before 1930," 23–78, and Ralph Eastman, "'Pitchin' up a Boogie': African-American Musicians, Nightlife, and Music Venues in Los Angeles, 1930–1945," 79–102; and Kyle Julien, "Sounding the City: Jazz, African American Nightlife, and the Articulation of Race in 1940s Los Angeles," PhD diss., University of California, Irvine, 2000.

28. Collette with Isoardi, UCCAS, September 13, 152.

29. Quoted in liner notes to *Charles "Baron" Mingus West Coast, 1945–49*, 8.

30. See Eastman, "Pitchin' up a Boogie."

31. See Bryant et al., *Central Avenue Sounds*, 12; Ingrid Monson, *Freedom Sounds: Civil Rights Call Out to Jazz and Africa* (New York: Oxford University Press), 29–65; Eastman, "Pitchin' up a Boogie," 81.

32. Quoted in Bryant et al., *Central Avenue Sounds*, 154. Also see Lee Young's reminiscences on p. 71.

33. Quoted in Bryant et al., *Central Avenue Sounds*, 113.

34. See Robert E. Sunenblick's liner notes to *Charles "Baron" Mingus West Coast, 1945–49*.

35. Quoted in Bryant et al., *Central Avenue Sounds*,175.

36. Ibid., 315–16.

37. Britt Woodman, quoted in Priestley, *Mingus*, 29.

38. Gioia, *West Coast Jazz*, 337.

39. "File for the Future," *Metronome*, December 1953, 18.

40. Collette with Isoardi, UCCAS, September 28, 1989 (vol. 1, tape 6, side 1), 325.

41. Ibid., 327.

42. Ibid., 328.

43. Gioia, *West Coast Jazz*, 337–38, 339.

44. Miles Davis with Quincy Troupe, *Miles: The Autobiography of Miles Davis* (New York: Simon and Schuster, 1989), 86.

45. Quoted in Bryant et al., *Central Avenue Sounds*, 175.

46. Hampton doesn't mention "Mingus Fingers," boasting only of bringing Mingus to

New York. Lionel Hampton with James Haskins, *Hamp: An Autobiography* (New York: Penguin, 1989), 92.

47. Liner notes to *Charles "Baron" Mingus*, 23.

48. Quoted in Bryant et al., *Central Avenue Sounds*, 160.

49. So convinced was he of the threat, Mingus wrote to President Eisenhower asking that an investigation be started into the predicaments facing musicians attempting to make an honest living. He insisted that he was the kind of man the President needed to keep an eye and ear on what was happening in cities across the United States. And even if Eisenhower never read the letter, Mingus wrote, he was confident that the seriousness of the situation would catch someone else's attention. Charles Mingus, letter to President Dwight Eisenhower, March 5, 1959, CMC. See also George Variale, Division of Employment, letter to Charles Mingus, July 23, 1958; George Variale, letter to Charles Mingus, October 9, 1958; Charles Mingus, letter to Mr. George Varriale [*sic*], October 10, 1959; J. S. Raff, U. S. Treasury Department, letter with enclosed mimeograph to Charles Mingus, April 22, 1959, all CMC.

50. Ralph Gleason, "Charlie Mingus: A Thinking Musician," *Down Beat*, June 1, 1951.

51. Ralph Gleason, "Red Norvo Set for Date at Frisco's Black Hawk," *Down Beat*, March 9, 1951, 7.

52. *Down Beat*, August 11, 1950. Norvo believed that Mingus's switch from wire strings to gut strings made him keep a faster tempo. Red Norvo interview with Loren Schoenberg, Jazz Oral History Project (JOHP), Smithsonian Institute, Institute of Jazz Studies, 216, 276.

53. Burt Korall, liner notes, *The Red Norvo Trio with Tal Farlow and Charles Mingus*. Savoy SV-0267.

54. Korall, liner notes, *The Red Norvo Trio*, and Norvo JOHP, 278.

55. Korall, liner notes, *The Red Norvo Trio*.

56. Mingus quoted in Korall liner notes, *The Red Norvo Trio*.

57. *Metronome*, July 1951, 26; *Metronome*, October 1951, 14, 19. Some reviewers felt the absence of the traditional rhythm section. See *Billboard*, February 3, 1951.

58. Korall, liner notes, *The Red Norvo Trio*.

59. Jack Kenney, "Red Norvo: Four Decades of Jazz Quality," *Metronome*, June 1960, 20–21, quote on p. 21.

60. Jack Tracy, "Red Norvo Trio 'Astounding, Impeccable,'" *Down Beat*, November 17, 1950, 4; J. Kenney, "Red Norvo: Four Decades of Jazz Quality," 20–24.

61. Korall, liner notes, *The Red Norvo Trio*.

62. Quoted in Bob Reisner, "The Titans VI. Charlie Mingus," *Village Voice*, November 6, 1957, 12.

63. Gioia, *West Coast Jazz*, 341; *The Red Norvo Trio with Tal Farlow and Charles Mingus*, Savoy SJL 2212.

64. *Beneath the Underdog*, 322–23; "Charlie Mingus Quits Norvo 3," *Down Beat*, No-

vember 2, 1951, 1. "Red Norvo Trio on Tormé's TVer," *Down Beat*, October 19, 1951, 3. Norvo JOHP, 278–84.

65. Murray Foreman, *One Night on TV is Worth Weeks at the Paramount: Popular Music on Early Television* (Durham, NC: Duke University Press, 2012), 255–58, 267–68, 259, 261.

66. George T. Simon, "The Twenty-One Inch Screen," *Metronome*, July 1955, 39, and "Steve Allen Presenting Jazz on Television," *Metronome*, July 1955; "Play Jazz & Make Money," *Metronome*, October 1957; Jack Maher, "Television Still Flirts With Jazz," *Metronome*, n.d.; George T. Simon, "Jazz on Television? Well . . . er . . . Let's See!," *Metronome*, October 1953. "TV's Only Network Jazz Program," *Metronome*, December 1958, 19, 29. "Stars of Jazz" on ABC began with the promise of only four weeks when it first aired in July 1956.

67. "Norvo Dropped from TVer; Hassel Begins," *Down Beat*, December 14, 1951, 1; "Red Norvo 3 Back on Tormé Show, but Dissension Continues to Flare," *Down Beat*, December 28, 1951, 3; "Color TV Stoppage Halts Tormé's Show," *Down Beat*, November 30, 1951, 3.

68. Celia Mingus, in Ira Gitler's liner notes to *Charles Mingus, The Complete Debut Recordings*, Fantasy 1990, 13.

69. Priestley, *Mingus*, 47.

70. Bob Summarisse, Seattle, Washington, to Charles Mingus, July 11, 1953, CMC.

71. Quoted in Neil Leonard, *Jazz and the White Americans* (Chicago: University of Chicago Press, 1962), 99.

72. Arnold Shaw, *52nd St. The Street of Jazz* (New York: Da Capo Press, 1971); DeVeaux, *The Birth of BeBop*, 285.

73. John Gennari, *Blowin' Hot and Cool* (Chicago: University of Chicago Press, 2006); Ron Welburn, "American Jazz Criticism, 1914–1940," PhD dissertation, New York University, 1983.

74. Tom Piazza, ed., *Setting the Tempo: Fifty Years of Great Jazz Liner Notes* (New York: Anchor Books Doubleday, 1996).

75. See letter from BJ and Karl Keinz, Cologne, West Germany, June 29, 1959, CMC.

76. *Down Beat*, June 7, 1962, 64.

77. *Autobiography in Jazz*, liner notes.

78. Charles Mingus and John La Porta, *Jazzical Moods*, Fantasy Records, OJCCD-1857-2; Charles Mingus, *The Black Saint and the Sinner Lady*, Impulse! IMPD-174; Charles Mingus, *Charles Mingus Presents Charles Mingus*, Candid CD9005; Charles Mingus, *Let My Children Hear Music*, Columbia CK 48910.

79. *Autobiography in Jazz*, liner notes.

80. Gary A. Soucie, letter to Debut Records, April 25, 1956, CMC.

81. Celia Mingus, letter to Gary A. Soucie, April 30, 1956, CMC. Soucie was not the only cadet to receive blank order forms; see letter from G. T. Bergman, New London, Connecticut, January 11, 1957, CMC.

82. Soucie letter to Mingus, November 5, 1956, CMC.

83. Charles Mingus, letter to Soucie, November 13, 1956, CMC. Mingus's papers contain no writing samples from Soucie, presumably because he returned them as requested.

84. Gary A. Soucie, letter to Charles Mingus, January 9, 1956 (1957), CMC

85. Ibid.

86. Charles Mingus, letter to Gary A. Soucie, February 22, 1957, CMC.

87. Nat Hentoff, "A Volcano Named Mingus," *HiFi/Stereo Review*, December 1964, 55.

88. Letter to the Editor, *Down Beat*, June 2, 1950.

89. Gary A. Soucie, letter to Charles Mingus, May 19, 1957, CMC.

90. Charles Mingus, letter to Gary A. Soucie, July 2, 1957, CMC.

91. Andrew Homzy, "Charles Mingus, the Atlantic Years," *Charles Mingus Passions of a Man, the Complete Atlantic Recordings, 1956–1961*, Rhino R2 72871, 45.

92. Mingus, "What Is a Jazz Composer?," in the liner notes to *Let My Children Hear Music*, Columbia CK 48910.

93. Mingus (as told to Diane Dorr-Dorynek), liner notes to album *Blues & Roots*, reissued on *Charles Mingus Passions of a Man, the Complete Atlantic Recordings, 1956–1961*, Rhino R2 72871, 98.

94. Quoted in Priestley, *Mingus*, 124–25.

95. Richmond quoted in Nat Hentoff's liner notes, *Charles Mingus Presents Charles Mingus*, Candid CD9005.

96. Steffano Zenni, "The Need to Tell a Story," in liner notes to *Charles Mingus Passions of a Man, the Complete Atlantic Recordings, 1956–1961*, Rhino R2 72871, 56.

97. Spillers, *Black, White, and in Color*, 426; Charles Mingus, letter to Jack Garrett, n.d., CMC.

98. Mingus, quoted in "A Jazz Summit Meeting," in *Keeping Time: Readings in Jazz History*, ed. Robert Walser (New York: Oxford University Press, 1998), 266.

99. Duke Ellington, "Swing Is My Beat!" in *The Duke Ellington Reader*, ed. Mark Tucker (New York: Oxford University Press, 1993), 249.

100. Mingus, quoted in "A Jazz Summit Meeting," in Walser, *Keeping Time*, 265; see also Nichole T. Rustin, "*Cante Hondo*: Charles Mingus, Nat Hentoff, and Jazz Racism," *Critical Sociology* 32.2–3 (2006): 309–31.

101. Charles Mingus, liner notes to *Pithecanthropus Erectus*; *Charles Mingus Passions of a Man, the Complete Atlantic Recordings, 1956–1961*, Rhino R2 72871, 87.

102. Charles Mingus, liner notes to *Blues & Roots*, 98.

103. Charles Mingus, liner notes to *Pithecanthropus Erectus*, 88.

104. Gene Santoro, "Town Hall Train Wreck: Why Charles Mingus Came to Grief in 1962," *Village Voice*, June 6, 2000, http://www.villagevoice.com/music/town-hall-train-wreck-6418362. Pepper Adams articulates the frustration some musicians may have felt with learning the compositions: "He wrote some marvelous things, and some other things

that just don't work out. A lot of it had to do with how slapdash he was. He hardly would ever complete an orchestration. He'd come to a rehearsal with something half-written, or more often with something completely unwritten and just try to make up something on the spot. Sometimes it would work. Sometimes it would work real well. Sometimes it was a disaster!" "Reminiscences: Charles Mingus," http://www.pepperadams.com/Pepper OnMingus/Page04.html, last accessed September 5, 2015.

105. Mingus, Jazz Oral History Project (JOHP), March 29, 1978, 42.

106. Quoted in "A Trombone Mouth," a profile of Knepper by Whitney Balliett, *New Yorker*, May 20, 1991.

107. Quoted in Bryant et al., *Central Avenue Sounds*, 139.

108. Alan Levin, "Court Frees Mingus; He Sits In on a Sit-In," *New York Post*, March 17, 1963. See also, Rustin, "*Cante Hondo*," and Porter, *What Is This Thing Called Jazz*.

109. Crouch in *1959: The Year That Changed Jazz*, a BBC documentary, dir. Paul Bernays, 2009.

110. Charles Mingus, *Charles Mingus Presents Charles Mingus*, Candid CD9005. To understand why musicians accepted the term "jazz" for their music, while rejecting being termed "jazz musicians," see Kevin Fellezs who describes genre terms like jazz as discursive shorthand, "active, invested signifying/signifyin(g) practices" (*Birds of Fire: Jazz, Rock, Funk, and the Creation of Fusion* [Durham, NC: Duke University Press, 2011], 7–8), and Wolfram Knauer, "'Jazz' or not 'Jazz' From Word to Non-Word and Back," in *Jazz Debates/Jazzdebatten*, ed. Wolfram Knauer, Darmstadt Studies in Jazz Research, vol. 13 (2014): 175–92.

111. Mingus, quoted in "A Jazz Summit Meeting," in Walser, *Keeping Time*, 279.

112. George Wein, quoted in John F. Goodman, *Mingus Speaks* (Berkeley: University of California Press, 2013), 174.

113. Quoted in Priestley, *Mingus*, 139.

114. Quoted in Bryant et al., *Central Avenue Sounds*, 139.

115. Collette with Isoardi, September 13, 1989, UCCAS (vol. 1, tape 3, side 1), 131.

116. Ted White, quoted in Priestley, *Mingus*, 139.

117. Morgenstern quoted in Goodman, *Mingus Speaks*, 205; Priestley, *Mingus*, 139.

118. Bill Coss, *Down Beat*, December 6, 1962, 40.

119. Quoted in Bryant et al., *Central Avenue Sounds*, 139.

120. Mingus JOHP, March 29, 1978, 42.

121. Quoted in Nat Hentoff, *The Jazz Life* (New York: Da Capo, 1975), 164.

122. Don DeMicheal, review of *Money Jungle* (United Artists 15017), *Down Beat*, March 28, 1963.

123. Roach quoted in Stanley Crouch, "Max Roach: Drums Unlimited," *Village Voice*, December 17, 1979. Clark Terry quoted in Wilmer, *Jazz People*, 110.

124. Peter Goddard, performance review, n.d., CMC.

125. Rafi Zabor, review of Mingus's album, *Cumbia & Jazz Fusion*, in *Musician*, October 1978, 74.

126. John S. Wilson, "Mingus' Best—Off Shelf at Last," *New York Times*, July 22, 1962.

127. Judith Mingus, letter to Mrs. Jeanne Atwell, Cornell University, February 11, 1964, CMC.

128. Shaw and Richmond quoted in Nat Hentoff, "A Volcano Named Mingus," *HiFi/Stereo Review*, December 1964, 52–55.

129. Curson and Richmond quoted in Brett Primack, "The Gospel according to Mingus," *Down Beat*, December 7, 1978, 39, 41. In his biography of Thelonious Monk, Robin D. G. Kelley describes in detail Monk's preference for teaching his musicians compositions by ear, the better for them to assimilate the music and to develop ideas about possibilities for improvisation. See Robin D. G. Kelley, *Thelonious Monk: The Life and Times of an American Original* (New York: The Free Press, 2009).

130. Liner notes to *The Black Saint and the Sinner Lady* (Impulse! IMPD-174), 17.

131. Ibid., 10.

132. Ibid., 18.

133. Ibid., 19.

134. Ibid., 19.

135. Ibid., 21–22. Critic Barry Ulanov echoes Pollack when he writes, "Alternately eloquent and tongue-tied with words, Mingus has the conviction that some day he can make his ideas perfectly clear on his own instrument or somebody else's. He knows, no matter how wispy these ideas may appear to him or to others, that some day it will be possible to give them musical definition—and in jazz." Ulanov, *A Handbook of Jazz* (Hutchinson of London, 1958), 39–40.

136. Bob Thiele, "Mingus Ho-Hum," *JAZZ*, n.d., 20–21, Mingus Clippings File, IJS.

137. Quoted in Max Gordon, *Live at the The Village Vanguard* (New York: Da Capo, 1982), 106.

138. Thiele, "Mingus Ho-Hum," 20. Mingus eventually signed an agreement bringing him an advance of $10,000 and a five-percent royalty. The second-year option raised the advance to $15,000. See Priestley, *Mingus*, 145.

139. Thiele, "Mingus Ho-Hum," 21.

140. Ibid., 20–21. Nat Hentoff, in the liner notes to Mingus's self-titled release on the independent label Candid, offered this description of working with Mingus: "A recording session with Mingus is somewhat similar to walking into a building tenanted by libertarians of all conceivable political and psychological bents, and pressing a floor number on the elevator without looking at it. You don't know where you are going to wind up, but the result is certainly going to be fiercely stimulating. My policy on a Mingus date is to give him complete freedom—not that he wouldn't take it anyway—because I have thorough

confidence in his bottomless drive to insist on the most honest and uninhibited emotions he can get from his musicians and from himself."

141. Dolphy, born in Los Angeles in 1928, moved to New York in 1959. A classically trained musician, he played alto saxophone, flute, and bass clarinet. Dolphy joined Mingus's band in December 1959 and continued working with him intermittently through 1964. During this period, he also led his own bands in recordings for the Prestige label, was frequently written up in the jazz press, and worked as a sideman. Remembered for his sweet nature and his generosity, he died in Berlin in June 1964 of complications from diabetes. See liner notes to *Eric Dolphy: The Complete Prestige Recordings*, Prestige 9PRCD-4418-2. See also, "In Tribute Eric Dolphy, 1928–1964," *Down Beat*, August 27, 1964, 10, and Nat Hentoff's column on page 40 of the same issue. Hentoff writes of how "acutely" important Dolphy became to Mingus because "Mingus could rely on him to understand what Mingus wanted while being able to fulfill that understanding in his own, strongly personal way." A classic example of their symbiotic relationship is "What Love" on the album *Charles Mingus Presents Charles Mingus*, Candid 9005.

142. See Nat Hentoff, "A Festival Triumph: *Mingus at Monterey*," *HiFi Stereo Review*, April 1965, 75. Also, "M and M at Monterey," *Newsweek*, October 5, 1964.

143. Charles Mingus, *Down Beat*, n.d., Mingus Clippings File, IJS.

144. Daniel Fischlin, Ajay Heble, and George Lipsitz, *The Fierce Urgency of Now: Improvisation, Rights, and the Ethics of Cocreation* (Durham, NH: Duke University Press, 2013); Priestley, *Mingus*, 66.

145. "Jazz Is to Hear, Not to Be Talked Against, Says Charlie Mingus," *Boston Globe*, May 15, 1960.

146. Mingus, *Playboy* Summit, 276–77; see also Eric Porter, *What Is This Thing Called Jazz*.

147. Rustin, "*Cante Hondo*."

148. Neil P. Hurley, "Toward a Sociology of Jazz," *Thought* 44 (1969): 219–46, 241.

149. Jeffrey Kastner, "'Negro Artists Exploited': Mingus Urges Investigation," *Toronto Daily Star*, October 31, 1964; Helen McNamara, "Mingus Out to Blast Color Bar in Music," *Toronto Telegraph*, November 2, 1964.

150. Mingus, quoted in Ira Gitler, "Mingus Speaks—And Bluntly," *Down Beat*, July 21, 1960, 30.

THREE "Invisible Lady"

Chapter epigraphs from Ira Gitler's liner notes to *Charles Mingus, The Complete Debut Recordings*, Fantasy 1990, 14; Charles Mingus letter to Jack Garret, November 21, 1952, CMC (Garret/Garrett used interchangeably in the letters); and "Miles Davis . . . a Candid Conversation with the Jazz World's Premier Iconoclast," *Playboy*, September 1962.

Epigraphs to section "'No Private Income Blues'" from Ross Russell, *Jazz Tempo* news-letter, May 1946, Mingus Clippings File, IJS; and Whitney Balliett, "Jazz Today," *Atlantic Monthly* 192.5 (November 1953): 76–81; https://www.theatlantic.com/past/docs/unbound /jazz/balliett.htm.

Epigraph to section *"Money Jungle"* from Charles Mingus, letter to Jack Garrett, n.d., CMC.

Epigraphs to section "'Celia'" from Mingus on his song "Celia," quoted in Nat Hentoff's liner notes to *East Coasting*, Bethlehem BS 6019; and Mingus interview with Sy Johnson, February 19–22, 1978, transcript of cassette 1–2, Jazz Oral History Project, Smithsonian Institute, 11.

1. "Mingus Starts Own Record Company," *Down Beat*, May 21, 1952.

2. Bill Coss, "Jazz Label: Debut," *Metronome*, December 1953.

3. Cheryl I. Harris, "Whiteness as Property," *Harvard Law Review* 106 (June 1993): 1713.

4. Mal Waldron, quoted by Ira Gitler, "Bass-ically Speaking," *Charles Mingus: The Complete Debut Recordings*, 13.

5. Herman Gray argues that there are three types of independent record labels. The "primary identity and commitment" of the ideological independent is "to maintaining jazz's cultural and aesthetic significance"; its functional reliance is upon interpersonal relationships. The structural independent is "distinguished by [its] search for large com-mercial markets," where "music is primarily a source of financial profits." The mixed independent is "concerned with achieving and maintaining commercial success and . . . operate[s] with ideological commitments to the importance of jazz, its tradition, and practitioners." Herman Gray, *Producing Jazz: The Experience of an Independent Record Company* (Philadelphia: Temple University Press, 1988), 10–13, and "Independent Cul-tural Production: The Case of a Jazz Recording Company," *Journal of Popular Music and Society* (Summer 1986): 1–16.

6. In other instances, music pitted family members against one another. Al Tinney told an interviewer that his mother was inspired by the Nicholas brothers to push her children into performing. See James Patrick, "Al Tinney, Monroe's Uptown House, and the Emergence of Modern Jazz in Harlem," *Annual Review of Jazz Studies* 2 (1983): 150–79; quotes on 153.

7. Gray, *Producing Jazz*, 100; Maxine Gordon quoted in Robin D. G. Kelley, "The Jazz Wives: Muse and Manager," *New York Times*, July 21, 2002.

8. Sherrie Tucker asks "What is the relationship between the gendering of certain jazz practices and the values placed on them by audiences, the music industry and histori-ans?" See Valerie Wilmer, *As Serious as Your Life: The Story of the New Jazz* (London: Allison and Busby, 1977); Angela Davis, "I Used to Be Your Sweet Mama: Ideology and Domesticity in Blues Culture," in *Blues Legacies and Black Feminism: Gertrude "Ma" Rainey, Bessie Smith, and Billie Holiday* (New York: Random House, 1997); and Sherrie

Tucker, "West Coast Women: A Jazz Genealogy," *Pacific Review of Ethnomusicology* 8.1 (Winter 1996/1997): 5–22.

9. Donald J. Mabry, "The Rise and Fall of Ace Records: A Case Study in the Independent Record Business," *Business History Review* 64 (Autumn 1990), 413, 415. See also Tom McCourt, "Bright Lights, Big City: A Brief History of Rhythm and Blues, 1945–1957," *Journal of Popular Music and Society*, and Brian Ward, *Just My Soul Responding: Rhythm and Blues, Black Consciousness, and Race Relations* (Berkeley: University of California Press, 1998).

10. H. J. Lengsfelder letters of December 20, 1954 and April 8, 1955, CMC. See also McCourt, "Bright Lights, Big City," and Mabry, "The Rise and Fall of Ace Records."

11. John Gennari, *Blowin' Hot and Cool*, 315. Unscrupulous recording practices weren't limited to Russell or to white owners. John Dolphin, a black businessman in Watts who owned the record store, Dolphin's of Hollywood, was a notorious figure. In addition to selling the music of other labels, he recorded musicians on his own label, Recorded In Hollywood (RIH), and set up deejays from local stations in the front window of his store (which was open twenty-four hours a day) to promote his records. He took advantage of his artists, leading to his fatal shooting by Percy Ivy in 1958.

12. Francis Newton (Eric Hobsbawm), *The Jazz Scene* [1959] (New York: Da Capo Press, 1975), 237. See also Dan Wakefield, *New York in the 50s* (New York: St. Martin's Griffin, 1992), 299, 300; Valerie Wilmer, *Mama Said There'd Be Days Like This: My Life in the Jazz World* (London: The Women's Press, 1989); Keir Keightley, "'Turn It Down!' She Shrieked: Gender, Domestic Space, and High Fidelity, 1948–59," *Popular Music* 15.2 (May 1996), 149–77.

13. Rick Kennedy and Randy McNutt, *Little Label—Big Sound* (Indianapolis: Indiana University Press, 1999), 108.

14. Newton, *The Jazz Scene*, 183.

15. Patrick Burke, "Oasis of Swing: The Onyx Club, Jazz, and White Masculinity in the Early 1930s," *American Music* 24.3 (Autumn 2006): 326, 335.

16. Gabler quoted in Ted Fox, *In the Groove: The People behind the Music* (New York: St. Martin's Press, 1986), 75–76.

17. "Milt Gabler Interview," by Dan Morgenstern (with Michael Cuscuna and Charlie Lourie) from the liner notes to *The Complete Commodore Jazz Recordings, Volumes I–III* (Mosaic Records), in Robert Gottlieb, ed., *Reading Jazz: A Gathering of Autobiography, Reportage, and Criticism from 1919 to Now* (New York: Pantheon Books), 217.

18. Alfred W. Lion, "Blue Note: Just Fans," *Metronome*, August 1956.

19. Russell's papers at the Harry Ransom Center, University of Texas at Austin, provide details of his struggles to make the label profitable.

20. Daniel Goldmark, "Slightly Left of Center: Atlantic Records and the Problems of Genre," in *Jazz/Not Jazz: The Music and Its Boundaries*, ed. David Ake, Charles Hiroshi Garrett, and Daniel Goldmark (Berkeley: University of California Press, 2012), 148–69. See

also Edward Komara, "The Dial Recordings of Charlie Parker," in *The BeBop Revolution in Words and Music*, ed. Dave Oliphant with an introduction by Richard Lawn (Austin: Harry Ranson Humanities Research Center, University of Texas, 1994), 78–103; J. Picardie and D. Wade, *Atlantic and the Godfathers of Rock and Roll*, revised edition (London: Fourth Estate, 1993); and Nesuhi Ertegun, "Atlantic Plans Future," *Metronome*, August 1956.

21. Bob Thiele as told to Bob Golden, *What a Wonderful World: A Lifetime of Recordings* (New York: Oxford University Press, 1995), 138–39.

22. "How to Have Healthier Music Business? Learn to Say No: Mitch Miller," *Down Beat*, November 3, 1950, 15.

23. Ozzie Cadena, "Savoy: Doing for Jazz," *Metronome*, August 1956.

24. James Hale, "How Blue Note Records Became the Biggest Brand in Jazz," http://music.cbc.ca/#/blogs/2012/11/How-Blue-Note-Records-became-the-biggest-brand-in-jazz, last accessed November 28, 2012.

25. Nat Hentoff, "Early Blue Note Jazz," *Wall Street Journal*, October 3, 1997.

26. Herbert Kimmel, "Jazz: West Grass Roots," *Metronome*, August 1956.

27. George Avakian, "George Avakian Discusses Jazz," *New York Post*, April 23, 1956.

28. Marili and Nesuhi Ertegun, letter to "Friend," January 15, 1952, and Nesuhi Ertegun, letter to George Hoeffer, January 31, 1952, Nesuhi Ertegun Collection, IJS.

29. "Jazz Record Companies—Two Independents," *Metronome*, September 1957, 27.

30. *The Blue Note Label: A Discography*, compiled by Michael Cuscuna and Michel Ruppli (New York: Greenwood Press, 1988); Dan Skea, "Rudy Van Gelder in Hackensack: Defining the Jazz Sound in the 1950s," *Current Musicology* 71–73 (Spring 2001–2002); 54, 56, 72; Goldmark, "Slightly Left of Center," 153.

31. Other African American labels in the postwar period are as important as Debut, not because of how many records they sold, but as examples of "among other things, cultural manifestations of racial self-sufficiency as well as cultural transmitters of social culture." David Sanjek, "One Size Does Not Fit All: The Precarious Position of the African American Entrepreneur in Post–World War II American Popular Music," *American Music* 15.4 (Winter 1997): 547, 554.

32. Quotes from Dizzy Gillespie with Al Fraser, *To Be, or Not . . . to Bop: Memoirs* (Garden City, NY: Doubleday, 1979), 370, 371; Brian Priestley, *Jazz on Record: A History* (London: Elm Tree Books, 1988), 90. Gillespie had left Billy Eckstine's band in 1944 to record for various independents; his partner in Dee Gee was Dave Usher. See also DeVeaux, *The Birth of Bebop*, 411–13.

33. Celia Mingus, quoted in Ira Gitler's liner notes to *Charles Mingus, The Complete Debut Recordings*, Fantasy 1990. She and Mingus also founded a publishing company, Chazz-Mar Inc.

34. Max Roach quoted in Gitler liner notes, *Complete Debut Recordings*.

35. See Gitler liner notes, *Complete Debut Recordings*. Lovette was a black attorney

based in New York. One of his many musician clients was Miles Davis, who described him as "cold," able to put fear into otherwise powerful nightclub owners. See Miles Davis with Quincy Troupe, *Miles: The Autobiography* (New York: A Touchstone Book, 1989), especially p. 202.

36. Dan Morgenstern, liner notes, *The Debut Story*, Fantasy Records 1997, 14–16. Another account suggests that three fans, Bill Brandt Jr., Larry Suttlehan, and Joe Mauro, approached Mingus with the idea of starting the label, then had to divest from the company because they were going into the armed services. "Debut," *Metronome*, August 1954. See also "Certificate of Partners," June 1, 1953, CMC, and "Statements of Investments by Max Roach and Charles Mingus," June 8, 1953, CMC, which indicate that William J. Brandt's shares were bought out by Roach and Mingus for $250 each.

37. Celia Mingus, letter to Bill (William J. Brandt), April 20, 1953, CMC.

38. "With my full-time job at Caltex Oil and the way DEBUT has been building up, plus the work I was doing on this Composer's Workshop, I have really had my hands full." Celia Mingus to Dick Wattam, February 25, 1954, CMC.

39. Roach quoted in Taylor, *Notes and Tones*, 113.

40. Quoted by Dan Morgenstern in liner notes to *The Debut Story*, 16.

41. Celia alludes here to the first Composer's Workshop concert, a cooperative venture between Mingus and the other "radical experimenters," Teo Marcero, John LaPorta, Don Butterfield, Teddy Charles, and Eddie Shaughnessy, held in New York in January 1954. The concert organizers wanted a venue that would both allow the musicians to see a profit and introduce their music to a new audience. Celia Mingus, letter to Boyd Raeburn, March 1, 1954, CMC.

Echoing other critics, Bill Coss, writing for *Metronome* and working with the musicians as secretary of the Workshop, concluded, "It is up to the jazz musician, with the help of the loyal jazz fan, to do something for himself and his art." Jazz independents believed that the music would not grow if not for their work in recording and promoting it. The Workshop members planned to keep the admission price low so as not to lose sight of one of their primary goals—making jazz accessible to a wide audience. They were confident that it was not their music, but the prices that club owners charged which audiences rejected. The financial and critical success of the concert proved Coss was right. Reviewers praised Mingus's compositions as "swinging," "modern," and "individual." Subsequent concerts were planned with the hope that a major label would record them. The organizers followed the lead of other efforts to make new venues accessible to audiences for the music. Joe Goldberg, *Jazz Masters of the '50s* [1965] (New York: Da Capo, 1983), 136. Bill Coss, "The November Revolution," *Metronome*, March 1954; Barry Ulanov, "Composer's Workshop Moves b.u.," *Metronome*, April 1954; "Jazz Concerts," *Metronome*, May 1954; George T. Simon, "Jazz Composers' Second Workshop Concert Extremely Impressive," *Metronome*, July 1954.

42. Dorothy Sachs, letter to Celia Mingus, May 3, 1956, CMC; Celia Mingus, letter to Dorothy Sachs, June 2, 1956, CMC. Charlie Mack, of Ad Lib Records, explained how much his label depended upon his wife's work. After deciding that he wanted to run a label, he talked it over with his wife and they "decided to plunge everything we had and could borrow into the venture. I would do the leg work and she would take care of the business end and of course that messy bookkeeping." "Ad Lib Improvises," *Metronome*, August 1956.

43. Harold Lovette, letter to Joe Oxman, Pan American Record Supply, April 19, 1954, CMC.

44. Ted Vincent argues that the short-lived but industrious black-owned label, Black Swan (1921–1923 and 180 records) could not overcome a fundamental class conflict between its musicians and the management. Black Swan's board of directors (including W. E. B. DuBois, Harlem realtor John E. Nail, and Dr. M. V. Boutte of Meharry Medical School, among others) and its president, Harry H. Pace, wanted the company to be representative of the better qualities of the race. During a time when jazz was widely associated with promiscuity and vice, they wanted the label to be known for its recordings of classical music by serious black artists. Though its success was predicated upon the sales of its blues artists, Black Swan privileged its classical artists in advertisements. Racial uplift and capitalism were not easily reconciled. Vincent, "The Social Context of Black Swan Records," *Living Blues*, May/June 1989, 34–40.
See also Susan M. Leonard, "An Introduction to Black Participation in the Early Recording Era, 1890–1920," *Annual Review of Jazz Studies* 4 (1988): 31–44, Nelson George, *The Death of Rhythm and Blues* (New York: Pantheon Books, 1988), 201.

45. Gioia, *West Coast Jazz*, 338, 339.

46. Tim Anderson, "'Buried under the Fecundity of His Own Creations': Reconsidering the Recording Bans of the American Federation of Musicians, 1942–1944 and 1948," *American Music* 22.2 (Summer 2004): 257.

47. William Barlow, *Voice Over: The Making of Black Radio* (Philadelphia: Temple University Press, 1999), 26.

48. Anderson, "'Buried under the Fecundity of His Own Creations,'" 249.

49. Richard A. Peterson, "Why 1955? Explaining the Advent of Rock Music," *Popular Music* 9.1 (1990): 97–115; "DJs One Reason Men Are Jobless," *Down Beat*, June 2, 1950. See Johnny Hutchinson, letter to Oscar (Pettiford), January 31, 1951, DEC. Hutchinson wrote, "I got a wonderful break about two weeks ago, when WAYS here in Charlotte (NC) hired me to do an hour-and-a-quarter afternoon disc show. Dig those 5,000 watts, man! Over a million and a half potential listeners in this area!"

50. Paul Cass, *Metronome*, October 1955, 10, 14.

51. Deejay Carl Ide explained that in the wake of negative reaction to bebop, he avoided using the term "bop" altogether when introducing new music. "Jumping Jockey," *Metronome*, May 1951, 21. The push by postwar deejays to educate their publics on what to

listen for in jazz, how to create opportunities for musicians to perform, and how to pursue jazz as a profession, reflects a parallel push to provide consumers with information about the developing television industry. See Murray Foreman, *One Night on Television is Worth Weeks at the Paramount: Popular Music on Early Television* (Durham, NC: Duke University Press, 2012).

52. *Metronome*, June 1956, 18, 28, and July 1956, 18–19.

53. *Metronome*, January 1951, 31.

54. *Metronome*, April 1951, 33.

55. *Metronome*, June 1956, 18, 28, and July 1956, 18–19.

56. Felix Grant of Washington, D.C.'s WMAL, asked, "Why do most jazz shows flop? Mainly because the disc jockeys kill them off. In a lot of cases, the shows are run by young guys with a built-in line of *hip* chatter. They make inane remarks which have little or nothing to do with the music and eventually get to the point where they're playing the show only for themselves and for *hip* listeners." *Metronome*, February 1958, 40–41.

57. *Metronome*, August 1957, 33.

58. *Jazz Review*, February 1959, 50.

59. Hal Holly, "Music Men Unhappy with Radio's Platter Spinners," *Down Beat*, September 8, 1950, 9; Milton Weiss, Milton Phono Records Co., letter to Mrs. Mingus, December 9, 1957, CMC. Congressional investigations into payola began in 1959 and resulted in a finding that indicted the whole music industry. Record labels, programmers, and disc jockeys were found guilty of numerous unethical practices, including bribery and tax evasion. The investigations led to a 1960 revision of the Communications Act of 1934, restricting payola by enhancing disclosure requirements. (Before the investigations, reporting had been very loosely defined.) Even with the new requirements, however, payola remained a fact of life for small labels trying to get their music played on the radio. One perhaps unanticipated result of the investigation was that deejays began losing control over programming, with station owners increasingly relying on the emerging Top 40 format to establish a uniform sound (according to the preferred genre) throughout the day. See Jerry Segrave, *Payola in the Music Industry* (Jefferson, NC: McFarland and Co., 1994); William Barlow, *Voice Over*, 187; Lauren J. Katunich, "Time to Quit Paying the Payola Piper: Why Music Industry Abuse Demands a Complete System Overhaul," *Loyola of Los Angeles Entertainment Law Review* 22 (2002): 643.

60. See Russell Sanjek and David Sanjek, *American Popular Music Business in the 20th Century* (New York: Oxford University Press, 1991); Andre Millard, *America on Record: A History of Recorded Sound* (New York: Cambridge University Press, 1995); and Robert D. Leiter, *The Musicians and Petrillo* (New York: Bookman Associates, 1953).

61. Robert Gannon, "Vibrations," *Metronome*, August 1957, 10.

62. Mimi Clar, "KNOB: Twenty-four Hours of Jazz a Day," *Jazz Review*, August 1959, 37. KNOB began broadcasting August 18, 1957, and received 1,100 pieces of mail in the

first week. "The music is wonderful. In fact, it's so great to hear jazz all day long, that my husband and I are both wondering if it can last," wrote one housewife. Musicians and deejays echoed her excitement about the station. Four major music stores attributed an increase in FM radio sales to the station. *Metronome*, March 1958, 30–31.

63. Mingus to Summarisse in June 1953; Bob Summarisse, to Charles Mingus Jr., June 23, 1953, CMC.

64. Bob Summarisse, letter to Debut Records, Attn: Mr. Charlie Mingus, July 11, 1953, CMC.

65. Debut, letter to Leon M. Banks Sr., "Music with Maggie" Radio Station KLUF, Galveston, Texas, December 14, 1953, CMC.

66. Bob Summarisse, letter to Charles Mingus Jr., June 23, 1952, CMC. Jack Garrett, letter to Charlie (Mingus), (c. 1952), CMC.

67. Garret, letter to Mingus, n.d.; Mingus, letter to Garret, n.d.; Mingus to Garret, October 30, 1953, CMC. Charles Mingus, letter to Don Williamson, n.d., CMC; E. E. Harvey, Commercial Music Company, letter to William J. Brandt, January 9, 1954; Debut Records, letter to Ed Harvey, February 25, 1954, CMC. Though Debut was interested in the popular field, they soon became discouraged from it. To Marcel Fleiss, Mingus explained that he regretted a recent venture into the field. Expenses for the date (for an album not named) rose considerably and their lack of experience made it difficult to push the recording. Mingus, letter to Marcel Fleiss, November 24, 1954, CMC.

68. E. E. Harvey, Commercial Music Company, letter to William J. Brandt, September 16, 1953, CMC.

69. Celia Mingus, letter to Flo Hansen, n.d., CMC. Charles Mingus and John LaPorta, *Jazzical Moods*, Fantasy OJCCD-1857–2; see also Krin Gabbard on Mingus's brief foray into "Third Stream" jazz, *Better Git It in Your Soul: An Interpretive Biography of Charles Mingus* (Berkeley: University of California Press, 2016).

70. Celia Mingus, letter to Flo Hansen, n.d., CMC.

71. Mingus, "What Is a Jazz Composer?," liner notes to *Let My Children Hear Music*, Columbia CK 48910.

72. Charles Mingus, letter to Charles Delauney, June 2, 1952, CMC. Mingus was attracted to singers who were able to hold their own against his challenging compositions, such as "Miss Bliss" and "Eclipse." "Eclipse" was written for Billie Holiday but never recorded by her.

73. Charles Mingus in Andrew Homzy, ed., *Mingus: More Than a Fake Book* (New York: Jazz Workshop, 1991), 111. Many appreciated Mingus's skill at writing lyrics; Hal Zogg described them as "perfection." Hal Zogg, letter to Charles Mingus, September 1, 1952, CMC.

74. Both versions appear in *The Debut Story*, Fantasy 1997, on discs 1 and 4, respectively.

75. Mingus also employed the strategy of explaining a recording when sending review copies to critics; see, for example, his May 9, 1953, letter to critic Barry Ulanov.

76. Celia Mingus, letter to Flo Hansen, n.d., CMC. Mingus also sent Summarisse these tracks. Bob Summarisse, letter to Charles Mingus Jr., July 11, 1953, CMC.

77. Hansen, letter to Celia Mingus, July 17, 1952, CMC.

78. Ibid.

79. Charles Mingus, letter to Hal Zogg, September 8, 1952, CMC.

80. Charles Mingus, letter to Don Williamson, n.d., CMC. Jackie McLean prescribed a similar tactic to those of his students embarking on broadcasting careers. See Kenneth Levis's documentary, *Jackie McLean on Mars* (1979).

81. Nat Hentoff, note to Charles Mingus, July 13, 1952, CMC.

82. Charles Delauney, letter to Charles Mingus, June 4, 1952, CMC.

83. Marcel Fleiss, letter to Charles Mingus, May 14, 1952, CMC.

84. Marcel Fleiss, letter to Charles Mingus, September 16, 1952, CMC.

85. Charles Mingus, letter to Gary A. Soucie, July 2, 1957, CMC.

86. Celia Mingus, letter to Henry Z. Cholinkski, Poland, February 7, 1958. See also letters from James Grof, Carbondale, Illinois, 1957, Ulysses B. Broadnax Jr., Hampton, Virginia, February 2, 1958, and Nelson Coluzzi, New York City, January 13, 1958; along with Celia's reply to Coluzzi on January 29, 1958.

87. See letters from Lou Larmay, Attleboro, Massachusetts, 1956, and Helen Rubens, Helena, Montana, January 19, 1957; with replies from Celia Mingus to Larmay on August 27 and September 14, 1956, and to Rubens on February 11, 1957.

88. See Beverly Slocum, Pennsylvania, letter, November 9, 1957, Celia Mingus, letter to Beverly Slocum, November 13, 1957 and Beatrice Nelson, El Dorado, AK, letter, December 12, 1957, Celia Mingus, letter to Beatrice Nelson, December 26, 1957, CMC.

89. Barry Ulanov, "Morality and Maturity in Jazz," *Metronome*, August 1954, 20; Barry Ulanov, *A Handbook of Jazz* (Hutchinson of London, 1958), 114.

90. Jerry M. Walker, letter, March 26, 1957, CMC.

91. John W. Brown to Debut Records, November 14, 1957, CMC.

92. Ed Michel, liner notes, *Debut Story*, Fantasy 1997, 5.

93. Liner notes to *Debut Story*, 12.

94. Celia Mingus, quoted in Ira Gitler's liner notes to *Charles Mingus: The Complete Debut Recordings*, Fantasy 1990, 13.

95. Ibid., 14.

96. Nat Hentoff, liner notes, *East Coasting*, Bethlehem BS 6019.

97. Elaine Tyler May, *Homeward Bound* (New York: Basic Books, 1988), 77.

98. In 1956, an editor at *Mademoiselle* contacted Celia, wanting to know if the increased listener base in the recording industry had produced more job opportunities for women. Celia responded that because the majority of jazz listeners were male, most of the jobs were held by them. Her entrée into the business was the result of her teenage interest in jazz and subsequent marriage to a musician. Dorothy Sachs, *Mademoiselle*, letter to Celia

Mingus, May 3, 1956, CMC; Celia Mingus, letter to Dorothy Sachs, June 2, 1956, CMC. Mary Cantwell recalled "a certain amateurishness, a beguiling raffishness to *Mademoiselle*" when she worked there in the 1950s. "*Mademoiselle* was the kind of place where you could make things up as you went along, not because anybody was ever thinking seriously about innovation or would even dream of using the word but because most of the staff was imbued with the spirit of a Mickey Rooney/Judy Garland musical." Mary Cantwell, *Manhattan, When I Was Young* (New York: Penguin, 1995), 170, 171.

99. Celia Mingus, letter to Bill (William J. Brandt), n.d., CMC. One woman defined being a secretary as having "the ability to write letters as the 'boss' thought he dictated." Angel Kwolek-Folland, *Engendering Business: Men and Women in the Corporate Office, 1870–1930* (Baltimore: Johns Hopkins University Press, 1994), 59.

100. Rob Gannon thanked the Minguses profusely for news, letter to "Mr. And Mrs. Mingus," February 12, 1953, and letter to Charles and Celia Mingus, March 2, 1953, CMC; Charles Mingus Jr., letter to Don Williamson, February 6, 1953, CMC.

101. Celia Mingus, letter to Rob Gannon, March 11, 1953, CMC.

102. Celia Mingus, letter to Seven Arts Book Society, August 12, 1957, CMC.

103. Ralph Gleason, letter to Celia and Charles, September 14, 1955, CMC. Not everyone was quick to take advantage of this network. Bob Purlongo, a writer at the *Voice*, missed his chance when Coss was looking to add more writers to *Metronome*'s staff. Celia then told Purlongo that she had heard a job at *Down Beat* might be opening up. Celia Mingus, letter to Bob Purlongo, June 4, 1956.

104. Ralph Gleason, letter to Celia Mingus, August 14, 1956, CMC; Celia Mingus, letter to Don Williamson, February 6, 1953, CMC. Fans also could be used to create openings. Seeking New England distribution, Mingus wrote Connecticut distributor Joe Rukin when Rukin's customers, after seeing Mingus perform, reported that Debut records were unavailable in the area. Mingus, letter to Joe Rukin, Record Shop, Waterbury, Connecticut, July 21, 1954. See also Henry F. Whiston, producer, Canadian Broadcasting Corporation, letter to Leonard Feather, October 30, 1950, Duke Ellington Collection, Smithsonian Institute.

105. Celia Mingus, letter to Tom Dexter, Dexter Distributing Co., August 6, 1955; Tom Dexter, letter to Celia Mingus, August 14, 1995; Celia Mingus, letter to Tom Dexter, August 19, 1955; Dick Maw, D & D Distributing Company, letter to Harold Lovette, January 14, 1955, CMC.

106. Hal Zogg, letter to Charles Mingus, September 1, 1952, CMC.

107. Charles Mingus, letter to Charles Heller, Columbia Music Company, February 4, 1953, CMC.

108. E. E. Harvey, Commercial Music Company, Inc., letter to William J. Brandt, September 16, 1953; Larry Kane, Lone Star Record Co., letter to M. Ferris, May 26, 1955; E. V. Mironko, Emco Distributors, letter to Debut Records, June 22, 1955; Paul O. Neves, Contemporary Distributing, letter to Charles Mingus, October 17, 1955; Celia Mingus,

letter to Bill (William Brandt), January 20, 1953; Leon M. Banks Sr., "Music with Maggie" Radio Station KLUF, Galveston, Texas, December 14 and 29, 1953; Bob Thoralson, Modern Music House, letter, December 7, 1953, CMC.

109. Celia Mingus, letter to Audrey Schwarz, June 18, 1952, CMC.

110. William J. Brandt, letter to Jack Levenson, College Music Distributing Co., September 19, 1952, CMC.

111. Letter to Celia Mingus, January 31, 1956, CMC.

112. William J. Brandt, letter to Jack Levenson, College Music Distributing Co., October 31, 1952, CMC.

113. William J. Brandt, letter to Jack Levenson, College Music Distributing Co., December 5, 1952, CMC. In January, Debut at last received a check from College Music, in the amount of $13.86. Levenson had deducted $6.30 for the 15 records he had used as promotion. "But 15 records out of 48 for promotion sounds pretty phoney so since Mingus was going to Boston he took the check with him and is going to find out the story." Celia Mingus, letter to Bill (William J. Brandt), January 20, 1953, CMC. Mingus was able to get an additional $3.62 from the company. Celia Mingus, letter to Bill (William J. Brandt), n.d., CMC. In December 1953, Debut at last received the remaining amount owed. The label then settled on an additional number of albums to be distributed by College Music. Celia Mingus, letter to Bill (William J. Brandt), December 12, 1953, CMC.

114. Celia Mingus, letter to Charles W. Mahaffay, Contemporary Distributing Co., April 3, 1957, CMC.

115. Thiele, *What a Wonderful World*, 30–31, 38; Thiele quoted in Ted Fox, *In the Groove* (New York: St. Martin's Press, 1986), 213. Duke Ellington's label, Mercer Records, was headed by his son Mercer Ellington and critic Leonard Feather, during the 1950s. Mercer was distributed by Prestige for a while. See Business Records, Duke Ellington Collection, Smithsonian Institution (hereafter cited as DEC).

116. Celia Mingus, letter to Commercial Music Company, June 12, 1957, CMC.

117. Celia Mingus, letter to Cecil Steen, June 11, 1957, CMC. Levister, who had just recorded the album *Manhattan Melodrama*, decided to use a "personal touch" in promoting his record by "hitch-hiking his way" from coast to coast. See Celia Mingus to Bill Simon, June 21, 1957, CMC. Robert Sylvester's review of the album found it to be "the most unusual jazz, if it is jazz. . . . Much of it, including a long 'challenge' between cello and tympani, probably isn't jazz." *Daily News*, March 16, 1957.

118. M. Ferris, letter to Larry Kane, Lone Star Records, June 27, 1955, CMC.

119. Robert M. Chatton, letter to Charles Mingus, March 28, 1955, CMC.

120. Edward T. Hughes, Music Please & Record Co., letter to Debut Records, April 28, 1955; Harold E. Lovette, letter to Edward T. Hughes, May 3, 1955, CMC.

121. Tom Dexter, Dexter Distributing Co., letter to Celia Mingus, August 14, 1955; Celia Mingus, letter to Tom Spinosa, Dexter Distributing Co., September 3, 1955; Tom Spinosa,

letter to Celia Mingus, August 27, 1955, CMC. The price war had begun after World War II, and the new long-playing record had a tremendous ripple effect on the industry. See "Price-Slicing War Looms in LP Biz," *Down Beat*, June 30, 1950; "Record Cuts," *Metronome*, February 1955, 10; and Michael Hobson interview with George Avakian and Howard "Scotty" Scott, *Audiophile*, June 1998, 14.

122. Ralph Williams (a Victor salesman), letter to Celia Mingus, June 11, 1954, CMC; D. J. Finn, manager, Custom Record Sales, RCA Victor Division, letter to "All Custom Record Customers," August 9, 1954, CMC.

123. Charles Mingus, letter to Hal Zogg, n.d., CMC.

124. Celia Mingus, letter to Bill (William J. Brandt), March 17, 1953, CMC.

125. Helen Keane, as quoted in Linda Dahl's *Stormy Weather: The Music and Lives of a Century of Jazzwomen* (New York: Limelight Editions, 1984), 246, 247.

126. Wilmer, *As Serious As Your Life*, 192

127. At least that's what David Rosenthal suggests when he argues that the short life and career of trumpeter Lee Morgan sounded the death knell of hard bop. Rosenthal recounts Morgan's murder in a bar by an older woman, Helen More, with whom he had been involved. Her jealousy over Morgan's new girl—"a younger girl, very pretty; she looked like Angela Davis," according to a friend—led her to shoot him when he flaunted the new woman around town. Rosenthal argues that Morgan's death was "spectacular in jazz not so much because he was young as because it involved a woman instead of drugs." Rosenthal's account of More ends with the sound of her screaming, "What have I done?" Because Rosenthal then launches into the story of hard bop, we are left to wonder whether More was shocked by the fact she had shot a man, or that she had killed jazz. To Rosenthal, the answer seems clear. David Rosenthal, *Hard Bop: Jazz and Black Music, 1955–1965* (Oxford University Press, 1992), 3.

128. "The High Mark of the Lionel Hamptons . . . ," *Color* 7.1 (February 1951): 31. See also, for example, Wallace Terry, "His Love, Pain . . . and All That Jazz," *Parade Magazine*, June 16, 1991, 6, 7, 9, 16; and Lewis K. McMillan Jr., "Good Vibes from Hamp," *Down Beat*, April 27, 1972 (12–13, 26).

129. Lionel Hampton as told to Bernard Seeman, "Me and Benny Goodman," *Saturday Evening Post*, n.d. Lionel Hampton Clippings File, IJS. Bandleader Arnold Shaw recalled that it was difficult getting black wives down to 52nd Street to socialize. See his *52nd Street* (New York: Da Capo, 1977), 246–48.

130. Terry, "His Love, Pain . . . and All That Jazz," 8.

131. *The Autobiography of Malcolm X*, as told to Alex Haley (New York: Grove Press, 1964), 116. See also, among others, Hal Mitchell in Gary Carner, "Conversation with Hal Mitchell: Jazz Patriarch of Newark," *Black Perspective in Music* 17 (1989): 109–34.

132. See Harold McGhee quoted in DeVeaux, *The Birth of Bebop*, 197–98; Joe Wilder quoted in Chip Deffaa, *In the Mainstream: Eighteen Portraits in Jazz* (Metuchen, NJ:

Scarecrow Press and Institute of Jazz Studies, Rutgers University), 254; Cecil McNeely quoted in Bryant et al., *Central Avenue Sounds*, 188.

133. Marshall Royal also recalls how the low wages the Hamptons paid their band members translated into a greater nest egg for themselves. In spite of the other bandmembers being on a "starvation circuit . . . money was being made because Gladys . . . was buying a thousand-dollar bond every week." Quoted in Bryant et al., *Central Avenue Sounds*, 45.

134. Gillespie, *To Be, or Not . . . to Bop*, 122.

135. Leonard Feather, *Inside Jazz* [J. J. Robbins and Sons, 1949] (New York: Da Capo, 1977), 22.

136. Gillespie quoted in Taylor, *Notes and Tones*, 131.

137. Wilmer, *As Serious As Your Life*, 195.

138. Gillespie, *To Be, or Not . . . to Bop*, 120–27, 401.

139. Dizzy Gillespie, "My Wife Lets Me Play," February 1952, 29, Gillespie Clippings File, IJS.

140. See Rustin, "'Mary Lou Williams Plays Like a Man!'"; *Mary Lou Williams: The Lady who Swings the Band*, dir. Carol Bash, 2015; Farah Jasmine Griffin, *Harlem Nocturne: Women Artists & Progressive Politics during World War II* (New York: Basic Civitas, 2013); Ruth Feldstein, *How It Feels to Be Free: Black Women Entertainers and the Civil Rights Movement* (Oxford University Press, 2013); Benjamin Piekut, "New Thing? Gender and Sexuality in the Jazz Composers Guild," *American Quarterly* 62.1 (March 2010): 25–48; Eric Porter, *What Is This Thing Called Jazz? African American Musicians as Artists, Critics, and Activists* (Berkeley: University of California Press, 2002); Eric Porter, "Jeanne Lee's Voice," *Critical Studies in Improvisation* 2.1 (2006), http://www.criticalimprov.com/article /view/53/184, last accessed June 6, 2016.

141. Phil Carter, "Hazel Scott Demonstrates Versatile Talents on Coast," *Atlanta Daily World*, September 5, 1945, 4.

142. "Congressman Powell, Hazel Scott, Marry," *Chicago Defender*, October 4, 1945, 1.

143. Wil Haygood, *King of the Cats: The Life and Times of Adam Clayton Powell, Jr.* (New York: Houghton Mifflin, 1993), 127–31.

144. She remembers feeling at times, however, that she wished they were either both black or both white. Celia quoted in Gitler's liner notes to *Complete Debut Recordings*, 16.

145. Quoted in Priestley, *Mingus*, 95. She concluded, "Marriage with Mingus didn't work out for many reasons, but I think he saw the potential in me. He didn't realize it was going to take a long time. He was by far the most spiritual man I was ever with, and all the values I have now are values I could have shared at that time with him, but I was in my learning process. Also, he was very difficult. You know how moody he was. But my ability to laugh and be light—he liked that. That offset his—I used to tickle him (not literally) because he had a hard time laughing. . . . You never really heard Mingus laugh, the belly laugh." Quoted in Gitler's liner notes to *Complete Debut Recordings*, 16.

146. Quoted in Priestley, *Mingus*, 133.

147. Max and Sol Weiss founded Fantasy in San Francisco in 1949. Zaentz started as a salesman in 1955; in 1967 he purchased the label. Celia Zaentz to Charles Mingus, May 7, 1971, CMC.

148. See Dianne Dorr-Dorynek to Buddy Collette, August 5, 1958, and Buddy Collette to Diane and Charles, August 20, 1958, CMC.

149. Sue Graham Mingus explores this in her memoir, *Tonight at Noon* (New York: DaCapo Press, 2003).

150. Arnold Shaw, *52nd St. The Street of Jazz* (New York: Da Capo Press, 1971); Patrick Burke, *Come In and Hear the Truth: Jazz and Race on 52nd Street* (Chicago: University of Chicago, 2008); DeVeaux, *The Birth of BeBop*, 285.

151. See Amiri Baraka, "Jazz and the White Critic," in *The Jazz Cadence of American Culture*, ed. Robert G. O'Meally (New York: Columbia University Press, 1998), 137–42; DeVeaux, "Constructing the Jazz Tradition," in O'Meally, ed., *The Jazz Cadence of American Culture*, 483–512; John Gennari, "Jazz Criticism: Its Development and Ideologies," *Black American Literature Forum* 25 (Fall 1991): 449–523; and Bernie Gendron, "'Moldy Figs' and Modernists: Jazz at War (1942–1946)," in *Jazz among the Discourses*, ed. Krin Gabbard (Durham, NC: Duke University Press, 1995).

152. Mingus had relationships with several of the magazine's critics over the period, including Bill Coss and Nat Hentoff, both of whom would write liner notes for Debut releases as well as profile Mingus numerous times. Some readers were even irritated by his coverage, linking it to a general failure on the part of the magazine to present a broad picture of the jazz scene. One wrote in complaining that a "guy you overwork is Charlie Mingus. You have a very narrow-minded staff down there at metronome." "over-hall-ing," *Metronome*, August 1954.

FOUR "Eclipse"

Chapter epigraphs from Michael Brooks's liner notes to *The Quintessential Billie Holiday*, vol. 8 (1939–40), Columbia CK 47030, 1991; and LeRoi Jones, *Blues People* (New York: Morrow Quill Paperbacks, 1963), 218.

Epigraphs to section "'Devil Woman'" from Zora Neale Hurston, "Characteristics of Negro Expression," in *African America Literary Theory: A Reader*, ed. Winston Napier (New York: New York University Press, 2000), 41; Billie Holiday interview with Dave Dexter, *Down Beat*, November 1939, quoted in Barney Josephson, *Café Society: The Wrong Place for the Right People* (Urbana: University of Illinois Press, 2009), 52; and Hazel Scott in Taylor, *Notes and Tones*, 262–63. The section title is from a song on Mingus's album *Oh Yeah*, Atlantic SD 1377.

Epigraphs to section "'Showbiz, God, and the Race'" from Betty Carter, in Taylor, *Notes and Tones*, 280; and Hazel Scott, in Taylor, *Notes and Tones*, 259.

Epigraph to section "The Hazel Scott Incident" from "Dewey Criticizes D.A.R. in Scott Case," *New York Times*, October 16, 1945, 25.

1. "Hazel Scott for the March of Dimes," https://www.youtube.com/watch?v=Nt BMXE9mJV4, last accessed September 8, 2015.

2. Josephson, *Café Society*, 126.

3. Monica Hairston, "The Wrong Place for the Right People? Café Society, Gender and Jazz, 1938–1947," PhD dissertation, New York University, 2009, 200.

4. Hairston defines "strategic cosmopolitanism" as reflecting how black women's "hybrid art combined the vocabulary of the vaudeville, nightclub and Broadway stages, concert, folk, and vernacular forms. In doing so, they articulated, mediated, and negotiated important social processes, including migration, immigration, and urbanization. Perhaps most importantly, by sonically and visually mapping out geographical and historical routes and centers of black movement, their performances laid the groundwork and registered the shift from representations of primitivism to diasporal—particularly as regards the black female body." Hairston, "The Wrong Place for the Right People?," 236–37.

5. Hazel Scott quoted in Taylor, *Notes and Tones*, 264.

6. Ibid., 263.

7. Carby, *Race Men*, 4.

8. Hazel Carby finds that "artistic creativity" and "sexual longing" are inextricably intertwined in memoirs of black male artists like Miles Davis and Samuel Delany. *Race Men*, 137.

9. See George E. Lewis, "Improvised Music after 1950: Afrological and Eurological Perspectives," in *The Other Side of Nowhere: Jazz, Improvisation, and Communities in Dialogue*, ed. Daniel Fischlin and Ajay Heble (Middletown, CT: Wesleyan University Press, 2004), 131–72; Julie Dawn Smith, "Playing Like a Girl: The Queer Laughter of the Feminist Improvising Group," in Fischlin and Heble, *The Other Side of Nowhere*, 224–43; and Sherrie Tucker, "Bordering on Community: Improvising Women Improvising Women-in-Jazz," in Fischlin and Heble, *The Other Side of Nowhere*, 244–67.

10. See Gillian Siddall, "'I wanted to live in that music': Blues, Bessie Smith and Improvised Identities in Ann-Marie MacDonald's *Fall on Your Knees*," *Critical Studies in Improvisation/Etudes critiques en improvisation* 1.2 (2005), http://www.criticalimprov .com/article/viewArticle/16/45, last accessed September 9, 2012.

11. Arna Bontemps, "A Pianist with a Mind of Her Own—Hazel Scott," *Senior Scholastic*, March 5, 1945.

12. "Current Biography: Hazel Scott," August 1943, Hazel Scott Clippings File, Schomburg Center for Research in Black Culture (SCRBC). Scott's father, R. Thomas Scott, was

the king's architect on Trinidad; when the family moved to the United States, he took a teaching job in the South. He died when Scott was fourteen. Robert Sullivan, "She Sure Plays Piano," November 8, 1942, Hazel Scott Clippings File, SCRBC.

13. Bontemps, "A Pianist with a Mind of Her Own." See also "New Fem Batoneer, Only 18, Sings Pop Tunes Seven Ways!," 1938; "Stars with Coleman Hawkins," December 1, 1939; and Robert Sullivan, "She Sure Plays Piano," November 8, 1942 (all Hazel Scott Clippings File, IJS); and Schomburg; "Fashion Queen of Harlem," n.d., Hazel Scott Clippings File, SCRBC.

14. See Lewis Erenberg, *Swingin' the Dream: Big Band Jazz and the Rebirth of American Culture* (Chicago: University of Chicago Press, 1998), and Sherrie Tucker, *Swing Shift: All Girl Bands of the 1940s* (Durham, NC: Duke University Press, 2000), which both explore these themes in greater detail.

15. Ted Gioia, *The History of Jazz* (New York: Oxford University Press, 1997), 101; Barry Ulanov, *A History of Jazz in America* [1950] (New York: Viking, 1952), 63–64, 122–23, 213–14; Ira Gitler, *Jazz Masters of the 40s* [1966] (New York: Da Capo, 1983); Hairston, "The Wrong Place for the Right People?"

16. Leonard Feather, "Notes on Hazel Scott," liner notes, *Hazel Scott: Vol. 2*, Decca No. A-321.

17. Nora Holt, "Or Hazel Scott Doing Chores at Carnegie Hall," *New York Amsterdam News*, December 8, 1945.

18. Feather, "Notes on Hazel Scott"; "Hot Classicist," *Time*, October 5, 1942, 88, 90.

19. See, for example, Gypsie Cooper, "Can Women Swing?," *The Metronome*, September 1936, 30; "Why Women Musicians Are Inferior," *Down Beat*, February 1938, 4; Ted Toll, "The Gal Yippers Have No Place in Our Jazz Bands," *Down Beat*, October 15, 1939, 16; and Sherrie Tucker, *Swing Shift: All-Girl Bands of the 1940s* (Duke University Press, 2000).

20. Elizabeth Hawes, "Elizabeth Hawes Applauds This Torch Singer's Clothes," *PM*, November 12, 1940; Adam Clayton Powell Jr., *Adam by Adam* [1971] (New York: Dafina Books, 2002), 225.

21. Seymour Peck, *Time*, 1954, Tuskegee Clippings File.

22. Ruth Feldstein, *How It Feels to Be Free: Black Women Entertainers and the Civil Rights Movement* (New York: Oxford University Press, 2013), 12. See also Ruth Feldstein, *Motherhood in Black and White: Race and Sex in American Liberalism, 1930–1965* (Ithaca: Cornell University Press, 2000).

23. See also Farah Jasmine Griffin, *Harlem Nocturne: Women Artists & Progressive Politics during World War II* (New York: Basic Civitas, 2013), 1–18.

24. See reviews of the film and Scott and Horne's performance in *Time*, November 29, 1943, 92; *New York Times*, November 11, 1943, 29; and *Commonweal*, November 5, 1943, 72–74.

25. Horne quoted in Michael Denning, *The Cultural Front: The Laboring of American Culture in the Twentieth Century* (New York: Verso, 1996), 348.

26. Barney Josephson writes that Scott came to Café Society Downtown, where Lena was having a drink with several musicians. "Some words were exchanged. Hazel called Lena a whore, and a fight ensued. Hazel had short hair very close to her scalp. Lena had beautiful long hair, shoulder length. Somehow they began pulling each other's hair." *Café Society*, 126.

27. Hairston, "The Wrong Place for the Right People?," 78. "Did Hazel Scott and Helena Horne, two of the prettiest sepia performers settle it via the hair-pulling route at Downtown Café Society?," *New York News*, September 1, 1941. Ivan Black Papers, 1887–1979, New York Public Library, Performing Arts Collection.

28. Josephson, *Café Society*, 127.

29. Lena Horne, *Lena* (New York: Doubleday, 1965), 177, 178–79, 192.

30. Lena Horne as told to Audreen Buffalo, "Lena!" *Essence* (May 1985): 150, quoted in Josephson, *Café Society*, 122.

31. Scott in Taylor, *Notes and Tones*, 255.

32. Ibid., 262–63.

33. Holiday, *Lady Sings the Blues*, 91.

34. Josephson, *Café Society*, 122.

35. Josephson, *Café Society*, 188–93.

36. "Hazel Faints in Dressing Room," *New York Amsterdam News*, November 11, 1945; *New York Times*, August 2, 1945, Hazel Scott Clippings File, SCRBC. See also Powell, *Adam by Adam*; "Powell Weds Hazel Scott," *Daily Worker*, August 2, 1945, FBI files on Adam Clayton Powell, reel 3; Carl Dunbar Laurence, "Adam, Hazel Honeymoon on L.I.," *New York Amsterdam News*, August 4, 1945.

37. "Ex-Mrs. Powell Moves into Her Summer Home," *Atlanta Daily World*, August 2, 1945.

38. Powell, *Adam by Adam*, 224.

39. Carolyn Dixon, "Carolyn Dixon Rides Again; Dopes Out Adam-Hazel Tift," *New York Amsterdam News*, November 17, 1945, 2.

40. Ibid.

41. Edgar G. Brown, "Hazel Scott's Baptism Is Almost Kept as a Secret," *New York Amsterdam News*, December 22, 1945, 8.

42. Hazel Scott, "How He Proposed," *Tan Confessions*, 1951, 5, 52. Powell, *Adam by Adam*, 226. Untitled clipping, 1945, Hazel Scott Clippings File, IJS. An article titled, "Do Career Women Make Good Wives," *Jet*, April 17, 1952, discussed Scott, Horne and others. Pauli Murray, "Why Negro Women Stay Single," *Negro Digest*, 1947.

43. Powell, *Adam by Adam*, 227–28.

44. Hazel Scott, "How I Found God in Show Business," *Ebony*, May 1956, 40–49. Letters to the editor about the article appeared in the next several issues. Readers opined on her relevance as a role model, ranging from complete adoration of and support for Scott to reminders that one cannot uplift the race by advocating service to both God and mammon. See "What Kind of Women Should Ministers Marry?," and "God and Show Business," letters to the editor, *Ebony*, July 1956 and August 1956.

45. James Booker, "Hazel (Scott) Says She 'Digs' Adam," *New York Amsterdam News*, November 23, 1957; "Final Decree," *New York Post*, November 24, 1960; 'I'll Talk When I Get My Divorce,' Says Hazel Scott," Hazel Scott Clippings File, IJS; Hazel Scott, letters to Mary Lou Williams, 1960s, Mary Lou Williams Collection, IJS.

46. "Charges Racial Bias: Agent for Hazel Scott Cites Constitution Hall, in Capital," *New York Times*, October 1, 1945, 14. Wil Haygood suggests that Powell and Scott orchestrated the scheme to mark Scott's introduction to Washington, both as an artist and as his wife. Haygood, *King of the Cats*, 128.

47. Marian Anderson, *My Lord, What a Morning: An Autobiography* (New York: Viking, 1956), 189; see also Raymond Arsenault, *The Sound of Freedom: Marian Anderson, the Lincoln Memorial, and the Concert That Awakened America* (Bloomsbury Press, 2009).

48. Richard Iton, *In Search of the Black Fantastic* (New York: Oxford University Press, 2008), 9.

49. Bess Truman had already been invited to the tea before the denial of permission to perform at Constitution Hall was made. Truman felt the two incidents had little to do with one another, and therefore there was no reason for her to break her promise to attend. Robert J. Donovan, *Conflict and Crisis: The Presidency of Harry S. Truman, 1945–1948* (Columbia: University of Missouri Press, 1996), 147–48.

50. "Protests Mount against Group," *Afro-American*, October 20, 1945, 2; Powell, *Adam by Adam*, 79; Haygood, *King of the Cats*, 128–31; William R. Shields, Letter to the Editor, *New York Amsterdam News*, November 10, 1945, 8.

51. "Tea Attendance Rapped by Hazel," *Afro-American*, October 20, 1945, 1–2.

52. See also Andrew S. Berish, *Lonesome Roads and Streets of Dreams: Place, Mobility, and Race in Jazz of the 1930s and '40s* (Chicago: University of Chicago Press, 2012), 13; Jennifer Stoever-Ackerman, "The Contours of the Sonic Color-Line: Slavery, Segregation, and the Cultural Politics of Listening," University of Southern California, PhD dissertation, 2007.

53. Donovan, *Conflict and Crisis*, 148.

54. D. M. Giangreco and Kathryn Moore, *Dear Harry— : Truman's Mailroom* (Mechanicsburg, PA: Stackpole Books, 1999), 40.

55. Ibid., 36, 38.

56. "Political Hodge Podge over DAR," *New York Times*, October 27, 1945, 3; Dan Gardner, *New York Amsterdam News*, November 3, 1945, 12; "The D.A.R. Auditorium,"

Pittsburgh Courier, October 20, 1945, 6; "D.A.R. Controversy Continues," *Pittsburgh Courier*, October 27, 1945, 6; A. V. Copeland, letter to the editor, *New York Amsterdam News*, November 10, 1945, 8.

57. "A Word about the DAR," *Afro-American*, October 20, 1945, 4.

58. "Anti-DAR Laws Set for House," *New York Amsterdam News*, October 27, 1945, 23; "Celler Seeks Revocation of DAR Charter," *Washington Post*, October 19, 1945; "House Bill to Void DAR Charter Filed," *New York Times*, October 19, 1945, 15; "DAR Ban Asked in 2 House Bills," *Afro-American*, October 27, 1945, 1.

59. "Pres. Truman, First Lady Rebuke DAR," *Atlanta Daily World*, October 14, 1945; "Trumans Condemn D.A.R. Negro Ban," *New York Times*, October 13, 1945, 17; "President Asked to Act in DAR Constitution Bar to Hazel Scott," *Atlanta Daily World*, October 3, 1945; "Congress Debates D.A.R. Hall Row," *New York Times*, October 17, 1945, 21; "DAR Praised, Hit in House," *Atlanta Daily World*, October 17, 1945, 1; "DAR May Reconsider Barring of Hazel Scott," *Afro-American*, October 13, 1945, 1.

60. "Protests Mount against Group," *Afro-American*, October 20, 1945, 2; "DAR Ban Asked in 2 House Bills," *Afro-American*, October 27, 1945, 21; Theodore G. Bilbo, *Take Your Choice: Separation or Mongrelization* (Poplarville, MI: Dream House Publishing Co., 1947), 100.

61. "People's DAR Formed to Push Action in Hazel Scott's Case," *Atlanta Daily World*, October 24, 1945, 1.

62. "Powell Sets Up People's DAR," *Afro-American*, October 20, 1945, 1, 2; "Morris Discusses D.A.R. in Harlem," *New York Times*, October 22, 1945, 9; "Hazel Scott, Pianist, in Varied Program," *New York Times*, November 27, 1945, 18.

63. "Dewey Criticizes D.A.R. in Scott Case," *New York Times*, October 16, 1945, 25.

64. "ALP Asks Inquiry in Capital on D.A.R.," *Afro-American*, October 14, 1945, 46.

65. "DAR Compared with Axis Agents," *Afro-American*, October 20, 1945, 2.

66. Ibid.

67. Edlee Webster, "Here Is the Inside Story of the D.A.R.," *Afro-American*, October 27, 1945, 5.

68. Clare Boothe Luce, letter to President Truman, June 29, 1946, Box 575, Folder 7, Library of Congress (LC).

69. "Mrs. Luce's Action Fails to Sway D.A.R.," *New York Times*, November 2, 1945, 21.

70. News clipping quoting Luce, sent to her with postcard from R. Prendergart, December 22, 1945, Box 508, Folder 8, LC; "Mrs. Luce Quits Greenwich DARs," *Pittsburgh Courier*, November 10, 1945; "Mrs. Luce to Change DAR Chapter," *New York Times*, November 29, 1945, 19; "Clare Luce to Shift Membership in D.A.R.," *New York Times*, November 3, 1945, 10.

71. "Outline of D.A.R. Speech," Papers of Edward L. Bernays, Box 227, Clare Boothe Luce, Miscellany, November 1945, LC.

72. Ibid. As interested as Bernays was in the "Negro situation," Luce's turn to him clearly provoked some questions on her part, as she asked him to help her rationalize why she would need him. Their relationship lasted the few short months following the Scott incident and coincided with Luce developing positions on atomic energy, among other concerns. He and his team created a well-researched, issue-based strategy for a variety of Luce's interests. (He wanted her to focus on the issue of censorship.) Bernays had been active during World War I in the Department of Propaganda and had written about the relationship between democracy and public participation—the power of a few to shape the opinions of many was an ideal of his.

73. Mrs. Julius Y. Talmadge, "The President General's Report," *National Historical Magazine*, May 1945, 235.

74. Ibid., 237.

75. Mabel Alston, "DAR Action by No Means Final, Observers Assert," *Afro-American*, October 20, 1945, 2. Luce herself claimed that the descendants of Attucks were eligible, considering that the constitution of the DAR had no provisions against including black female members. The labyrinthine process of applying for membership, including the presentation of valid papers and affidavits, was even more handicapped by, as Luce described it, "the civil status of the Negro in Washington's time." However, she "would be most eager to see a Negro woman, with her papers in order, make the attempt." Clare Boothe Luce, letter to John Roy Carlson, April 22, 1947, LC.

76. Minutes, National Board of Management, Regular Meeting, *National Historical Magazine*, July 1945, p. 413.

77. Clare Boothe Luce to Mrs. Edward Sandreuter, December 6, 1945, Box 511, Folder 20, LC.

78. Clipping, *PM*, n.d., Papers of Edward Bernays, LC.

79. "Ban Opposed by DAR Chapter," *New York Times*, October 19, 1945, 15; "DAR Chapter Decries Hazel Scott Action," *New York Times*, October 20, 1945, 7; "D.A.R. Unit against Race Ban," *New York Times*, November 22, 1945, 25. While some chapters voted to uphold the ban, some members of those chapters followed Luce's lead and resigned from them. "Stamford D.A.R. Votes," *New York Times*, November 21, 1945, 23; "Quits D.A.R. over Hazel Scott," *New York Times*, December 10, 1945, 24; "Clarifies Stand on D.A.R.," *New York Times*, October 25, 1945, 3.

80. Clare Boothe Luce to Mrs. Helen Roosevelt Robinson, December 12, 1945, Box 484, Folder 2, LC.

81. Clare Boothe Luce, unused speech, February 21, 1946, Box 680, Folder 6, LC, and speech delivered on radio, February 21, 1946, Box 680, Folder 7, LC.

82. The DAR pointed to the recent appeals case, *Mays vs. Burgess* (1945), in which a black female government employee purchased a home through a straw agent in a northwest part of the District of Columbia bound by a restrictive covenant against black residents,

to support its claim. The court found that Mays had both constructive and actual notice of the covenant, thus negating any claim that she was a valid purchaser of the property. The court maintained that the only way to legitimize her purchase was to document that the value of the land had depreciated prior to the sale or that the neighborhoods adjacent to the contested property had been subject to the "constant penetration . . . of colored person." In other words, the court was loath to devalue the property of the white homeowners by permitting the plaintiff to breach the covenant; 147 F.2d 869, Court of Appeals, Dist. of Columbia Circuit (1945); "Protests Mount against Group," *Afro-American*, October 20, 1945, 2; "D.A.R. Refuses Auditorium to Hazel Scott; Constitution Hall for 'White Artists Only,'" *New York Times*, October 12, 1945, 25.

83. "White Artists Only," *New York Times*, October 13, 1945, 14.

84. Clare Boothe Luce, February 21, 1946, Box 680, Folder 7, LC. The draft of the speech likened Scott to the heroic figure of Dorie Miller, who received a posthumous Navy Cross after taking up arms in defense of his ship when all the white sailors had been either killed or wounded during the attack on Pearl Harbor. Luce suggests that it is only a "minority faction" within the membership that supports the discrimination clause; February 21, 1946, Box 680, Folder 6, LC.

85. Adam Clayton Powell Jr., letter to Clare Boothe Luce, October 17, 1945, Box 508, Folder 6, LC; Sarah Povill, letter to Clare Boothe Luce, October 20, 1945; Fred B. Putnam, letter to Clare Boothe Luce, November 7, 1945, Box 508, Folder 16, LC; Saul Richman, letter to Clare Boothe Luce, November 5, 1945, Box 510, Folder 2, LC; D. Ryan, postcard to Clare Boothe Luce, October 14, 1945, Box 511, Folder 7, LC.

86. Wilson B. Roberts, letter to Clare Boothe Luce, October 17, 1945, Box 510, Folder 9, LC.

87. Emma Bugbee, "Head of D.A.R. Is Bitter at Foes of Racial Ban," *Herald Tribune*, May 21, 1946; Eleanor Morehead, "DAR Votes to Gag Critics of Anti-Negro Practice," *PM*, May 22, 1946, 11; Louis D. Clark, "Hats Off to Mrs. Talmadge," Letter to the Editor, *Hartford Courant*, May 29, 1946; Martha Strayer, "It's Not Easy to Buck the Daughters," *Washington Post*, April 24, 1953; Samuel Wallach, president, Teacher's Union, letter to Andrew G. Clauson Jr., president, Board of Education, New York, June 4, 1946, LC. Wallach's proposal that New York City schools refuse any medals given to students from the DAR did see some result. The Girl's High School of Brooklyn, an integrated school, refused to accept the annual American History award that a New York chapter regularly gave. Principal Edith M. Ward explained that the students, "were upset at the discrimination shown by the Washington Chapter of the DAR in the case of Hazel Scott, and earlier, Marian Anderson." And because the Battle Pass Chapter refused to comment on the school's decision, Ward severed ties with the chapter, commenting, "To evade a stand is equivalent to agreement with those who would deny to the Negro his Americanism." Memo/Press Release, February 8, 1946, NAACP papers, LC.

88. "DAR May Reconsider Barring of Hazel Scott," *Baltimore Afro-American*, October 13, 1945, 1; "Hazel Scott 'Not Great Artist' Says DAR Head," *Atlanta Daily World*, October 7, 1945.

89. Exceptions to the ban were made both before and after the Scott incident, including when the DAR invited Marian Anderson to sing in 1941 as a part of the organization's war relief effort, and in 1951 when Dorothy Maynor, a soprano, performed at the hall with the National Symphony Orchestra. The DAR rationalized Maynor's appearance by arguing that the contract had been made with the orchestra and not with Maynor. The NAACP received inquiries about Maynor's appearance, but was unable to respond definitively as to whether or not the "white artists only" clause had been rescinded. But the DAR had made no change to the rules of management. "DARs Bar Hazel Scott," *Pittsburgh Courier*, October 6, 1945, 1; "D.A.R. Hall Open to Negro Soprano," "DAR OK's Negro Star at Constitution Hall," *Sunday News*, April 22, 1951; Roberta M. Robinson, letter to Roy Wilkins, April 14, 1955, and Henry Lee Moon, letter to Roberta M. Robinson, May 6, 1955, Records of the NAACP, Group 11, Box A 373, LC.

90. Earnest E. Johnson, "Hazel Scott to Appear for Nat'l Press Club; Newsmen Aroused," *Atlanta Daily World*, November 7, 1945, 1.

91. "Hazel Scott Changes Mind; Won't Play for Lily-White Press Club," *Afro-American*, November 17, 1945, 11; "Lifting Race Bar Urged," *New York Times*, November 12, 1945, 19.

92. "Hazel Scott Has the Key to the City," *Daily Compass*, March 2, 1950.

93. Hugh Deane, "'Redlist' Costs Hazel Scott Job," *Daily Compass*, September 17, 1950.

94. See Carole Stabile, "The Typhoid Marys of the Left: Gender, Race, and the Broadcast Blacklist," *Communication and Critical/Cultural Studies* 8.3 (September 2011): 266–85; and Dwayne Mack, "Hazel Scott: A Career Curtailed," *Journal of African American History* 91.2 (Spring 2006): 153–70.

95. Hugh Deane, "'Redlist' Costs Hazel Scott Job," *Daily Compass*, September 17, 1950.

96. Iton, *In Search of the Black Fantastic*, 37.

97. "Josh White Sings 'Strange Fruit' before Activities Committee," September 1950, Tuskegee Clippings File; Walter White, "The Strange Case of Paul Robeson," *Ebony*, February 1951, 78–84.

98. See "Negro Groups Warned against Anti-Communist Hysteria" and "Branded by Un-American Committee," 1950, Tuskegee Clippings File.

99. Quoted in Iton, *In Search of the Black Fantastic*, 34.

100. Reports include "Hazel Scott Asks Union Boycott of 'Unfair' Stations," *New York Post*, September 24, 1950; "Hazel Scott Hits Back at Counterattack," *Daily Compass*, September 15, 1950; "Hazel Scott Makes Denials at Inquiry," *New York Times*, September 23, 1950; "Hazel Scott Denies Any Red Sympathies," *New York Times*, September 16, 1950; "Hazel Scott Tells House Inquiry She Is Not Red," *Herald Tribune*, September 23, 1950; "Pianist Hazel Scott Denies 'Red' Charges," September 24, 1950, Hazel Scott Clippings File, Tuskegee.

101. Hazel Scott's FBI file posted on Carole Stabile's blog, http://cstabile.files.wordpress
.com/2010/08/hazel-scott-fbi-files.pdf, last accessed November 18, 2012.

102. See Mark Naison, *Communists in Harlem during the Depression* (New York: Grove,
1985), and Cheryl Greenberg, *"Or Does It Explode"? Black Harlem during the Depression*
(New York: Oxford, 1997).

103. Fredi Washington, "New Type of Night Club Gives Artists a Break," *People's Voice*,
January 8, 1944; FBI files of Adam Clayton Powell Jr. , reel 2.

104. House Committee on Un-American Activities, "Testimony of Hazel Scott Powell,"
September 22, 1950, p. 3612.

105. "Puts Hazel Scott on Jim Crow Bus Down in Missouri," *New York Amsterdam
News*, October 27, 1945, 23.

106. Robert D. Dean explores the "purge the perverts" period of the HUAC era in his
Imperial Brotherhood (Amherst: University of Massachusetts, 2003).

107. "Testimony of Hazel Scott Powell," p. 3620.

108. Scott, in Taylor, *Notes and Tones*, 256–57, 258.

109. Ibid., 257, 255–56, 263, 259.

110. Ibid., 259.

111. Ibid., 267–68.

FIVE "The Chill of Death"

Chapter epigraphs from Janet Coleman and Al Young, *Mingus/Mingus: Two Memoirs*
(Berkeley: Creative Arts Book Company, 1989), 160; and Nina Simone, quoted in Robert
Lucas, "Nina Simone, A Girl with Guts," *Negro Digest*, February 1962, 23–24.

Epigraphs to section "'God Must Be a Boogie Man'" from Joni Mitchell, quoted in
Fellezs, *Birds of Fire*, 169; and Mitchell's liner notes to *Mingus* (1979), http://jonimitchell
.com/music/album.cfm?id=12, last accessed March 20, 2012.

Epigraphs to section *"Passions of a Man"* from William Matthews in Yusef Komunyakaa
and William Matthews, "Jazz and Poetry: A Conversation," moderated by Robert Kelley,
Georgia Review 46.4 (Winter 1992): 647 [emphasis in the text]; and Janet Coleman in Janet
Coleman and Al Young. *Mingus/Mingus: Two Memoirs* (Berkeley: Creative Arts, 1989), 65.

Epigraph to section *"Epitaph"* from Nat Hentoff's liner notes to *Blues & Roots*, Atlantic
(F) 50232.

1. Hal Willner, liner notes, *Hal Willner Presents Weird Nightmare: Meditations on
Mingus*, Columbia 472467-2 (1992), 13.

2. Charles Mingus, liner notes, *Let My Children Hear Music*, Columbia CK 48920.

3. Ingrid Monson, *Freedom Sounds: Civil Rights Call Out to Jazz and Africa* (New York:
Oxford University Press, 2007), 19.

4. Paul Allen Anderson explores an aspect of this public fascination with feeling, es-

pecially the poignancy associated with Bill Evans, in jazz. "'My Foolish Heart': Bill Evans and the Public Life of Feelings," *Jazz Perspectives* 7.3 (2013): 205–49.

5. Mingus, "What Is a Jazz Composer?," liner notes to *Let My Children Hear Music*, Columbia CK 48910.

6. Duke Ellington, "The 'Jazz Fakers' Can't Make It Now," *Negro Digest*, November 1961, 78.

7. Ibid. These are ideas that Mingus explored elsewhere over the years, including in his 1973 essay, "An Open Letter to the Avant-Garde," published in *Changes* magazine. Mingus stressed musicianship as key to the expression of musical ideas. He argued that some contemporary musicians who were called avant-garde seriously lacked the skill to actually be avant-garde. Nor in fact did the contemporary jazz press understand the demands of the music enough to write perceptively about these so-called avant-garde musicians. Perhaps the grumblings of a bitter man, the essay nevertheless expresses Mingus's lasting desire to explain his theories about music, musicianship, and the importance of feeling in jazz.

8. Leonard Feather, "Joni Mitchell Has Her Mojo Working," *Los Angeles Times*, June 10, 1979.

9. Joni Mitchell, lyrics, "God Must Be a Boogie-Man!," recorded on *Mingus* (1979), http://jonimitchell.com/music/song.cfm?id=120, last accessed February 9, 2012.

10. Mitchell, liner notes, *Mingus*.

11. Joni Mitchell, quoted in Feather, "Joni Mitchell Has Her Mojo Working."

12. Fellezs, *Birds of Fire*, 14, 150.

13. Ibid., 148.

14. Bob Longino, "'Reckless Daughter' Too 'Weird,'" *High Point Enterprises*, January 29, 1978.

15. Wesley Strick, "Joni Mitchell Meets Don Juan's Reckless Daughter," March 2, 1978, http://jonimitchell.com/library/view.cfm?id=715, last accessed March 19, 2012.

16. John Rockwell, "Joni Mitchell Is Still Going Her Way," *New York Times*, December 16, 1977.

17. Dave Surratt, "Replay: Don Juan's Reckless Daughter," September 23, 2004, http://jonimitchell.com/library/view.cfm?id=1174, last accessed March 19, 2012.

18. Rockwell, "Joni Mitchell Is Still Going Her Way."

19. Janet Maslin, "Joni Mitchell's Reckless and Shapeless 'Daughter,'" *Rolling Stone*, March 9, 1978.

20. Steven Holden, "Madam Joni Almost Pulls It Off," *Village Voice*, December 19, 1977.

21. Mark Kernis, "Daughter: Bitterness with a Steely Edge," *Washington Post*, January 11, 1978.

22. Mitchell, quoted in Fellezs, *Birds of Fire*, 150.

23. Angela LaGreca, "The Making of the Don Juan's Reckless Daughter Cover," *Rock Photo*, 1985.

24. Tony Mitchell, "Joni's Enigmatic Innervisions," *Sounds*, December 24, 1977.

25. Fellezs, *Birds of Fire*, 157.

26. Leonard Feather, *Mingus, Down Beat*, August 9, 1979. Mitchell's performance of black masculinity traded on its sanctification, argues Sandy Robertson, who described the "reverential tone" of "the little white girl in awe of the big black man," as a "beautifully recorded, self-consciously precious, . . . maddeningly white attempt at blackness" and a sincere failure of execution. Sandy Robertson, "Scared to Dance," *Sounds*, June 30, 1979. Michael Watts, writing in *Melody Maker*, agreed, finding that Mitchell tried too hard to make jazz despite her best efforts. "Joni . . . er . . . um," June 16, 1979.

27. Feather, "Joni Mitchell Has Her Mojo Working"; John Rockwell, "Joni Mitchell's New Disc Includes Mingus's Music," *Milwaukee Journal*, August 22, 1979.

28. Neil Strauss, "The Hissing of a Living Legend," *New York Times*, October 4, 1998, http://www.nytimes.com/1998/10/04/magazine/the-hissing-of-a-living-legend.html, last accessed February 25, 2012.

29. Joni Mitchell, quoted in Larry Kart, "Mitchell and Mingus in an Unlikely Merger," *Chicago Tribune*, August 22, 1979; Neil Coppage, "Joni's Mingus," *Stereo Review*, October 1979; Mary Jo Santili, "Celebrating a Jazz Master and a Bold New Style," *Daily Collegian*, September 14, 1979.

30. Adrian Piper, "On Wearing Three Hats," 1996, "http://www.adrianpiper.com/docs /WebsiteNGBK3Hats.pdf.

31. Adrian Piper, *Out of Order, Out of Sight, Volume 1: Selected Writings on Meta Art, 1968–1992* (Boston: MIT Press, 1999), 115, emphasis in the original, 112.

32. Cherisse Smith, *Enacting Others: Politics of Identity in Eleanor Antin, Nikki S. Lee, Adrian Piper, and Anna DeVeare Smith* (Durham, NC: Duke University Press, 2011), 23.

33. Sidonie Smith and Julia Watson, eds., *Interfaces: Women, Autobiography, Image, Performance* (Ann Arbor: University of Michigan Press, 2002), 223.

34. Ibid., 5. Coleman reports that after seeing the manuscript again in the mid-1960s, "it had been altered, whitened up beyond repair" (8).

35. Ibid., 87.

36. Al Young, *Drowning in the Sea of Love: Musical Memoirs* (Hopewell, NJ: Ecco Press, 1981).

37. Coleman and Young, *Mingus/Mingus*, 123, 164.

38. Young, *Drowning in the Sea of Love*, 199. See also Amiri Baraka, *The Autobiography of Leroi Jones*, Chester Himes, *If He Hollers, Let Him Go* (New York: Thunder's Mouth, 1986), and Clarence Major, *All Night Visitors* [1969] (Boston: Northeastern University Press, 1998).

39. Coleman and Young, *Mingus/Mingus*, 108, 109.

40. Ibid., 116.

41. Komunyakaa and Matthews, "Jazz and Poetry," 650.

42. "Blindfold Test," *Down Beat*, April 28, 1960, http://mingusmingusmingus.com/mingus/blindfold-test, last accessed May 7, 2013.

43. Ibid.

44. The piece was recorded as Charles Mingus, *Epitaph*, Columbia C2K 45428.

45. All quotes from Don McGlynn's documentary film, *Charles Mingus: Triumph of the Underdog* (1998).

46. Coleman and Young, *Mingus/Mingus*, 20.

47. Mingus, quoted in *Mingus 1968*, Rhapsody Films, d. Thomas Reichman, May 1968.

48. Carolyn (Keki) Mingus, quoted in Gene Santoro, *Myself When I'm Real: The Life and Music of Charles Mingus* (New York: Oxford University Press, 2001), 265.

49. Judy Starkey Mingus McGrath, quoted in Santoro, *Myself When I'm Real*, 274.

50. Collette with Isoardi, UCCAS, tape no. 15, side 2, January 5, 1990, 735.

51. Ibid., 740–742. Grace and Vivian Mingus resented not having the opportunity to be with Mingus either at his death or his cremation, *The Mingus Sisters Speak*.

52. Mingus, "Chill of Death," *Let My Children Hear Music*.

BIBLIOGRAPHY

Collections

Papers of Edward L. Bernays, Library of Congress (LC)

Ivan Black Papers, 1887–1979, New York Public Library, Performing Arts Collection

Central Avenue Sounds Oral History Collection, University of California, Los Angeles

Duke Ellington Collection (DEC), Smithsonian Institute

Jazz Oral History Project (JOHP), Smithsonian Institute, Institute of Jazz Studies (IJS), Rutgers University

Charles Mingus Collection (CMC), Library of Congress

Charles Mingus Clippings File, IJS, Rutgers University

Records of the NAACP, Library of Congress

Papers of Clare Boothe Luce, Library of Congress

Hazel Scott, Clippings File, IJS, Rutgers University

Hazel Scott Clippings File, Schomburg Center for Research in Black Culture (SCRBC)

Tuskegee Institute News Clippings File

Mary Lou Williams Collection, IJS, Rutgers University

Mingus Discography

Charles Mingus. *A Modern Jazz Symposium of Music and Poetry with Charles Mingus.* Bethlehem 20–40092, 1957.

———. *East Coasting,* Bethlehem BS 6019, 1957.

———. *Charles Mingus Presents Charles Mingus.* Candid CD9005, 1960.

———. *Blues & Roots.* Atlantic (F) 50232, 1960; reissued on Atlantic R2 72871.

———. *Mingus/Oh Yeah.* Atlantic, 1961.

———. *The Black Saint and the Sinner Lady.* Impulse! IMPD-174, 1963.

———. *Mingus Plays Piano.* Impulse! IMPD-217, 1963.

———. *Let My Children Hear Music.* Columbia CK 48910, 1972.

———. *Charles Mingus and Friends in Concert.* Columbia 1973, reissued 1996.

———. *Charles Mingus—The Complete Debut Recordings.* Debut 12DCD 4402–2, 1990.

———. *Charles Mingus Passions of a Man, the Complete Atlantic Recordings 1956–1961.* Rhino R2 72871, 1997.

Charles Mingus and John La Porta. *Jazzical Moods* [1955]. Fantasy Records, OJCCD-1857–2, 1995.

Other Artists

Eric Dolphy. *Eric Dolphy: The Complete Prestige Recordings.* Prestige 9PRCD-4418–2, 1995.

Billie Holiday. *The Quintessential Billie Holiday, Volume 8 (1939–1940).* Columbia CK 47030, 1991.

Darryl A. Lewis. *The Mingus Sisters Speak.* Lacecap Records, 2008.

Joni Mitchell. *Don Juan's Reckless Daughter.* Asylum BB-701, 1977.

———. *Mingus.* Asylum 5E-505, 1979.

Red Norvo. *The Red Norvo Trio with Tal Farlow and Charles Mingus.* Savoy SV-0267, 1950.

Hazel Scott. *Relaxed Piano Moods.* Debut, 1955; reissued OJCCD-1702-2, 1992.

Newspapers and Magazines

Atlanta Daily World

Baltimore Afro-American

Boston Globe

Chicago Defender

Commonweal

Daily Compass

Daily Worker

Down Beat

Ebony

Hartford Courant

Herald Tribune

Jet

Metronome

National Historical Magazine [DAR]

New York Amsterdam News

New Yorker

New York Post

Playboy

PM

People's Voice

Pittsburgh Courier

Sunday News

Tan Confessions

Washington Post

Books, Articles, Dissertations

Ahmed, Sara. *Queer Phenomenology: Orientations, Objects, Others.* Durham: Duke University Press, 2006.

Alexander, Elizabeth. *The Black Interior: Essays.* Minneapolis: Graywolf Press, 2004.

Anderson, Tim. "'Buried under the Fecundity of His Own Creations'": Reconsidering the Recording Bans of the American Federation of Musicians, 1942–1944 and 1948." *American Music* 22.2 (Summer 2004): 231–69.

Annfelt, Trine. "Jazz as Masculine Space." Kilden Information Centre for Gender Research in Norway, eng.kilden.forskningsradet.no/c52778/nyet/vis.html?tid=53517, last accessed October 16, 2013.

Arsenault, Raymond. *The Sound of Freedom: Marian Anderson, the Lincoln Memorial, and the Concert that Awakened America.* New York: Bloomsbury Press, 2009.

Baraka, Imamu Amiri. *The Autobiography of LeRoi Jones.* Chicago: Lawrence Hill Books, 1997.

——. "The 'Blues Aesthetic' and the 'Black Aesthetic': Aesthetics as the Continuing Political History of a Culture." *Black Music Research Journal* 11.2 (Autumn 1991): 101–9.

—— (LeRoi Jones). *Blues People: Negro Music in White America* [1963]. New York: Quill William Morrow, 1999.

——. "The Dark Lady of the Sonnets." In *Setting the Tempo,* ed. Tom Piazza, 230. New York: Anchor Books Doubleday, 1996.

——. "Homage to Miles Davis." In *Miles Davis Companion: Four Decades of Commentary,* ed. Gary Carner, 41–51. London: Omnibus Press, 1996.

——. "Jazz and the White Critic." In *The Jazz Cadence of American Culture,* ed. Robert G. O'Meally, 137–42. New York: Columbia University Press, 1998.

——. "Numbers, Letters," in *The Black Poets,* ed. Dudley Randall (New York: Bantam Books, 1971).

Bakan, Michael B. "Way Out West on Central: Jazz in the African-American Community of Los Angeles before 1930." In *California Soul: Music of African Americans in the West,* ed. Jacqueline Cogdell DjeDje and Eddie S. Meadows, 23–78. Berkeley: University of California Press, 1998.

Barlow, William. *Voice Over: The Making of Black Radio.* Philadelphia: Temple University Press, 1999.

Barthes, Roland. *A Lover's Discourse: Fragments.* New York: Hill and Wang, 1979.

Battersby, Christine. *Gender and Genius: Towards a Feminist Aesthetics.* Bloomington and Indianapolis: Indiana University Press, 1989.

Berger, Harris M. *Stance: Emotion, Style, and Meaning for the Study of Expressive Culture.* Middletown, CT: Wesleyan University Press, 2011.

Berish, Andrew S. *Lonesome Roads and Streets of Dreams: Place, Mobility, and Race in Jazz of the 1930s and '40s.* Chicago: University of Chicago Press, 2012.

Berliner, Paul F. *Thinking in Jazz: The Infinite Art of Improvisation.* Chicago: University of Chicago Press, 1994.

Bilbo, Theodore G. *Take Your Choice: Separation or Mongrelization.* Poplarville, MI: Dream House Publishing Co., 1947.

Bontemps, Arna. "A Pianist with a Mind of Her Own—Hazel Scott." *Senior Scholastic,* March 5, 1945.

Bowles, John P. *Adrian Piper: Race, Gender, Embodiment.* Durham: Duke University Press, 2011.

Braxton, Joanne M. *Black Women Writing Autobiography: A Tradition within a Tradition.* Philadelphia: Temple University Press, 1989.

Brooks, Daphne. *Bodies in Dissent: Spectacular Performances of Race and Freedom, 1850–1910.* Durham: Duke University Press, 2006.

Brown, Elsa Barkley. "'What Has Happened Here': The Politics of Difference in Women's History and Feminist Politics." *Feminist Studies* 18.2 (Summer 1992): 295–312.

Bryant, Clora, et al. *Central Avenue Sounds: Jazz in Los Angeles.* Berkeley: University of California Press, 1997.

Burke, Patrick. "Oasis of Swing: The Onyx Club, Jazz, and White Masculinity in the Early 1930s." *American Music* 24.3 (Autumn 2006): 320–46.

Butterfield, Stephen. *Black Autobiography in America.* Amherst: University of Massachusetts Press, 1974.

Byrd, Rudolph. "The Tradition of John: A Mode of Black Masculinity." In *Traps: African American Men on Gender and Sexuality,* ed. Rudolph P. Byrd and Beverly Guy-Sheftall, 1–24. Indianapolis: Indiana University Press, 2001.

Callender, Red, and Elaine Cohen. *Unfinished Dream: The Musical World of Red Callender.* London: Quartet Books, 1986.

Carby, Hazel. "'It Jus Be's Dat Way Sometime': The Sexual Politics of Women's Blues." *Radical America* 20.4 (1986): 9–24.

———. *Race Men.* Cambridge: Harvard University Press, 1998.

Carmichael, Thomas. "*Beneath the Underdog*: Charles Mingus, Representation, and Jazz Autobiography." *Canadian Review of American Studies* 25.3 (Fall 1995): 29–41.

Carner, Gary. "Conversation with Hal Mitchell: Jazz Patriarch of Newark." *Black Perspective in Music* 17 (1989): 109–34.

Chevan, David. "The Double Bass as a Solo Instrument in Early Jazz." *The Black Perspective in Music* 17 (1989): 73–92.

Clarke, Donald. *Billie Holiday: Wishing on The Moon.* New York: Viking, 1994.

Cleage, Pearl. *Deals with the Devil: And Other Reasons to Riot.* New York: Ballantine, 1994.

Coleman, Janet, and Al Young. *Mingus/Mingus: Two Memoirs.* Berkeley: Creative Arts, 1989.

Collette, Buddy, with Steven Isoardi. *Jazz Generations: A Life in American Music and Society.* London: Continuum, 2000.

Crouch, Stanley. "Max Roach: Drums Unlimited." *Village Voice,* December 17, 1979.

Cuscuna, Michael, and Michel Ruppli. *The Blue Note Label: A Discography.* New York: Greenwood Press, 1988.

Dahl, Linda. *Stormy Weather: The Music and Lives of a Century of Jazzwomen*. New York: Limelight Editions, 1984.

Davis, Angela. *Blues Legacies and Black Feminisms: Gertrude "Ma" Rainey, Bessie Smith, and Billie Holiday*. New York: Vintage, 1999.

Davis, Miles, with Quincy Troupe. *Miles: The Autobiography of Miles Davis*. New York: Simon and Schuster, 1989.

Dean, Robert D. *Imperial Brotherhood: Gender and the Making of Cold War Foreign Policy*. Amherst: University of Massachusetts, 2003.

Deffaa, Chip. *In the Mainstream: Eighteen Portraits in Jazz*. Metuchen, NJ: Scarecrow Press and Institute of Jazz Studies, Rutgers University, 1992.

Denning, Michael. *The Cultural Front: The Laboring of American Culture in the Twentieth Century*. New York: Verso, 1998.

DeVeaux, Scott. *The Birth of Bebop: A Social and Musical History*. Berkeley: University of California Press, 1997.

———. "Constructing the Jazz Tradition." In *The Jazz Cadence of American Culture*, ed. Robert G. O'Meally, 483–512. New York: Columbia University Press, 1998.

Donovan, Robert J. *Conflict and Crisis: The Presidency of Harry S. Truman, 1945–1948*. Columbia: University of Missouri Press, 1996.

DuBois, W.E.B. *The Souls of Black Folk*. Chicago: A.C. McClurg and Co., 1903.

Dudley, David I. *My Father's Shadow: Intergenerational Conflict in African American Men's Autobiography*. Philadelphia: University of Pennsylvania Press, 1991.

Early, Gerald. "'I Just Adored that Man': Interview with Quincy Jones." In *Miles Davis and American Culture*, ed. Gerald Early, 42–43. St. Louis: Missouri Historical Society Press, 2001.

———. "On Miles Davis, Vince Lombardi, and the Crisis in Masculinity in Mid-century America." *Daedulus* 131.1 (Winter 2002): 154–59.

Eastman, Ralph. "'Pitchin' Up a Boogie': African-American Musicians, Nightlife, and Music Venues in Los Angeles, 1930–1945." In *California Soul: Music of African Americans in the West*, ed. Jacqueline Cogdell DjeDje and Eddie S. Meadows, 79–102. Berkeley: University of California Press, 1998.

Eldridge, Roy, as told to James Goodrich. "Jim Crow Is Killing Jazz." *Negro Digest*, October 1950, 44–49.

Erenberg, Lewis. *Swingin' the Dream: Big Band Jazz and the Rebirth of American Culture*. Chicago: University of Chicago Press, 1998.

Fanon, Frantz. *Black Skins, White Masks*. Translated by Constance Farrington. New York: Grove Press, 1994.

Feather, Leonard. *Inside Jazz* [1949]. New York: Da Capo, 1977.

———. "Joni Mitchell Has Her Mojo Working." *Los Angeles Times*, June 10, 1979.

———. "Mingus Blindfold Test." *Down Beat*, April 28, 1960.

Feldstein, Ruth. "'I Don't Trust You Anymore': Nina Simone, Culture, and Black Activism in the 1960s." *Journal of American History* 91.4 (March 2005): 1349–79.

Fellezs, Kevin. *Birds of Fire: Jazz, Rock, Funk, and the Creation of Fusion.* Durham: Duke University Press, 2011.

Fischlin, Daniel, Ajay Heble, and George Lipsitz. *The Fierce Urgency of Now: Improvisation, Rights, and the Ethics of Cocreation.* Durham: Duke University Press, 2013.

Foreman, Murray. *One Night on TV is Worth Weeks at the Paramount: Popular Music on Early Television.* Durham: Duke University Press, 2012.

Foucault, Michel. *The Use of Pleasure (The History of Sexuality Vol. 2).* New York: Vintage Books, 1986.

Fox, Ted. *In the Groove: The People behind the Music.* New York: St. Martin's Press, 1986.

Gendron, Bernie. "'Moldy Figs' and Modernists: Jazz at War (1942–1946)." In *Jazz among the Discourses,* ed. Krin Gabbard, 31–56. Durham: Duke University Press, 1995.

Gennari, John. *Blowin' Hot and Cool: Jazz and Its Critics.* Chicago: University of Chicago Press, 2006.

———. "Jazz Criticism: Its Development and Ideologies." *Black American Literature Forum* 25 (Fall 1991): 449–523.

George, Nelson. *The Death of Rhythm and Blues.* New York: Pantheon Books, 1988.

Giangreco, D. M., and Kathryn Moore. *Dear Harry— : Truman's Mailroom.* Mechanicsburg, PA: Stackpole Books, 1999.

Gibson, Maya C. "Alternate Takes: Billie Holiday at the Intersection of Black Cultural Studies and Historical Musicology." PhD dissertation, University of Wisconsin-Madison, 2008.

Gillespie, Dizzy, with Al Fraser. *To Be, or Not . . . to Bop: Memoirs.* Garden City, NY: Doubleday, 1979.

Gilman, Sander. *Difference and Pathology: Stereotypes of Sexuality, Race, and Madness.* Ithaca: Cornell University Press, 1985.

Gioia, Ted. *The History of Jazz.* New York: Oxford University Press, 1997.

———. *West Coast Jazz: Modern Jazz in California, 1945–1960.* Berkeley: University of California Press, 1992.

Gitler, Ira. *Jazz Masters of the 40s* [1966]. New York: Da Capo, 1983.

———. "Mingus Speaks—And Bluntly." *Down Beat,* July 21, 1960, 30.

Gleason, Ralph. "Charlie Mingus: A Thinking Musician." *Down Beat,* June 1, 1951.

Goldberg, Joe. *Jazz Masters of the '50s* [1965]. New York: Da Capo, 1983.

Goldmark, Daniel. "Slightly Left of Center: Atlantic Records and the Problems of Genre," In *Jazz/Not Jazz: The Music and Its Boundaries,* ed. David Ake, Charles Hiroshi Garrett, and Daniel Goldmark, 148–69. Berkeley: University of California Press, 2012.

Goodman, John F. *Mingus Speaks.* Berkeley: University of California Press, 2013.

Gordon, Max. *Live at The Village Vanguard.* New York: Da Capo, 1982.

Gray, Herman. "Black Masculinity and Visual Culture." *Callaloo* 18.2 (1995): 401–5.

——. "Independent Cultural Production: The Case of a Jazz Recording Company." *Journal of Popular Music and Society* (Summer 1986): 1–16.

——. *Producing Jazz: The Experience of an Independent Record Company*. Philadelphia: Temple University Press, 1988.

Green, Benny. *The Reluctant Art: Five Studies in the Growth of Jazz*. New York: Horizon, 1963.

Greenberg, Cheryl. *"Or Does It Explode?" Black Harlem in the Depression*. New York: Oxford University Press, 1997.

Griffin, Farah Jasmine. "Baraka's Billie Holiday as a Blues Poet of Black Longing." *African American Review* 37.2–3 (Summer–Autumn, 2003), 313–20.

——. *If You Can't Be Free, Be a Mystery: In Search of Billie Holiday*. New York: One World/Ballantine, 2002.

Guillory, Monique. "Black Bodies Swingin': Race, Gender, and Jazz." In *Soul: Black Power, Politics, and Pleasure*, ed. Monique Guillory and Richard C. Green, 191–215. New York: New York University Press, 1998.

Hairston, Monica. "The Wrong Place for the Right People? Café Society, Gender and Jazz 1938–1947," PhD dissertation, New York University, 2009.

Halberstam, Judith. "The Good, the Bad, and the Ugly: Men, Women, and Masculinity." In *Masculinity Studies & Feminist Theory*, ed. Judith Kegan Gardiner, 344–68. Urbana: University of Illinois Press, 2009.

Hale, James. "How Blue Note Records Became the Biggest Brand in Jazz." http://music .cbc.ca/#/blogs/2012/11/How-Blue-Note-Records-became-the-biggest-brand-in-jazz, last accessed November 28, 2012.

Hamlin, Jesse. "Billie Holiday's Bio, "Lady Sings the Blues," May Be Full of Lies but It Gets at Jazz's Great Core." *San Francisco Chronicle*, September 18, 2006.

Hamm, Charles. *Putting Popular Music in Its Place*. Cambridge: Cambridge University Press, 1995.

Hampton, Lionel, with James Haskins. *Hamp: An Autobiography*. New York: Penguin, 1989.

Harlos, Christopher. "Jazz Autobiography: Theory, Practice, Politics." In *Representing Jazz*, ed. Krin Gabbard, 131–66. Durham: Duke University Press, 1995.

Harris, Cheryl I. "Whiteness as Property." *Harvard Law Review* 106 (June 1993): 1709–91.

Haygood, Wil. *King of the Cats: The Life and Times of Adam Clayton Powell, Jr.* New York: Houghton Mifflin, 1993.

Heble, Ajay. *Landing on the Wrong Note: Jazz, Dissonance, and Critical Practice*. New York: Routledge, 2000.

Hentoff, Nat. "Early Blue Note Jazz." *Wall Street Journal*, October 3, 1997.

——. "A Festival Triumph: *Mingus at Monterey*." *HiFi Stereo Review*, April 1965, 75.

——. *The Jazz Life*. New York: Da Capo, 1975.

———. "A Jazz Summit." In *Keeping Time: Readings in Jazz History*, ed. Rob Walser, 265–69. New York: Oxford University Press, 1999.

———. "M and M at Monterey." *Newsweek*, October 5, 1964.

———. "Mingus Dynasties." *Village Voice*, March 22, 1979, 34.

———. "Mingus in Job Dilemma, Vows 'No Compromise.'" *Down Beat*, May 6, 1953.

———. "A Volcano Named Mingus." *HiFi Stereo Review*, December 1964, 53.

Higginbotham, Evelyn Brooks. "African American Women's History and the Metalanguage of Race." *Signs* (Winter 1992): 251–74.

Himes, Chester. *If He Hollers, Let Him Go*. New York: Thunder's Mouth, 1986.

Holden, Steven. "Madam Joni Almost Pulls It Off." *Village Voice*. December 19, 1977.

Holiday, Billie, and William Dufty. *Lady Sings the Blues*. New York: Doubleday, 1956.

Homzy, Andrew, ed. *Mingus: More Than a Fake Book*. New York: Jazz Workshop, 1991.

Horne, Lena. *Lena*. New York: Doubleday, 1965.

hooks, bell. *Ain't I a Woman? Black Women and Feminism*. Boston: South End Press, 1981.

———. *Feminist Theory: From Margin to Center*. Boston: South End Press, 1984.

———. *Yearning: Race, Gender, and Cultural Politics*. Boston: South End Press, 1990.

House Committee on Un-American Activities. "Testimony of Hazel Scott Powell." September 22, 1950.

Hurley, Neil P. "Toward a Sociology of Jazz." *Thought* 44 (1969): 219–46.

Hurston, Zora Neale. "Characteristics of Negro Expression." In *African America Literary Theory: A Reader*, ed. Winston Napier, 41. New York: New York University Press, 2000.

Isoardi, Steven. *Songs of the Unsung: The Musical and Social Journey of Horace Tapscott*. Durham: Duke University Press, 2001.

Iton, Richard. *In Search of the Black Fantastic: Politics and Popular Culture in the Post-Civil Rights Era*. New York: Oxford University Press, 2008.

Jackson, Jr., John L. "A Little Black Magic." *South Atlantic Quarterly* 104.3 (Summer 2005): 395–402.

James, Clive. "Jim Crow in the Jazz World." *Observer*, August 15, 1971.

Jay, Martin. *Songs of Experience: Modern American and European Variations on a Universal Theme*. Berkeley: University of California Press, 2005.

Josephson, Barney. *Café Society: The Wrong Place for the Right People*. Urbana: University of Illinois Press, 2009.

Johnson, Charles S. "A Phenomenology of the Black Body." In *Traps: African American Men on Gender and Sexuality*, ed. Rudolph P. Byrd and Beverly Guy-Sheftall, 223–35. Indianapolis: Indiana University Press, 2001.

Johnson, E. Patrick. "Queer Theory." In *The Cambridge Companion to Performance Studies*, ed. Tracy C. Davis, 161–81. Cambridge: Cambridge University Press, 2008.

Julien, Kyle. "Sounding the City: Jazz, African American Nightlife, and the Articulation of Race in 1940s Los Angeles." PhD dissertation, University of California, Irvine, 2000.

Kaplan, E. Ann. "Is the Gaze Male?" In *Powers of Desire: The Politics of Sexuality*, ed. Ann Snitnow, Christine Stansell, and Sharon Thompson, 309–27. New York: Monthly Review Press, 1983.

Kastner, Jeffrey. "'Negro Artists Exploited': Mingus Urges Investigation." *Toronto Daily Star*, October 31, 1964.

Katunich, Lauren J. "Time to Quit Paying the Payola Piper: Why Music Industry Abuse Demand a Complete System Overhaul." *Loyola of Los Angeles Entertainment Law Review* 22 (2002): 643–85.

Keightley, Keir. "'Turn It Down!' She Shrieked: Gender, Domestic Space, and High Fidelity, 1948–59." *Popular Music* 15.2 (May 1996): 149–77.

Kelley, Robin D. G. "The Jazz Wives: Muse and Manager." *New York Times*, July 21, 2002.

———. "Miles Davis: The Chameleon of Cool; A Jazz Genius in the Guise of a Hustler." *New York Times*, May 13, 2001.

———. *Thelonious Monk: The Life and Times of An American Original.* New York: The Free Press, 2009.

Kennedy, Rick, and Randy McNutt. *Little Label—Big Sound.* Indianapolis: Indiana University Press, 1999.

Kenney III, William H. "Negotiating the Color Line: Louis Armstrong's Autobiographies." In *Jazz in Mind: Essays on the History and Meaning of Jazz*, ed. Reginald T. Buckner and Steven Weiland, 38–59. Detroit: Wayne State University Press, 1991.

Kernis, Mark. "Daughter: Bitterness With a Steely Edge." *Washington Post*, January 11, 1978.

Komara, Edward. "The Dial Recordings of Charlie Parker." In *The BeBop Revolution in Words and Music,"* ed. Dave Oliphant with an introduction by Richard Lawn, 78–103. Austin: Harry Ranson Humanities Research Center, University of Texas, 1994.

Komunyakaa, Yusef. "Copacetic Mingus." In *Pleasure Dome: New and Collected Poems*, 111. Middletown, CT: Wesleyan University Press, 2001.

Komunyakaa, Yusef, and William Matthews. "Jazz and Poetry: A Conversation," moderated by Robert Kelley. *Georgia Review* 46.4 (Winter 1992): 645–61.

Kwolek-Folland, Angel. *Engendering Business: Men and Women in the Corporate Office, 1870–1930.* Baltimore: Johns Hopkins University Press, 1994.

LaGreca, Angela. "The Making of the Don Juan's Reckless Daughter Cover." *Rock Photo*, 1985.

Leiter, Robert D. *The Musicians and Petrillo.* New York: Bookman Associates, 1953.

Leonard, Neil. *Jazz and the White Americans.* Chicago: University of Chicago Press, 1962.

Leonard, Susan M. "An Introduction to Black Participation in the Early Recording Era, 1890–1920." *Annual Review of Jazz Studies* 4 (1988): 31–44.

Levin, Alan. "Court Frees Mingus; He Sits In on a Sit-in." *New York Post*, March 17, 1963.

Levis, Kenneth. Director. *Jackie McLean on Mars* (1979).

Lewis, George E. "Improvised Music after 1950: Afrological and Eurological Perspectives."

In *The Other Side of Nowhere: Jazz, Improvisation, and Communities in Dialogue.* ed. Daniel Fischlin and Ajay Heble, 131–72. Middleton, CT: Wesleyan University Press, 2004.

Livingson, Jerrold. "Emotion in Response to Art." In *Emotion and the Arts*, ed. Mette Hjort and Sue Laver, 20–36. New York: Oxford, 1997.

Longino, Bob. "'Reckless Daughter' Too 'Weird.'" *High Point Enterprises*, January 29, 1978.

Lorde, Audre. *Zami: A New Spelling of My Name—A Biomythography.* Freedom, CA: The Crossing Press, 1982.

Lott, Eric. *Love and Theft: Blackface Minstrelsy and the American Working Class.* New York: Oxford University Press, 1993.

Lubiano, Wahneema. "But Compared to What? Reading Realism, Representation, and Essentialism in *School Daze, Do the Right Thing* and the Spike Lee Discourse." *Black American Literature Forum* 25.2 (1991): 253–82.

Mabry, Donald J. "The Rise and Fall of Ace Records: A Case Study in the Independent Record Business." *Business History Review* 64 (Autumn 1990): 411–50.

Madison, D. Soyini. "The Dialogic Performative in Critical Ethnography." *Text and Performance Quarterly* 26.4 (2006): 320–24.

Major, Clarence. *All Night Visitors* [1969]. Boston: Northeastern University Press, 1998.

Marsalis, Wynton, with Selwyn Sefu Hinds. *To a Young Jazz Musician: Letters from the Road.* New York: Random House, 2005.

Maslin, Janet. "Joni Mitchell's Reckless and Shapeless 'Daughter.'" *Rolling Stone*, March 9, 1978.

Matthews, William. "Mingus in Diaspora." In *Search Party: Collected Poems of William Matthews.* New York: Houghton Mifflin Harcourt Publishing Company, 2004.

May, Elaine Tyler. *Homeward Bound: American Families in the Cold War Era.* New York: Basic Books, 1988.

McClary, Susan. *Feminine Endings: Music, Gender, and Sexuality.* Minneapolis: University of Minnesota Press, 1991.

McCourt, Tom. "Bright Lights, Big City: A Brief History of Rhythm and Blues 1945–1957." *Journal of Popular Music and Society* 9.2 (1983): 1–18.

McDowell, Deborah. "Pecs and Reps: Muscling in on Race and the Subject of Masculinities." In *Race and the Subject of Masculinities*, ed. Harry Stecopoulus and Michael Uebel, 361–86. Durham: Duke University Press, 1997.

McMullen, Tracy. "Identity for Sale: Glenn Miller, Wynton Marsalis, and Cultural Replay in Music." In *Big Ears: Listening for Gender in Jazz Studies*, ed. Nichole T. Rustin and Sherrie Tucker, 129–54. Durham: Duke University Press, 2008.

McNamara, Helen. "Mingus Out to Blast Color Bar in Music." *Toronto Telegraph*, November 2, 1964.

McNeilly, Kevin. "Charles Mingus Splits, or, All the Things You Could Be by Now If

Sigmund Freud's Wife Was Your Mother." *Canadian Review of American Studies* 27.2 (1997): 45–70.

Mercer, Kobena. *Welcome to the Jungle: Identity and Diversity in Postmodern Politics: New Positions in Black Cultural Studies.* New York: Routledge, 1994.

Meyer, Leonard. *Emotion and Meaning in Music.* Chicago: University of Chicago Press, 1961.

Millard, Andre. *America on Record: A History of Recorded Sound.* New York: Cambridge University Press, 1995.

Mingus, Charles. "Open Letter to Miles Davis." *Down Beat,* November 30, 1955.

———. *Beneath the Underdog* [1971]. New York: Vintage, 1991.

Mitchell, Tony. "Joni's Enigmatic Innervisions." *Sounds,* December 24, 1977.

Monson, Ingrid. *Freedom Sounds: Civil Rights Call Out to Jazz and Africa.* New York: Oxford University Press, 2010.

———. "The Problem with White Hipness: Race, Gender, and Cultural Conceptions in Jazz Historical Discourse." *Journal of the American Musicological Society.* 48.3 (Fall 1995): 396–422.

Morgenstern, Dan, with Michael Cuscuna and Charlie Lourie. "Milt Gabler Interview." From the liner notes to *The Complete Commodore Jazz Recordings, Volumes I–III.* In *Reading Jazz: A Gathering of Autobiography, Reportage, and Criticism from 1919 to Now,* ed. Robert Gottlieb, 214–42. New York: Vintage, 1996.

Murray, Albert, and John F. Callahan, eds. *Trading Twelves: The Selected Letters of Ralph Ellison and Albert Murray.* New York: Modern Library, 2000.

Naison, Mark. *Communists in Harlem During the Depression.* New York: Grove, 1985.

Neal, Mark Anthony. *Looking for LeRoy: Illegible Black Masculinities.* New York: New York University Press, 2013.

Newton, Francis (Eric Hobsbawm). *The Jazz Scene* [1959]. New York: Da Capo Press, 1975.

Nicholson, Stuart. *Billie Holiday.* Boston: Northeastern University Press, 1995.

1959: The Year that Changed Jazz. Documentary film. BBC, 2009.

Nussbaum, Martha. *Upheavals of Thought: On the Intelligence of Emotions.* Cambridge: Cambridge University Press, 2001.

Ogren, Kathy. "'Jazz Isn't Just Me': Jazz Autobiographies as Performance Personas." In *Jazz in Mind: Essays on the History and Meaning of Jazz,* ed. Reginald T. Buckner and Steven Weiland, 112–27. Detroit: Wayne State University Press, 1991.

Ondaatje, Michael. *Coming through Slaughter.* New York: Vintage, 1976.

Patrick, James. "Al Tinney, Monroe's Uptown House, and the Emergence of Modern Jazz in Harlem." *Annual Review of Jazz Studies* 2 (1983): 150–79.

Pellegrinelli, Lara. "Separated at 'Birth': Singing and the History of Jazz." In *Big Ears: Listening for Gender in Jazz Studies,* ed. Nichole T. Rustin and Sherrie Tucker, 31–47. Durham: Duke University Press, 2008.

Penn, Donna. "Sexualized Woman: the Lesbian, the Prostitute, and the Containment of Female Sexuality in Postwar America." In *Not June Cleaver: Women and Gender in Postwar America, 1945–1960*, ed. Joanne Meyerowitz, 358–81. Philadelphia: University of Pennsylvania Press, 1994.

Peterson, Richard A. "Why 1955? Explaining the advent of Rock Music." *Popular Music* 9.1 (1990): 97–115.

Picardie, J., and D. Wade. *Atlantic and the Godfathers of Rock and Roll*, revised edition. London: Fourth Estate, 1993.

Piazza, Tom, ed. *Setting the Tempo: Fifty Years of Great Jazz Liner Notes*. New York: Anchor Books Doubleday, 1996.

Piper, Adrian. *Out of Order, Out of Sight, Volume 1: Selected Writings on Meta Art 1968–1992*. Boston: MIT Press, 1999.

———. "On Wearing Three Hats," 1996. http://www.adrianpiper.com/docs/WebsiteNG BK3Hats.pdf.

Porter, Eric. "'Born Out of Jazz . . . Yet Embracing All Music': Race, Gender, and Technology in George Russell's Lydian Chromatic Concept." In *Big Ears: Listening for Gender in Jazz Studies*, ed. Nichole T. Rustin and Sherrie Tucker, 210–34. Durham: Duke University Press, 2008.

———. "'It's About That Time': The Response to Miles Davis' Electronic Turn." In *Miles Davis and American Culture*, ed. Gerald Early, 130–47. St. Louis: Missouri Historical Society, 2001.

———. *What Is This Thing Called Jazz? African American Musicians as Artists, Critics, and Activists*. Berkeley: University of California Press, 2002.

Powell, Jr., Adam Clayton. *Adam by Adam*. [1971]. New York: Dafina Books, 2002.

Priestley, Brian. *Jazz on Record: A History*. London: Elm Tree Books, 1988.

———. *Mingus: A Critical Biography*. New York: Da Capo Press, 1982.

Queely, Andrea. "Hip Hop and the Aesthetics of Criminalization." *Souls* 5.1 (2003): 1–15.

Radano, Ronald. "The Jazz Avant-Garde and the Jazz Community: Action and Reaction." *Annual Review of Jazz Studies* 3 (1985): 71–79.

———. *Lying Up a Nation: Race and Black Music*. Chicago: University of Chicago Press, 2004.

———. *New Musical Figurations: Anthony Braxton's Cultural Critique*. Chicago: University of Chicago Press, 1994.

Ramsey, Guthrie P. *The Amazing Bud Powell: Black Genius, Jazz History and the Challenge of Bebop*. Berkeley: University of California Press, 2013.

———. *Race Music: Black Cultures from Bebop to Hip Hop*. Berkeley: University of California Press, 2003.

———. "Them There Eyes: On Connections and the Visual." In *Eye-Minded: Living and*

Writing Contemporary Art, ed. Kellie Jones, 349–51. Durham: Duke University Press, 2011.

Rasula, Jed. "The Media of Memory: The Seductive Menace of Records in Jazz History." In *Jazz among the Discourses*, ed. Krin Gabbard, 134–62. Durham: Duke University Press, 1995.

Robertson, Sandy. "Scared to Dance." *Sounds*, June 30, 1979.

Rockwell, John. "Joni Mitchell Is Still Going Her Way." *New York Times*, December 16, 1977.

Rosenthal, David. *Hard Bop: Jazz and Black Music, 1955–1965*. New York: Oxford University Press, 1992.

Ross, Marlon. "White Fantasies of Desire: James Baldwin and the Racial Identities of Sexuality." In *James Baldwin Now*, ed. Dwight A. McBride, 13-55. New York: New York University Press, 1999.

Russell, Ross. "The Legacy of Fats Navaro." *Down Beat*, February 19, 1970, 14–16, 33.

Rustin, Nichole T. "'Blow Man, Blow!': Representing Gender, White Primitives, and Jazz Melodrama Through *A Young Man with a Horn*. In *Big Ears: Listening for Gender in Jazz Studies*, ed. Nichole T. Rustin and Sherrie Tucker, 361–92. Durham: Duke University Press, 2008.

———. "*Cante Hondo*: Charles Mingus, Nat Hentoff, and Jazz Racism." *Critical Sociology* 32.2–3 (2006): 309–31.

———. "'Mary Lou Williams Plays Like a Man!' Gender, Genius, and Difference in Black Music Discourse.'" *South Atlantic Quarterly* 104.3 (Summer 2005): 445–62.

Rustin, Nichole T., and Sherrie Tucker, eds. *Big Ears: Listening for Gender in Jazz Studies*. Durham: Duke University Press, 2008.

Sanjek, Russell, and David Sanjek. *American Popular Music Business in the 20th Century*. New York: Oxford University Press, 1991.

Santoro, Gene. *Myself When I'm Real: The Life and Music of Charles Mingus*. New York: Oxford University Press, 2001.

———. "Town Hall Train Wreck: Why Charles Mingus Came to Grief in 1962." *Village Voice*, June 6, 2000.

Sartwell, Crispin. *Act Like You Know: African-American Autobiography and White Identity*. Chicago: University of Chicago Press, 1998.

Saul, Scott. *Freedom Is, Freedom Ain't: Jazz and the Making of the Sixties*. Cambridge: Harvard University Press, 2003.

Scott, Joan W. "The Evidence of Experience." *Critical Inquiry* 17 (Summer 1991): 773–97.

———. "History in Crisis: The Others' Side of the Story." *American Historical Review* 94.3 (June 1989): 680–92.

Segrave, Jerry. *Payola in the Music Industry*. Jefferson, NC: McFarland and Co., 1994.

Shaw, Arnold. *52nd St. The Street of Jazz*. New York: Da Capo Press, 1971.

Siddall, Gillian. "'I Wanted to Live in That Music': Blues, Bessie Smith and Improvised Identities in Ann-Marie MacDonald's *Fall on Your Knees*." *Critical Studies in Improvisation/Etudes critiques en improvisation* 1.2 (2005): 10–19.

Sidran, Ben. *Black Talk* [1971]. New York: Da Capo Press, 1983.

Skea, Dan. "Rudy Van Gelder in Hackensack: Defining the Jazz Sound in the 1950s." *Current Musicology* 71–73 (Spring 2001–2002): 54–76.

Smith, Cherisse. *Enacting Others: Politics of Identity in Eleanor Antin, Nikki S. Lee, Adrian Piper, and Anna DeVeare Smith*. Durham: Duke University Press, 2011.

Smith, Julie Dawn. "Playing Like a Girl: The Queer Laughter of the Feminist Improvising Group." In *The Other Side of Nowhere: Jazz, Improvisation, and Communities in Dialogue*, ed. Daniel Fischlin and Ajay Heble, 224–43. Middleton, CT: Wesleyan University Press, 2004.

Smith, Sidonie, and Julie Ann Watson, eds. *Interfaces: Women, Autobiography, Image, Performance*. Ann Arbor: University of Michigan Press, 2002.

Solie, Ruth, ed. *Musicology and Difference*. Berkeley: University of California, 1995.

Spellman, A. B. *Four Lives in the Bebop Business* [1966]. New York: Limelight Editions, 1994.

Spillers, Hortense J. *Black, White, and in Color: Essays on American Literature and Culture*. Chicago: University of Chicago Press, 2003.

Stabile, Carole. "The Typhoid Marys of the Left: Gender, Race, and the Broadcast Blacklist." *Communication and Critical/Cultural Studies* 8.3 (2011): 266–85.

Stein, Daniel. *Music Is My Life: Louis Armstrong, Autobiography, and American Jazz*. Ann Arbor: University of Michigan Press, 2012.

Steptoe, Robert. *Beyond the Veil*. Urbana: University of Illinois Press, 1991.

Stoever-Ackerman, Jennifer. "The Contours of the Sonic Color-Line: Slavery, Segregation, and the Cultural Politics of Listening." PhD dissertation, University of Southern California, 2007.

Strange Fruit. Documentary film. California Newsreel, 2002.

Strauss, Neil. "The Hissing of a Living Legend." *New York Times*, October 4, 1998.

Strick, Wesley. "Joni Mitchell Meets Don Juan's Reckless Daughter." March 2, 1978, http://jonimitchell.com/library/view.cfm?id=715, last accessed March 19, 2012.

Surratt, Dave. "Replay: Don Juan's Reckless Daughter." September 23, 2004, http://jonimitchell.com/library/view.cfm?id=1174, last accessed March 19, 2012.

Tate, Claudia. "Freud and His 'Negro': Psychoanalysis as Ally and Enemy of African Americans." *Journal for the Psychoanalysis of Culture & Society* 1.1 (Spring 1996): 53–62.

Taylor, Arthur. *Notes and Tones: Musician to Musician Interviews*. New York: Perigee Books, 1977.

Thiele, Bob, as told to Bob Golden. *What a Wonderful World: A Lifetime of Recordings*. New York: Oxford University Press, 1995.

Tucker, Sherrie. "Bordering on Community: Improvising Women Improvising Women-in-Jazz." In *The Other Side of Nowhere: Jazz, Improvisation, and Communities in Dialogue,* ed. Daniel Fischlin and Ajay Heble, 244–67. Middleton, CT: Wesleyan University Press, 2004.

———. *Swing Shift: "All-Girl" Bands of the 1940s.* Durham: Duke University Press, 2000.

———. "West Coast Women: A Jazz Genealogy." *Pacific Review of Ethnomusicology* 8.1 (Winter 1996/1997): 5–22.

———. "When Did Jazz Go Straight?: A Queer Question for Jazz Studies." *Critical Studies in Improvisation* 4.2 (2008): 1–16.

Uebel, Michael. "Men in Color: Introducing Race and the Subject of Masculinities." In *Race and the Subject of Masculinities,* ed. Harry Stecopolous and Michael Uebel, 1–16. Durham: Duke University Press, 1997.

Ulanov, Barry. *A Handbook of Jazz.* Hutchinson of London, 1958.

———. "Morality and Maturity in Jazz." *Metronome,* August 1954, 20.

Vincent, Ted. "The Social Context of Black Swan Records." *Living Blues,* May/June 1989, 34–40.

Von Eschen, Penny. *Satchmo Blows Up the World! Jazz Ambassadors Play the Cold War.* Cambridge: Harvard University Press, 2006.

Wakefield, Dan. *New York in the 50s.* New York: St. Martin's Griffin, 1992.

Walser, Robert, ed. *Keeping Time: Readings in Jazz History.* New York: Oxford University Press, 1998.

Ward, Brian. *Just My Soul Responding: Rhythm and Blues, Black Consciousness, and Race Relations.* Berkeley: University of California Press, 1998.

Watts, Jerry Gafio. *Amiri Baraka: The Politics and Art of a Black Intellectual.* New York: New York University Press, 1991.

Watts, Michael. "Joni . . . er . . . um." *Melody Maker,* June 16, 1979.

Weiss, Milton. *Payola in the Music Industry.* Jefferson, NC: McFarland and Co., 1994.

Welburn, Ron. "American Jazz Criticism, 1914–1940." PhD dissertation, New York University, 1983.

West, Hollie I. "Bass Viol Book." *Washington Post,* May 15, 1971.

Wilmer, Valerie. *As Serious as Your Life: The Story of the New Jazz.* London: Allison and Busby, 1977.

———. *Jazz People.* New York: Da Capo, 1970.

———. *Mama Said There'd Be Days Like This: My Life in the Jazz World.* London: The Women's Press, 1989.

Wilson, Olly. "The Black American Composer and the Orchestra in the Twentieth Century." *The Black Perspective in Music* (1985): 26–34.

Whitworth, Bill. "The Rich Full Life of Charlie Mingus." *New York Herald Tribune,* November 1, 1964, 13–16, 41.

Whyton, Tony. "Crosscurrents: The Cultural Dynamics of Jazz." In *Jazz Debates/Jazz-debatten*, ed. Wolfram Knauer, 165–74. Darmstadt Studies in Jazz Research, vol. 13, Jazzinstitut Darmstadt, 2014.

Wolfe, George C. *Jelly's Last Jam*. New York: Theatre Communications Group, 1993.

Wright, Richard. "Psychiatry Comes to Harlem." *Free World*, September 1946, 45–51.

X, Malcolm, as told to Alex Haley. *The Autobiography of Malcolm X*. New York: Grove Press, 1964.

Young, Al. *Drowning in the Sea of Love: Musical Memoirs*. Hopewell, NJ: Ecco Press, 1981.

——. Review of *Beneath the Underdog*. *Rolling Stone*, June 10, 1971, 52.

INDEX

of the American Revolution (DAR):
Constitution Hall and whites-only
policy; Horne, Lena; Josephson,
Barney; Powell, Adam Clayton, Jr.
Segovia, Andrés, 64, 66
"Self-Portrait" (Mingus): performance of
emotion and experience in, 1
sexuality, 16–17, 22, 25, 37–38, 44–48, 53,
163. *See also* Al Young
Sketches of Spain (Miles Davis), 10
Simon, George T., 76
Smith, Sidonie, 166
Solie, Ruth, 6
Sons of the American Revolution, 147
Spellman, A. B., 12
Spillers, Hortense, 45, 83, 185n50
"Stars of Swing": modeling
jazzmasculinity, 69–70

Talmadge, May Erwin (Mrs. Julius Y.),
146–47. *See also* Daughters of the
American Revolution (DAR)
Tate, Claudia, 45–46
Tatum, Art, x, 159
Taylor, Arthur, 154
Taylor, Billy, x, 77, 79, 96
Taylor, Farwell, 26–27
television: changes in performance style,
76
Thiele, Bob, 89; conflict as producer,
90–92, 102, 119. See also *The Black
Saint and the Sinner Lady* (Mingus)
Thompson, Lucky, 69–70
Thurlow, Janet, 21
Tijuana Moods (Mingus), x
Tizol, Juan, 27, 87
Tormé, Mel, 75
Trenier, Claude, 68
Tristano, Lenny, 102
Truman, Bess, 142–43, 144

Truman, Harry, 124, 142–43, 146, 212n49
Tucker, Sherrie, 18, 45

Ulanov, Barry, 194n135

Van Gelder, Rudy: sound engineering
and emotion, 104
vinyl, 120–21

Waldron, Mal, x, 97, 98
WAMH (Amherst College), 8, 10
Washington, Isabel, 138–39
Wein, George, 84, 86
Weinstock, Bob, 102, 107
Weird Nightmare: Meditations on Mingus
(Willner), 156–57
White, Josh: and HUAC, 151–52
Whitworth, Bill, 42
Whyton, Tony, 6
Wiggins, Gerald, 68
Williams, Mary Lou, 13, 17;
jazzmasculinity and, 16–17
Willner, Hal, 156–57
Wilmer, Val, 121
Women musicians: jazzmasculinity and,
17–19. *See also,* Holiday, Billie; Horne,
Lena; Scott, Hazel; Williams, Mary
Lou
Woodman, Britt, x, 62, 64, 68, 69
Woodman, Brother (William), 62, 67
Woodman, Coney, 31, 61

Young, Al, xiii, becoming a jazzman and,
168–69
Young, Coleman, 152
Young, Lee, x, 68
Young, Lester, 57, 164

Zaentz, Saul, 124–25
Zenni, Stefano, 82

Frances Aparicio
*Listening to Salsa: Gender, Latin Popular
Music, and Puerto Rican Cultures*

Paul Austerlitz
*Jazz Consciousness: Music, Race,
and Humanity*

Harris M. Berger
*Metal, Rock, and Jazz: Perception and the
Phenomenology of Musical Experience*

Harris M. Berger
*Stance: Ideas about Emotion, Style,
and Meaning for the Study
of Expressive Culture*

Harris M. Berger and
Giovanna P. Del Negro
*Identity and Everyday Life: Essays
in the Study of Folklore, Music,
and Popular Culture*

Franya J. Berkman
*Monument Eternal: The Music of Alice
Coltrane*

Dick Blau, Angeliki Vellou Keil
and Charles Keil
*Bright Balkan Morning: Romani Lives and
the Power of Music in Greek Macedonia*

Susan Boynton and Roe-Min Kok, editors
*Musical Childhoods and the
Cultures of Youth*

James Buhler, Caryl Flinn and David
Neumeyer, editors
Music and Cinema

Thomas Burkhalter, Kay Dickinson,
and Benjamin J. Harbert, editors
*The Arab Avant-Garde:
Music, Politics, Modernity*

Patrick Burkart
Music and Cyberliberties

Julia Byl
*Antiphonal Histories: Resonant Pasts
in the Toba Batak Musical Present*

Daniel Cavicchi
*Listening and Longing: Music Lovers
in the Age of Barnum*

Mark Slobin
Subcultural Sounds:
Micromusics of the West

Mark Slobin, editor
Global Soundtracks: Worlds of Film Music

Christopher Small
The Christopher Small Reader

Christopher Small
Music of the Common Tongue:
Survival and Celebration in
African American Music

Christopher Small
Music, Society, Education

Christopher Small
Musicking: The Meanings
of Performing and Listening

Regina M. Sweeney
Singing Our Way to Victory:
French Cultural Politics and Music
during the Great War

Colin Symes
Setting the Record Straight: A Material
History of Classical Recording

Steven Taylor
False Prophet: Fieldnotes from the
Punk Underground

Paul Théberge
Any Sound You Can Imagine: Making
Music/Consuming Technology

Sarah Thornton
Club Cultures: Music, Media
and Sub-cultural Capital

Michael E. Veal
Dub: Songscape and Shattered Songs
in Jamaican Reggae

Michael E. Veal and
E. Tammy Kim, editors
Punk Ethnography: Artists and Scholars
Listen to Sublime Frequencies

Robert Walser
Running with the Devil: Power, Gender,
and Madness in Heavy Metal Music

Dennis Waring
Manufacturing the Muse:
Estey Organs and Consumer Culture
in Victorian America

Lise A. Waxer
The City of Musical Memory:
Salsa, Record Grooves, and Popular
Culture in Cali, Colombia

Mina Yang
Planet Beethoven: Classical Music
at the Turn of the Millennium

ABOUT THE AUTHOR

Nichole Rustin-Paschal earned a JD from the University of Virginia and a PhD from New York University. She is coeditor of *Big Ears: Listening for Gender in Jazz Studies* (Duke University Press, 2008).